C000102549

OLIVE LEAF TEA

TIME TO SETTLE

SABINA OSTROWSKA

Copyright © 2023 Sabina Ostrowska

This book is a memoir and, as such, should be treated as a work of fiction rather than testimony. It reflects the author's recollections of experiences over time. Most names have been changed. People's characteristics may have been exaggerated for comic or dramatic effect, and some events have been rearranged in order to tell a story. The dialogues have been recreated from memory.

No part of this book may be reproduced, or stored in a retrieval system, or transmitted in any form or by any means, electronic, mechanical, photocopying, recording, or otherwise, without express written permission of the author.

ISBN: 978-84-09-52901-8

Cover art by Sally Campbell

Chapters 1, 4 and 17 artwork by John Lachlan Campbell, reprinted with the permission of his estate.

Artwork in the remaining chapters by Sabina Ostrowska

Formatting www.antpress.org

To receive updates about new books and to read additional chapters of my books, subscribe to my website or follow me on social media:

sabinaostrowska.com

Facebook @sabinawriter

Instagram @sabina.author

Published by:

textworkshop.org

WHAT READERS AND AUTHORS SAY ABOUT SABINA'S BOOKS

Unexpectedly absorbing!

A wonderful, humorous read

Stressful, Clueless, but Entertaining

Quite the Adventure!

A Witty Journey of Transformation

It's funny, cringe-worthy, and brave!

"When I started this book, I thought it was going to be another good life tale, wrong! It is a "warts and all" telling of this couple's start in a life that they were ill-prepared for."

"A most entertaining book. I enjoyed her earlier book *The Crinkle Crankle Wall*, but enjoyed *A Hoopoe on the Nispero Tree* even more. She writes with lively good humour whilst telling it 'how it is' - if you've ever thought of escaping to rural Spain and setting up an accommodation business, be sure to read this book first. Am looking forward to her next book already."

"This is an incredibly entertaining read and, if, like me, you are a fan of *Driving Over Lemons* by Chris Stewart, you will absolutely love this book."

"I felt like I was visiting an old friend since I read and enjoyed the previous book. Charming, interesting, and well-written. I felt like I was there with her…"

"For all you lovers of programmes like *Grand Designs*, *A Place in the Sun*, *DIY SOS* etc., this is for You!!"

To my kind and talented nieces and nephew, in order of appearance, Kosma, Zoja, and Gaja.

"Man is condemned to be free; because once thrown into the world, he is responsible for everything he does. It is up to you to give [life] a meaning."
Jean-Paul Sartre

CONTENTS

PREFACE

AT A CROSSROADS

Most decisions we make every day are inconsequential. What kind of breakfast I eat in the morning, what T-shirt I wear, or where I walk my dog are unlikely to influence my future significantly. They are incredibly unlikely to change the course of my life, not to mention the course of history. We fill our days with minutiae which affect nothing and interest no one. Whether I take the stairs or the lift, eat soup for lunch or have a sandwich, or watch a film or a series is extremely unlikely to affect my future. Not every flap of a butterfly's wings causes a typhoon. As we drown in prosaic trivia and banality, it is impossible to see when we stand at a fork in our life journey; when we are faced with a decision that may seem of little importance but turns out to be life-changing.

As I sat inside my car, watching the snow rapidly cover the windshield, I was oblivious to the fact that I was at a point where my life path was about to diverge. Every few minutes, I'd turn on the windshield wipers to remove the snow to see if Robert was coming in the four-by-four to rescue me from the mountain between Alcalá la Real and Montefrio. I had left home earlier that day to attend a job interview in Alcalá. It was the first week in January 2018, and just a few days earlier, we had hosted a barbecue with our friends to celebrate Epiphany.

I turned on the wipers again and saw yet another car skid down the road out of control, descending the hill in front of me. The driver must have been shocked by how little control he had over his car because, like me, he slowed down and parked on the side of the road to wait out the blizzard. There was now a long line of cars in front and behind me, all with our hazard lights blinking. By now, I had lived in Andalusia for almost four years and had only seen snow here once before. That first February, when we opened our little remote guest house, the guests woke to a white blanket covering the olive hills and their rental cars. But watching the snow gently fall through the window of one's cottage while sitting next to a cosy fireplace is one thing. Sitting in a freezing cold car on the side of a mountain while steadily being entombed in the snow is quite another experience.

I learned how to drive in the United Arab Emirates, where the roads are predominantly straight, flat, and wide. Only once during those years did I find myself in a difficult driving situation. It was in 2012 when I agreed to drive our four-by-four American pick-up truck as a support vehicle across a small section of the Empty Quarter. Robert and his friend, Justin, put their dirt bikes in the back of the pick-up, and we drove south of Al Ain, along the Oman border and past Al Quaa towards Um Al Zumoul until we reached a gate into the desert that we had used on previous desert camping trips. From this point, Robert and Justin left on their bikes across the desert towards Liwa Oasis. While they went straight across the dunes, I was to follow in their general direction on a desert road that we had used many times before. We were supposed to meet in Liwa about five hours later.

As the dust kicked up by the departing bikes settled on the horizon, I proceeded to drive along the compacted desert track for several kilometres until the sand got soft. It was time to deflate the truck's tyres, so I stopped by a small, presumably abandoned shack with a large veranda to work in the shade. A short man in uniform appeared in the doorway of the humble abode as I was checking the pressure in each tyre.

'Are you lost?' he asked.

'No,' I assured him. 'I'm following two bikes to Liwa.'

'To Liwa? It's quite far. No?'

'I've done this trip many times,' I understood that seeing a solo woman in an oversized American pick-up truck setting off into the endless ocean of the Empty Quarter must have raised his concern, so I chatted with him for a while.

I learned that he was from Nepal and was working for a sheikh guarding the entrance to this section of the desert. It emerged from our conversation that he led a very solitary life, and several days would go by without him seeing anyone.

'I wish I had some magazines or books to give you. Next time we come here, we will bring something for you to read.'

'That would be very nice.'

It was time for me to leave. I took a sip of water and said goodbye.

'Just be careful. Call me if you need help,' were his parting words. He had informed me that a middle-aged couple from France had gone down the same route a month earlier and had got stuck in the sand, thus necessitating their rescue by the local police. He gave me his mobile phone number, just in case.

I felt pretty smug for the first hour or so of my journey across the desert.

Look at me! I thought to myself. I was in my mid-thirties and driving a three-tonne GMC pickup truck across the biggest sand desert in the Arabian Peninsula, somewhere between Oman and Saudi Arabia. I'd stop every now and then, admire the stunning red dunes that contrasted against the deep blue sky, and take some photos to share on my social media accounts as soon as I could get a signal on my mobile phone. Little did I know how much my luck was about to change.

I arrived at a crossroads and, for the life of me, could not remember which way to go. The problem was that the last time Robert and I had driven that route, this area of the desert was completely empty, but now I could see several temporary buildings in the shape of shipping containers scattered around and an asphalt road that miraculously began in the middle of the sand track.

This must be a construction site for an oil well, I thought to myself. Not wanting to get into trouble for driving across someone's precious oil field, I turned left. But after driving for another half an hour, nothing in the desert looked familiar.

Where is the oryx sanctuary? Where are the gazelles?

The highlight of my planned route was to see oryx and gazelles grazing under an irrigated forest of acacia trees, but I had not come across the forest on the track I was following. The dunes I found myself in seemed different, too, choppier and showing no sign that a vehicle had passed through. I consulted my GPS receiver, which, in those days, provided only very basic information about my longitude and latitude, and noticed that I was driving away from the Liwa Oasis in the Emirates and heading towards Saudi Arabia. It was 2012, and women in Saudi were banned from driving, not to mention driving in shorts and a T-shirt with their hair flowing out of a vehicle's open window. Talking to a strange man without my dear husband's permission might have added a few more lashes according to Shariah law, which is so piously concerned with a women's modesty, purity, and general well-being.

I pondered how *Locked Up Abroad* might title my story. *Girl Gone* would work well and fit nicely between *Dangerous Liaison*, a story of a gay male nurse arrested by the religious police, and *Saudi Bootlegger*, the latter being self-explanatory. As I was making light of my predicament, I noticed that the sun had started to set. I checked the information in the battery-driven GPS and noted that I had about forty-five minutes before it would be dark outside. I zoomed in on the grey-scale map on the GPS and searched for a road. There was a very small dotted line, suggesting the presence of a road not far from where I was. I drove across a flat area in the desert in the general direction indicated by a small arrow on the GPS and soon joined a single-lane asphalt road that ran next to a very high fence topped with barbed wire and security cameras. As I glimpsed at the stunning sunset unfolding ahead of me over the giant dunes, I wanted to cry. My only hope was that I was still on the Emirati side of the border and had not inadvertently crossed over into Saudi during my meandering drive earlier that afternoon.

With no better idea in mind and no mobile signal to call anyone, I resigned myself to continue down the asphalt road. Even though I had never seen this track before, I convinced myself it must lead somewhere. I was certain that, by now, Robert and Justin were at the hotel in Liwa where we were supposed to meet. They would be sorely missing the supply of wine and brandy that I had packed on the back seat, as well as their clean clothes and Justin's insulin that was in a small fridge next to the wine. Few things in life can make you feel as totally useless as when you fail to deliver insulin to a person with diabetes, but I knew once the sun had set, I could not drive in the pitch black across the dunes. I resigned myself to the idea of spending the night alone, drinking wine and smoking cigarettes, as these were the only provisions that I had in the vehicle.

Since I was alone and with no one around to judge me, I was about to turn on the waterworks when suddenly, in the distance ahead, I saw an official-looking four-by-four heading towards me.

How bad can a Saudi prison be? I weighed my options. *Surely, they will let me go after a day or two or a few lashes. Hopefully, someone from the university's HR team will inquire about me.* I was not going to let this car drive past without asking for directions.

I put on all the truck's lights, including the hazard lights, and got out of the car so that they could see that I was alone and unarmed. I waved frantically at the approaching car. To my relief, it was the Emirati border patrol with two friendly police officers inside. Highly amused by my story, they kindly said they'd lead me to a junction in the desert from where I could follow a road to Liwa Oasis without getting lost. I drove behind them for half an hour or so until we reached the crossroads where I had taken a wrong turn earlier that afternoon. They told me that what I had assumed to be an oil field was a construction site for a new road. After thanking the officers for their assistance, I drove off into the darkness, and after another half an hour, I was on a main road that I knew led to Liwa Oasis. As soon as I had a telephone signal on my mobile phone, I saw that I had received dozens of missed phone calls and messages from Robert, who had arrived at the hotel two hours earlier and had been sitting at the bar in his sweaty motorcycle gear, wondering where I was.

I recalled my little automotive desert adventure as I now sat stuck in a blizzard only half an hour from my house. The blizzard was getting worse, but Robert promised to collect me in the four-by-four. The sedan which I had driven that morning to the job interview was not going to make it through the ice and snow. Since I did not fancy falling down a roadside cliff, I had prudently stopped and waited. However, I didn't want to use up my phone's battery reading mindless social media posts, so I looked at the white windscreen and reflected on my current situation instead.

It had been almost four years since we packed up everything we owned, including two Arabian street cats, and relocated from Abu Dhabi to southern Spain. Fuelled by romantic dreams of a pastoral Mediterranean lifestyle and with no road map to follow, we set off to start a new life among the olive groves. In the first two years, we renovated an old farmhouse, or *cortijo*, and turned parts of it into rental apartments for tourists. We now had experienced two seasons of paying guests, but there were still many improvements that we had to make to our house. This wasn't helped by the fact that we did not hold steady jobs, making our new life quite stressful and difficult to predict at times. To help with our finances, Robert had travelled to Oman to help a former student open a private school while I stayed in an empty house, looking after guests. This was very different from what we had imagined our lives in Andalusia might be like.

By January 2018, I had been alone, on and off, in my dream house for almost ten months and decided that I had had enough.

There must be better ways to make some money than travelling across continents every few months. I questioned our Ratonero Bodeguero —

an Andalusian breed of dog used in the past to protect wine cellars from rodents. In all fairness, Bobby had never travelled beyond the vet's office in Alcalá and was unable to comment on the rest of the planet.

And that's how I ended up accepting a job interview at a local language school in the nearby town of Alcalá la Real. I thought that if I had a steady teaching job, combined with the holiday rentals, my writing, and Robert's translation work, we might be able to live together again.

'If you like these conditions, you can start on Monday,' Belén, the manager of the language school, announced. She was sitting on the opposite side of her desk in a mustard-coloured office. We had just discussed my teaching career and what I had been doing in Andalusia for the last four years. Belén spoke excellent English, even though she unconsciously switched between a somewhat forced version of the Queen's English and her normal English, which was marked by a slight Spanish accent. I felt that she had put on the Queen's English for me, which was strange because I was Polish and did not particularly care about English accents.

Was she trying to impress ME? I wondered because it was me who was supposed to impress *her*.

'Thank you,' I said before leaving the school. 'I will think about it and get back to you later.'

'Can you let me know this afternoon? It's because I really need someone to start as soon as possible. My old teacher has passed her *oposiciones*, and she has to travel to Cádiz for her new post.'

At that time, I didn't understand what Belén was referring to, but I let it pass.

'OK, I will send you a WhatsApp message later today.'

'Perfect.'

I bade her farewell and, while leaving, cast my eye over the brown walls of the school's corridors and the dark, burgundy waiting room. I wasn't over the moon at the prospect of going back to teaching, but I also wasn't excited about spending another winter alone in the middle of nowhere.

Maybe I should go back to Oman with Robert and teach at Samira's school. I thought to myself as I appraised the brown and beige stripes that decorated the school's interior. *Did Belén decorate this school?* I wondered. It looked as if the colour scheme in every room at the school was taken straight from the 1970s Manchester set of *Life on Mars*, a depressing and strange mud-inspired combination of various shades of brown.

As I returned to my car, I weighed my options. Admit defeat, go to Oman, and be miserable. Or teach in an outdated local language school in a small town and earn peanuts. By the time I was stuck in the blizzard on my way home from the job interview, I knew where my heart was.

But for a moment, dear reader, let's stop here and rewind to seven months earlier when I was alone in my house, learning how to drive a manual car, recovering from a fall that had left me slightly concussed and with a broken arm, attending to paying guests and trying to make new friends.

ONE
THE PANADERÍA

I was staring down a steep hill which appeared to take a sharp turn into a river. Had I known how steep the hills in and out of Sarah's little valley were, I might have reconsidered my visit. She was a new acquaintance whom I had met through Trish, another local English woman who drove me to the shops and to the health centre after I had broken my arm earlier that spring.

I had instantly taken to Sarah and her artsy nature and so I decided to pay her a visit. I was also feeling quite lonely being by myself in the middle of nowhere for several months at a time, so even though my arm was still hurting and using the manual gearbox was particularly difficult, I ventured out in search of new friends. However, this was not as easy as one might imagine because of my limited experience of driving a car with a manual gearbox on mountainous roads. Thus, each escapade had to be planned carefully.

Before I left the house, I made sure no steep hills were involved in my journey, or if there were, that there was no audience to watch me stall the car. While Trish helped me with the longer trips to Mercadona or on other errands in and about Alcalá, I did a weekly drive to Montefrio's post office to enquire about my Polish driving licence. As my International Driver's Licence was due to expire in a few months, I was desperate to get the EU licence.

I had been jumping through bureaucratic hoops to get the EU licence since I had returned from visiting Robert in Oman in March and had decided that I did not possess enough patience to deal with any more Workaways or volunteer workers who might drive me around. After a few fruitless visits to *tráfico*, the Spanish traffic police, where a young recruit looked at my Emirati document, which was in Arabic and English, with a great deal of bewilderment and bemusement (as if I had handed him a scrap of toilet paper with my name written on it), I took matters into my own hands. I dedicated several evenings to studying the issue online by reading up on various European Union treaties and agreements with foreign countries, including the United Arab Emirates, where my licence was issued. Once I had become a legal scholar on the topic of converting driving licences from a non-European Union country to a European Union country, I was confident that I could skip a whole lot of Spanish paperwork — probably saving a small forest in the process — by simply exchanging my Emirati licence into a Polish one. This EU licence could then be readily changed for a Spanish one.

Being aware of the fact that the red tape at any embassy can entangle the simplest of applications and that documents take months to get looked at and signed by his or her highness, the ambassador, I asked my mum, who lives in Poland and who is an expert at nagging, to give the embassy's secretary a call once a week just to check how my case was progressing. This had the desired effect in that it only took a month or so for the ambassador's assistant to have a look at my paperwork and give my application his seal of approval. But from there, things slowed down. Eventually, my new Polish licence was sent to my mum's house, who then forwarded it by express mail to Montefrio.

As the weeks passed, I regularly checked my post-box for an *aviso* to collect the licence from the post office, but nothing had arrived. I started to suspect that my legendarily cheap mother wasn't telling me the whole truth and had, in fact, sent the licence by regular mail instead of using the more expensive registered mail service I had requested.

After a few heated arguments over Skype, where harsh words of criticism were exchanged, and I accused her of penny-pinching and in return, was reminded of what an ungrateful daughter I was, I decided to investigate the case of the missing letter at the *correos*, the local post office. This was easier said than done because Montefrio's post office lies at the heart of the medieval maze of narrow precipitous streets that constitute the village centre. Instead of traditional Roman city planning, where streets are conveniently organised in a logical grid pattern, an Escher sketch of a nightmarish, never-ending staircase was used as a model for the streets of Montefrio.

They make no sense — they start and end in randomly selected places, some loop back on themselves, and others take such sharp turns that no modern vehicle can navigate from one street to the next. The village streets are also located at various levels on the two main hills of Montefrio, with startling degrees of incline and decline. In summary, not a single straight line was used to plan our little village.

In addition to the somewhat surreal and chaotic street layout of Montefrio, I was also put off visiting the *correos* by car because it is situated right next to a *panadería*, the bread shop and a *frutería*, a greengrocer, both of which are extremely popular with the local ladies, who queue outside on the pavement and linger around for social reasons. Were I to stall the car there, I was sure to have a critical audience eager to impart advice and shout words of encouragement. The local housewives would talk about the incident of the repeatedly stalled car for weeks to come and gasp at the foreigner's inability to navigate through the village.

'I don't know who gave this woman a licence,' a heavyset middle-aged mum would whisper to her neighbour while I tried for the tenth time to inch the car uphill in an attempt to park outside the post office.

'I have news for you ladies,' I imagined myself saying something sassy as I managed to park the giant 4x4 on the tiny one-way medieval street. However, even in my wildest imagination, I had no clue what I could have said to counter the humiliation. In reality, I found the group of women gossiping in the bread shop rather intimidating.

Standing at a corner shop and chatting with neighbours is a popular Andalusian pastime that people engage in after breakfast and before lunch. During that period, time stretches in Andalusian villages to Proustian dimensions. Visitors or tourists soon become antsy when they stop by a small village shop in the morning. You can see them fidgeting, exploring their fingers, and swearing under their breath.

'Just get your bread and go home. What the Hell? Why is it taking so long? What is there to talk about?' they mutter to no one in particular and threaten murder with their eyes.

The time required to buy basic victuals in a shop varies around the world. Being a Central European, I assume that the amount of time we take to complete a transaction is the most accurate and the only acceptable one. To put it into perspective, if I were to travel to New York, I might find the speed that customers are dealt with a tad fast. I'd say three to four times faster than what I'm used to. Andalusia, on the other hand, lies on the other end of the spectrum. Here things slow down by a magnitude of two or three times to what I am used to. As you can imagine, a New Yorker visiting Andalusia might think that nothing is really happening. He or she would call us all country bumpkins and tell us to move on. All they'd see would be some middle-aged, corpulent women leaning on the baker's counter and making comments about a foreign woman trying to park her oversized car outside the post office.

To avoid the drama and inevitable derision, I parked the car outside a supermarket on the outskirts of Montefrio and walked all the way up to the post office. It was a steady climb. Even though I was moving briskly, I was being overtaken by *señoras* twice my age with heavy shopping bags in both hands. Once I got to the post office, I stood outside for a minute to catch my breath. I looked towards the and the *fruitería*. The regular bevy of matrons and young mums in their leggings occupied the pavement and spilt out onto the road.

Inside the post office, I started to interrogate the postman, a slightly balding young man who was always keen to practice his English with foreign residents. I tried both in English and Spanish, but he seemed adamant that no registered mail had arrived for Cortijo Berruguilla. I gave him a stern look even though it was not his fault.

'Maybe next week,' he suggested, and so I added a futile trip to the post office to my weekly errands.

Going to the post office to check whether my licence had arrived wasn't my only caper. Tired of solitude, I embarked on a couple of cheeky trips to Keith and Delia's house in Venta Valero and to Lucas and Arie's house a few kilometres away from my house. I usually arrived giddy with adrenaline and giggling hysterically until the time when I had to fire up the engine again and drive back down to my valley.

'I *can* drive,' I assured sceptical Lucas on my first visit to his house after he observed my amateurish parking manoeuvres outside his cottage. 'I just hate driving manual cars. I get very stressed changing gears on these hills.'

'I drive a semi-automatic,' he told me sympathetically while rolling himself a cigarette.

'Semi-automatic? What's that?' I thought perhaps this was another type of vehicle that I had never heard of.

'I put my car in third gear and never change it,' he grinned, pleased with his little joke, but little did he know that I thought it was great advice.

'I don't mind making a fool of myself,' I lied a little. 'It's better than driving one of those licence-less cars.'

I had learned about 'licence-less cars' from my neighbour, Rafa, after I had explained to him that the *tráfico* did not want to convert my licence. At first, I wasn't sure if I had heard him correctly.

'*Coche sin carnet?*' I repeated his Spanish words, *a car without a licence*. It seemed too good to be true. *Why don't I get one of those?* I wondered why Robert, who is a petrolhead, had never mentioned this option to me.

But soon, my enthusiasm for the concept of a 'licence-less car' faded when I realised that I had indeed seen them on the road many times before. They were tiny automobiles, ugly in shape and design, and often brightly coloured. But most importantly, they were driven predominantly by two types of drivers: oblivious-to-the-world-around-them-nonagenarians-with-Coke-bottle-spectacles (and ear trumpets) or raging alcoholics who had long lost their right to be on the road. Since these cars were two-seaters and could only reach a top speed of 45 kilometres per hour, or twenty-eight miles per hour, the harm they posed to other drivers was relatively small.

This must have been the excuse given by whatever authority had permitted their presence on the road. As if the option of being taken for a chronically drunk grandma wasn't enough of a deterrent to buying a licence-less car, the other obstacle was their price. In my initial excitement about the vehicle, I looked up its value online and quickly closed the window. The five-figure price tag was exorbitant for what, in reality, was a moped with a plastic tent around it. I decided to wait for my shiny new Polish licence to arrive.

As I stopped the car at the top of the hill, I saw Sarah's house at the bottom, and I contemplated for a few minutes whether I should drive down the valley and continue along the *barranco* or park somewhere by the road and walk to her cottage. The dirt track leading down to the dry river bed was particularly steep, and as far as my basic understanding of geology went, once I went down the ravine, I'd have to drive back up and stop on the steep incline before joining the main road. But soon, the decision was made for me, as a car stopped immediately behind me and waited patiently for me to continue down the slope. I couldn't turn back now, so I continued on the unpaved road until I saw Sarah's cottage. It has two formidable cypresses guarding the front of the house and a magnificent weeping willow in the garden.

As I approached the house, I saw Sarah walk down her driveway towards me, gesticulating towards where I should park the car. Because the car took up most of the lane, there was not much room to manoeuvre it, and inevitably, I ended up crashing gently into the white brick wall surrounding her property.

'Don't worry about that,' I heard Sarah say as I disembarked.

We were both standing in front of the car, assessing the damage. The bumper had a tiny scratch, and the wall was missing a chunk of plaster.

'I'm so sorry,' I apologised, and for the gazillionth time this spring, explained my aversion to manual gearboxes.

'I was planning to touch this wall up anyway,' she said as if it were normal for guests to crash land outside her cottage. But in truth, she must have been annoyed because she reminded me of this incident for years to come whenever she could fabricate a reason to do so.

As we approached the house entrance, I was greeted by cascades of red and pink geraniums carefully positioned all around the front door, hanging in flower baskets, and a row of splendid flowering yuccas. But what really attracted my attention was the colourful mural on the side wall. It depicted a sleepy white village street scene showing houses with winding entrance stairs and blue window shutters.

'This is lovely. Did you paint this?'

'I'm glad you like it. I copied it from a book. I'll show you. I was a bit tired of looking at the olives and the wheat fields whenever I sat on the patio.'

The mural was a valiant attempt at *trompe-l'œil*, a trick of the eye. It wasn't perfect, but from the right viewing angle, one might think there was a small village immediately behind Sarah's cottage.

'Are you an artist?'

'No, I just paint a little. Since James passed away, I've been trying to keep myself busy. It's something to do. It was my husband who was the artist. I'll show you.'

From the patio, we entered a small rustic kitchen decorated with dark wooden railway sleepers, hand-painted tiles, and James' fabulous artwork. The house tour took over an hour as Sarah explained the significance of each work of art. Her home was a box of treasures. The cosy living room was a bohemian paradise, with paintings from wall to ceiling, more *trompe-l'œil* murals, pottery pieces, and handicrafts from various parts of Spain.

James' paintings, which decorated the walls, were of world-class quality. They could be best described as 'cubist-expressionist' and could easily feature in any art gallery in New York or London — that is to say, places where people have a lot of disposable income to pay for quality art. Admittedly, they were not exactly my cup of tea, the same way Picasso does not speak to my heart. But even an amateur like myself could see that these were works of a troubled soul with an eccentric's eye for the nuances inherent in everyday social interactions and with the masterful ability to capture these on two-dimensional canvases.

I was grateful to see that James' art was actually proper art because I had been worried before my visit that I'd have to lie to his widow from the start of our acquaintance and then probably keep lying about it for years to come. It had only been a week earlier when I visited Trish's house to drop off some guest bedsheets for ironing when she told me she wanted to show me something.

'I know you love art. I have something you might like.'

I followed her to what looked like her home office.

'What do you think?' she pointed to a painting over the desk. 'I got it at a flea market in Wales when I was young. It's been with us for many years.'

I suddenly felt like an unwilling host at the *Antiques Roadshow* — just like many people who bring trash from grandma's attic to the experts in the show — Trish stood there expecting me to gasp in admiration for this purported work of art. I wasn't sure what she wanted me to say about the painting. Perhaps it was a long-lost Rembrandt or a Gainsborough.

'I like the Jack Russell,' I pointed at the little dog in the picture. 'He's very lively.'

This painting included everything I hated in amateur art. One did not need to be an art connoisseur to see that the painting was trash. My eyes hurt just looking at it. It depicted a horse gauchely leaning in to kiss (or sniff) a small terrier dog. Both animals were situated in a meadow by a lake with stylised pine trees in the background. It was a very detailed depiction of an improbable scene of cross-species friendship.

The meadow and the lake did not make any sense to me since horses and Jack Russells usually frequent barns or are accompanied by people. And finally, the piece depicted pine trees, my least favourite subject in the visual arts. The execution was somewhat correct, but it had no soul, no intriguing brushstrokes, no depth, no love, no light, or colour. It was dull and a senseless waste of the paint that was used.

Real art emanates from the artist's heart; it lives with you and inspires you. It allows you to see deep into your own soul. This type of living room décor makes you want to abandon all hope. But how can you tell the owner of a dull piece of kitsch that you hate it so much that you wish you were blind? I mumbled some fake compliments and wished her good luck trying to sell it online, as this was something she was planning on doing. I could not really evaluate this piece, I told her. Perhaps it was priceless.

After this experience with 'the horsey and the doggy on the lakeshore', I was worried that I would have to repeat the charade of lying and pretending to be amazed by the artist's work. But instead, I was taken aback by how good James' art was. While his work was excellent, I still preferred Sarah's art. After decades of being the artist's wife and muse, some of his skills must have rubbed off on her via some form of artistic osmosis. In the years after her life partner's death, she had covered almost every inch of the house with colourful artwork, including colourful patterns and designs on every cushion, curtain, and blanket, exquisite *art nouveau* murals, and copies of famous expressionist and naïve paintings.

'I usually select one of James' art books and copy a painting that I like,' she said, not realising how good her copies were and perhaps, in some sense, better than the originals.

'This picture is one of my favourites,' she pointed at what looked like one of James' canvasses. 'I had to touch it up because when James got dementia, he would walk around the house destroying his paintings. He smeared some blue paint all over this one. I cleaned it up and redid the faces, but it was never the same.'

The small painting depicted four people sitting on a sofa in a living room; a mother, a father, and two children — two boys with messy red hair. The spots that Sarah had retouched were evident; the faces were somewhat distorted, and the skin tone did not precisely match that of the arms and legs.

'We were a lovely little family,' she said. 'My little boys were so good. We travelled in a caravan around Europe and lived in Ibiza. Then we moved to Cornwall.'

'Are they in England?' I asked.

'No, one of them lives in New York with his wife and a small daughter. He never comes here. The other one, Matthew, is a heroin addict. I've not heard from him in a year. I've reported him to the Salvation Army in case they find him. He lives on the streets,' Sarah presented this tragic chronicle of her family history matter-of-factly.

There was a pause in the conversation while I took in all this new information.

'Matthew has been on drugs since he was a teenager. He's almost fifty now. The last time we spoke, I said I would not send him any more money.'

I looked again at James' painting of his family — two parents on each side of the sofa protecting the little boys. Now the faces were mangled and blurred, almost grotesque. No matter how good an artist Sarah was herself, she could not replicate her husband's hand at capturing faces. I looked around at her treasure box of a home. Every surface was covered in colour and pattern that brought life to the rooms, the marks of a lonely woman re-living her life through art, making an intricate series of mementoes of who she once was. I had never been to Frida Kahlo's house, but I imagined it to be very much the same. Every blank wall would be filled with colour, emptiness conquered by pattern. It was a house of sorrow, the type of sorrow one needs to create true art.

As a child, you are surrounded by role models and people who might inspire you on your way. As an adult, it's not always easy to know which path to follow, especially if you isolate yourself from others through heartbreak and disappointment. I admired Sarah for not giving up on herself. Once a mother, a wife, a business owner and a traveller, she could have surrendered when these roles were no longer part of her identity. For some, it would have been time to wither away. But she didn't give in to this temptation; new adventures lay ahead.

Always out and about meeting people, open to new experiences, and learning new skills, she became my role model for life.

I was sure it was not what she had imagined on the day when her husband painted the family portrait forty years earlier. We all have high hopes in our middle age and can't fathom that illness or death will one day take our loved ones away from us. As I stood in front of the painting, still in my prime and filled with great expectations for the future, I was, after all, thirty years Sarah's junior, I wanted to learn from her to be ready for the inevitable.

TWO

BASIL FAWLTY AND A CHERRY THIEF

'We'd like to buy a leg of lamb and put it on a barbecue,' my guest, a friendly New Zealander called George, announced as I was sitting on my patio typing up an email. He had just returned from his morning jog to an abandoned cottage nearby.

George and his wife had recently retired and were doing 'the European tour', which meant they were spending several months in Europe, hopping from country to country to visit all the things they had ever wanted to see. During the Andalusian part of their sojourn, he had developed an appetite for chorizo and eggs in the morning and thick slices of sheep and goat cheese in the evening, washed down with bottles of *Syrah* which, according to his trim and sporty wife, was affecting his waist. Thus, every morning before he fried his chorizo, he was obliged to go for a long run among the olives while she dutifully did her yoga by the pool.

Their stay with me lasted almost three weeks, so it was inevitable that we had developed a semblance of a routine and a certain synergy in our day-to-day interactions. We'd take turns making a barbecue for each other and engage in long chats in the evening. I was pleasantly surprised that, for once, my choice of wine had not been snubbed and looked down at. It turned out that George and I had the same taste in wines. He loved my favourite *Syrah*, known in Australia as *Shiraz*, so much so that I had to dig an empty bottle out of the recycling box one morning so he could photograph the label before he went shopping at Mercadona.

While George was excellent company, a jovial and heart-on-his-sleeve type of person, I did not much care for his wife, Helen. She had a grimace meant to imitate a smile; the lower lip would stretch out, almost showing her back molars. Her dead eyes were typically fixed on an indiscernible point in the distance, and her elbows would be tucked in close to her body. It was a posture I had seen before on successful but incredibly insecure people. She never let go of the façade, constantly afraid she might stand out among other Europeans. The fear that someone would be able to detect from her mannerisms or speech that she was not from here, that she wasn't one of us, made her social interactions stilted and disingenuous.

George, on the other hand, did not seem to bother with what anyone thought.

'Here're some cherries for you,' he dropped a plastic bag of cherries on my patio table next to my laptop.

'That's nice. Thanks. Are they from the orchard?' I looked at him suspiciously.

I told him a day or so earlier that he should try the cherries in the nearby orchard during one of his morning runs, but I didn't expect him to fill shopping bags with the fruit.

'I brought another bag for us,' he chirped, pleased with his bounty.

I've groomed a scrumper, I thought to myself. *I have to go and offer to pay Pedro for his cherries.* I made a mental note.

It was one thing to take a handful or two as you walked past the orchard; that would be but a drop in the ocean. But scrumping two shopping bags of fruit and running away with it was a bit too close to stealing for my liking.

'Enjoy the cherries. I'm off to Montefrio for coffee.'

And off he went alone to spend the morning in a café on the main square in the shade of the round church, drinking coffee with anise, mixing with the old men, smelling their cigarettes and watching them play cards. If I had ever seen a foreigner take to Andalusia like a duck to water, it was George. He didn't even speak Spanish or smoke cigarettes, so I had no idea what he did on those mornings in Montefrio, but he clearly had fun. So, I was slightly startled when he announced his need for a leg of lamb, a cut of meat not very common in our province.

He must be feeling homesick, I thought. But then thought again. *It was Helen who was homesick.*

'You can get lamb chops in a supermarket,' I told him when he asked where to buy lamb. 'There are some frozen lamb legs, but they are much smaller than you might be used to.'

I knew for a fact that they were much smaller. During our days in the Emirates, we used to eat New Zealand lamb all the time. The lamb from New Zealand is fatter, juicer, and definitely bigger than the Andalusian variety. Also, the way lamb chops are cut in the two countries is drastically different. The lamb chops that most English, Australians, and New Zealanders are used to are relatively thick. They are usually served rare or medium-rare. Andalusian butchers cut their lamb chops so thin they end up being almost transparent. They are cooked quickly and are usually more crispy on the edges than juicy. I was sure the wafer-thin lamb chops we barbecue in southern Spain would only disappoint George and Helen.

'Perhaps you should go to the butcher's and ask them to cut the chops the way you like them. They might also have a fresh leg of lamb,' I suggested, even though I doubted that a butcher in Montefrio would have a leg of lamb for sale.

They returned that afternoon pleased with themselves and eager to share their triumphs with me.

'We got a leg of lamb in Montefrio!' Helen was very jolly. 'It was the last one, I think.'

Or the only one, I thought. *How strange that a butcher in Montefrio would have a fresh leg of lamb. It's not a popular piece of meat.*

'It was forty euros,' George blurted out.

I almost fell off my chair. *They saw you coming*, I wanted to say, but I didn't want the whole thing to turn into ashes in their mouths, so instead, I congratulated them.

'You were very fortunate.' I said. 'I don't think I have ever seen a fresh leg of lamb for sale around here.'

'Oh no,' Helen clarified. 'It's frozen. So, we can't have it tonight, but I'll prep it for a barbecue tomorrow. I'll cut the bone out for Bobby — would he like that?'

On hearing his name, Bobs stood up from underneath the patio table and started to wag his docked tail, expecting something good to come his way. He was being spoiled rotten by George, who usually shared his chorizo breakfast feast with him. That spring, Bobby had developed a habit of rotating between the two guest apartments every morning and scavenging for food. As a result, his previously athletic Bodeguero frame had become comically rotund, and he looked as if he was in the middle of a transformation into an English bulldog. I had just loosened his collar a few days prior to this conversation, which was a sure sign that we needed to reduce the number of meals he ate. Between his own food and the treats he managed to beg from kind-hearted visitors, he was eating for a Labrador, not a terrier-sized dog.

'I'm sure he'd love a lamb bone,' I assured Helen that Bobby's culinary preference need not be considered. *He snacks on his own poo*, I might have added to clarify that our Bobby was no Gordon Ramsey when it came to what he put in his mouth. In Bobby's defence, his coprophagy was not a persistent habit.

'We'd love you to join us,' Helen was bubbly and not her usual mannequin-like-self.

'Yes, of course, I'd love to try lamb cooked by New Zealanders.' It was a genuine comment. I promised myself never to tell this lovely couple that they had been ripped off and that they could have bought the same frozen leg of lamb at the supermarket for a third of the price. However, it bothered me that the shopkeeper where they had bought the meat would so blatantly steal money from innocent tourists. This small injustice made me incredibly angry, so I swore never to shop there.

'By the way,' I said as they were leaving to go back to their apartment. 'Can you move your car away from the driveway because I have a water truck coming in tomorrow morning at around ten o'clock? It may be a bit noisy, too, for thirty minutes. I'm sorry about that.'

Two weeks earlier, when I was still wearing my plaster cast, I realised that our well was dry once again. It was only the middle of May, so it hadn't occurred to me that we might not have any water in the well. When the well pump refused to start, I called our electrician. The poor guy spent a good half an hour checking the electrical connections, the voltage, and the fuse box, all the while scratching his head and talking to another electrician loudly on his phone. Until that is, he decided to look at the submerged element of the pump itself.

As soon as he opened the well lid, the case was solved. The well was dry, so the water pump would not start. I could not believe my eyes. For the previous two years, we had been able to use it until the end of July. We were only in mid-May. Perhaps, since I had been away for February and most of March, I did not realise how little it had rained. It was now the third year of the drought, which meant that the little rain that had fallen during the winter was insufficient to properly saturate the ground and replenish the groundwater levels.

I apologised profusely for wasting the electrician's time. He didn't charge me for his time since we were old customers, and he had rewired the whole house during its renovation.

'No problem. Recommend me to your friends,' he said as he drove away in his Ford Fiesta.

I went back to the house to check how much water was left in the white tank. There was enough for a week for one person with minimal laundry, and only if flushing the toilet was regulated by the 'yellow-mellow rule'. I then checked the giant reservoir that was supposed to be replenished by the rain. There were maybe twenty thousand litres left in that tank. That was something, but I was confident it would not last a whole summer season with guests. I topped up the white tank, so I would not have to worry about the immediate water supply and went back to the drawing board.

I had spent days thinking of what to do. I didn't want to cancel all the guest reservations. We now had a good number of excellent reviews from our first season, so summer bookings were coming in regularly, and guests were more confident to book longer stays. While deep in thought about the essence of life, I noticed that the swimming pool was getting cloudier by the day. I needed help, but I had a snowball's chance in Hell of finding someone willing to come to my cottage in the middle of nowhere.

By then, I had a long list of plumbing and other pool- and water-related problems that needed expert advice, so the cloudy pool was the last straw. I wrote down what I wanted to sort out and ventured into Alcalá to find a plumber. As I rolled up and down the hills in third gear at a moderate speed, letting everyone overtake me, the thought dawned on me that I should have prepared my list in Spanish. Now I would have to Google translate everything on the spot and look for pictures online to explain what I needed.

It was too late to return home, so I rehearsed the few plumbing-related words I knew while following slowly behind a tractor. As soon as I arrived on the outskirts of Alcalá, I turned right to go to the industrial area where one can find all sorts of trades, hardware stores, and repair shops all in one location. Unlike the town centre, which consists of narrow, steep streets often ending on a steep hill, the industrial area has only two gentle hills.

Inevitably, I stalled the car on the second hill and had to wave several truck drivers to pass me while I regained my composure and restarted the car. Coming to terms with the fact that I might soon stall the engine again, I parked the car at the first empty parking spot and went to a shop I had seen on one of our errands here. A display of robot pool cleaners and filters drew me to this particular establishment. Once I stepped over the threshold, I entered a world that was unfamiliar to me — a plumber's Narnia.

With my limited vocabulary, I could identify a mountain of 'pipes', but a plumber would see adaptors, barbs, couplings, crosses, double-tapped bushings, elbows, nipples, reducers, tees, valves, wyes, unions, plugs, and caps. In short, I didn't know what I was looking at, or looking for, but I was sure I was in the right place. The owner of the business, Fran, was a patient and thoughtful man. Somehow, from my amateurish drawings and limited plumbing vocabulary, he understood that I needed to transfer water from the giant tank behind the house to the smaller one that fed the house. He spent a good half an hour devising a system for me, glueing different connections and fitting them to a flexible pipe.

Once this was out of the way, I explained that my pool was starting to look 'like milk'.

'When was the last time you changed the filter?' he asked.

He might as well have spoken Mandarin because I had no idea what he was talking about, which, in hindsight, was quite shocking considering that we had been 'mostly' happy pool owners for almost three years at that time.

'You filter?' he looked at me quizzically.

'This thing?' I had no idea what he was on about, so I pointed to a metal barrel similar to the one we had in our pool pump room. I saw the price tag and was starting to feel dizzy. *How much is THIS going to cost?*

'This is not a filter?' he looked at me curiously.

Aha, I thought to myself. I would have sworn on my pets' lives that this was a filter.

'What is a filter?' I was looking at Fran for some clues or an explanation.

He read my mind.

'This one is just a container. You put a filter inside it.'

I was nodding and taking notes in my head. *How come I didn't know this?*

'What kind of filter do you have in your pool?' this was starting to resemble the Spanish Inquisition. He was asking me questions to which I had no answers.

'A normal one,' I went with what I imagined to be an uncontroversial response.

'What do you mean by 'normal'?'

Why don't I sign my confession already so we can finish this torture, please? I was about to say. *I'd prefer to be drowned, but being set on fire in front of a gaping crowd sounds good too. I'll sign anything as long as we no longer have to discuss the depths of my ignorance.*

'Is it sand, fibre, or glass?' he was turning the screw.

'To be honest, I have no idea,' I surrendered.

'Don't worry. I can come to check the pool filtration system and see how to fix it.'

I explained to him that I had a few other plumbing issues that I'd like him to have a look at since he was going to pay us a visit. All the time, I was eyeing the pool robot on display. I looked at the box it had been taken out of. There were photos of a pristine pool with crystal-clear water. The people by the pool, dressed in prim yachting-style clothes, were blissfully busy doing absolutely nothing. They were overtly happy — not a worry at all in their white-polo-shirt-and-blue-deck-shoes world.

The other people in the pictures were swimming in the cleanest of pools with no algae to cloud the water or any dead flies to decorate the bottom of the pool. I wanted that robot so much that I went home determined to convince Robert that our lives were worth nothing unless we got a Maytronics Dolphin M 700 Premier Robotic Pool Cleaner with Powerful Dual Scrubbing Brushes and Multiple Filter Options, including the Doppler 4000 should you end up at the bottom of the pool with heart palpitations.

Fran arrived a few days later in his plumber's van, which, just like his shop, was filled to the brim with thingamabobs, whatsits, and doodahs, but I also spotted some other items I didn't know the name of. To save him a lot of head-scratching, I showed him what I meant by the milky pool. I went to the pump room, turned the pool pump on with the 'filter' setting selected, and returned to the pool. Sure as eggs is eggs, the jets in the pool spouted an unsavoury milky-coloured liquid. The bottom of the pool was also a disgrace; it was covered in a layer of fine mud. I looked to Fran, hoping he knew how to fix the mess.

'Can you see it?' I asked a rhetorical question.

'Your filter needs changing. It's not cleaning the water.'

He then educated me for a good quarter of an hour on the various filters I could choose from. He did not seem to have a high opinion of sand filters, and from his tone of voice, I deduced that only a complete imbecile would choose that option. I looked at the state of my pool and decided to save the last grain of my dignity in the eyes of the pool maintenance expert.

'You're right,' I agreed as if we were discussing a topic I had often pondered. 'Sand does sound like a waste of time and money.'

'*Eso*,' he was pleased that I was getting his drift.

Eso is a demonstrative pronoun which means 'this' or 'it'. It has a somewhat nebulous meaning, but the way Fran used it meant 'that's right'. But the word signals something a little more than mere agreement. It carries an approving undertone as if the speaker has praised you for being so clever in understanding their complex argument, even though they had to drum it into your thick skull for the last half an hour.

Once I heard this word, I could not resist using it whenever I saw an opportunity. There were few occasions on which I could lecture about anything in Spanish, and even fewer when my listeners agreed with me wholeheartedly. But on those once-in-a-blue-moon situations, I had my *eso* ready. It was a human equivalent of 'good boy' or 'good girl'; that is to say, it was exquisitely patronising if uttered with the right tone of voice but not at all snobbish.

As Fran was dishing out his praise for my timely astuteness, I realised that in my desire to receive his next *eso*, I would soon agree to install the most expensive option, namely the glass filter material.

'Can you tell me more about the fibre filter?' I had to take control of the situation before the final bill became astronomical.

The day before, Robert had agreed that a pool robot was essential to our future life together. As I was describing to him all the tools and machines I had seen at the pool shop, he suggested that I also order a summer pool cover to conserve the pool water, which would evaporate seemingly in front of our very eyes during the hot summer months. With these two items added to Fran's bill, I did not think we could afford the Holy Grail of filters, namely, the glass filter.

Once Fran and I had agreed that a fibre filter was the second-best option for our pool, I directed him down to the tiny pump room underneath the swimming pool. Before I could warn him, Fran went down the steps and inevitably smacked his head on the low door frame. I was certain that this event didn't put him in the most jubilant of moods. I stayed outside because there was not enough space in the pump room for two people.

After watching Fran for a good twenty minutes fighting with the filter container's lid as he tried to get it open — we discovered that Robert and I had lost the unique key that opens it — and going back and forth to the van to get various tools to manufacture a home-made version of the key, it occurred to me that this job would have taken Robert and me a whole day of bickering and arguing, and several trips to the plumber's shop to ask for help, advice, and to purchase specialised tools. I was also confident that we would never have managed to close the filter box again without it leaking. As I watched poor Fran walk up and down from the pump room to his van and lose his body weight in sweat while working in the claustrophobic conditions, I congratulated myself that, for once, we were having the job done by someone else instead of trying to do it ourselves.

'This filter of yours is as good as nothing,' I heard Fran shout out from the dingy room below the pool. 'The sand has turned rock hard. It should have been changed two years ago.'

Watching him work so hard changed my outlook on life, at least for the moment. I became very congenial and was stripped of my usual compulsion to roll my eyes. I nodded in agreement with everything he said but then realised he could not see me from the tiny den he was labouring in. So, instead, I shouted out some words in broken Spanish to give him the incentive to persevere.

'You work good!'

'Well job!'

Had I spoken in complete sentences, I might have been able to express my ideas grammatically, but I wanted to sound casual, as if I were fluent in vernacular Spanish. As a result, I sounded like a broken Google translation machine.

'You job really good!'

'Good done!'

While I was racking my brain to remember what else one might say to cheer on someone doing work, I heard Fran ask for a glass of water. It was time for me to shut up and let the man do his job — and a dirty job it was too. First, he scooped out a bucketful of slimy mud that had settled on the top of the filter. Once he had completed that task, he removed the whole metal container from the pump room, turned it upside down, and shook it vigorously. He hoped that shaking the container would loosen up the sedimentary rock that had formed inside. But it didn't work. He had to chisel it all out in pieces and then scrape the bottom of the container clean. If it were me who was doing the work, I would have become disheartened by now and would have probably set the job aside for another day. But to his credit, nothing broke Fran's spirit, neither the petrified filter nor my constant inane chattering in broken Spanish. He remained professional, and the smile did not slip from his face. Perhaps, to stay calm, he was calculating the final bill in his head, a trick I have often used when dealing with difficult customers.

Once the filter container had been cleaned, Fran took his lunch break and drove back to Alcalá to eat and to bring back the balls of fibre filter to replace the sand. When he returned in the afternoon, he seemed like a new man. Perhaps it was the lunch or some encouragement from his family that restored his faith in humanity. I can only imagine the stories he told his wife and kids at the lunch table. *Dumb as a rock* might have been a justifiable expression that he used. It was an accurate and fitting description of our pool maintenance practices.

'I'm surprised this pool has not gone green already,' he might have said while getting a second helping of fried fish. Little did he know about our previous battle with the cesspit we had created when we first moved into the house.

While Fran was (probably) venting to his family and cooling off after the battle with the rock-solid filter, I stood on the threshing area where he had been conducting the work and admired the coagulated mess of rock that once constituted our pool filter. It was a marvel how we had managed to keep the water reasonably clean over the last two years. Once he returned, inserting the fibre balls and reinstating the filter box inside the tiny pump room did not take him very long. As he was leaving, Fran caught a glimpse of the pool.

'You need to vacuum out the bottom, but put it on 'waste' so it does not go through the new filter,' he instructed me.

Once again, he was speaking in tongues. By now, he could read the ignorance and bewilderment on my face. He put away his tools in the van and returned to show me how to vacuum the pool so that the dirty water bypassed the filter and drained out into the potato patch behind the pool. In twenty minutes that afternoon, I learned more about pool maintenance and the significance of the different settings on the pump than I had during my first two years as a pool owner.

I wish I had known all this when we first moved in. But I also knew that if I had bothered to search for an article about it online, my eyes would have immediately glazed over and got bored one minute into my research. The art of pool maintenance is one of those things you must be shown how to do if the relevant information is to sink in. And it did. In two days, my pool was as sparkling and pristine as the one on the side of the Dolphin box. But while the Dolphin-box people could sit back and sip a glass of cava while the poor robot collected debris from the bottom of their pool, I had another worry. I was running out of water.

The trick Fran had shown me, to use the 'waste' setting on the filter box to get rid of the dirty water quickly, was pure genius. But it was only meant for extreme situations like ours. Admittedly, his method removed the algae and sand that were slowly settling at the bottom and didn't soil the new filter. However, the downside of this technique was that I had to work very quickly because, during the process, water was rapidly draining out of the pool in real-time. I had to do two waste cycles, and while the pool was crystal clear, the water level had dropped enormously. I had lost five or six thousand litres, and the pool's skimming function wouldn't work anymore. I needed to replenish the pool but did not want to use the little resource I had left in the tank. Before we opened our rural guest house, not having water was a problem that Robert and I had managed in various ways. But now, I had to solve it while welcoming and entertaining guests. My transformation into Basil Fawlty was swift. Running the remote guest house on my own, the jobs were piling up every day, from house maintenance, serving breakfasts, constant cleaning, running chores, washing laundry, killing weeds, and trimming hedges, to admin, marketing and responding to guest inquiries.

While George and Helen were a regular feature in my house in the second part of May, other tourists would come and go, leaving divots and dents on my mind that would stay with me forever. Like the middle-aged German woman in her hand-knit thick cardigan who knocked on my door on the morning of their check-out and handed me a plastic bag filled with what looked like hand-rolled cigarette ends. Taken by surprise, I accepted the curious gift and left it on the shelf next to the house keys while I waved them goodbye. On closer inspection, the bag's contents turned out to be a collection of marijuana butts. To this day, I wonder if this is a German custom that I have never heard of before. Did she think I wanted to recycle and smoke her roaches?

Or the English woman with a grey bob and metal-framed glasses who came knocking on my door well after 11 pm to tell me that there was no hot water in the kitchen and they couldn't finish doing the dishes. It takes a lot of patience to be a hotelier and refrain from letting customers know what is really on your mind when they drag you from your sofa late in the evening because of some minutiae.

Could these dishes not have waited until the morning? What kind of maniac are you?

You want to berate them, but then remember that they have their holiday brains on and have become entirely dependent on you for their basic needs and wants. So, I put on my best smile, got a torch, and went to inspect the water heater. Once I had replaced the batteries, the woman's life was complete again.

Only after they had left did I find out that they had 'cooked' a pizza in the frying pan. It seemed she had enough audacity to bother me in the middle of the night about a lack of hot water, but she forgot to mention that they had got cheese permanently stuck to the frying pan because they were too 'shy' to ask to use my oven to heat it.

The place is wonderful, but the kitchen is not well-equipped for a long stay. She wrote in her review. I couldn't agree more. I would not recommend my place to anyone planning to prepare a Thanksgiving dinner or a wedding buffet. She and her husband only stayed for one night, so I felt immensely grateful that she felt like warning other tourists of this possible downside.

THREE
THE SECOND YEAR OF DROUGHT

Between the odd behaviour of some of our guests and the constant fear of receiving a bad review, my days were spent fluffing up pillows on the sun loungers, continually removing leaves out of the pool, running the robot, fixing Wi-Fi problems, booking Alhambra tickets, researching fun things to see and do for my visitors, and checking whether there was enough water in the tank. It was during one of my tank inspections that a solution to the dry spell occurred to me. I couldn't believe why I had not thought of it before.

'I should call Santiago,' I informed Bobby, who was always shadowing me around the house.

Santiago was a man with a very deep borehole that never ran dry. I imagined that one very arid August afternoon, Santiago was sitting on his patio watching the farmers dragging their trailers with cubes of *aqua* from the municipal tap to their cottages when he realised he was sitting on a gold mine. He purchased a large truck that could carry ten thousand litres at a time, registered his business, and started driving up and down the steep hills of Montefrio, delivering H2O. His business model might seem straightforward, but driving that load on curvy mountain roads is not for the fainthearted. I wouldn't have called him out of the blue if he hadn't paid us a visit during our first year. His truck was quite long, and if I hadn't known, I would have assumed that he couldn't make the abrupt turn off from the dirt track up our driveway. But he did.

We first met a month or so into our renovation project three years earlier. The constant churning of the cement mixer to make a seemingly endless supply of cement meant that after a few weeks, our well was almost dry. Worried that not having water might stop the work on the new roof before the cold winter set in, we asked our English builder for some advice. At that stage of our relationship, we still trusted his judgement.

'I'll ask Manu to call Santiago to bring water for the well,' he told us.

It should have been a warning sign that, after living for a decade in Spain, our builder still could not make a simple phone call to order a truck of water. But we had so many other concerns in those days that we overlooked the writing on the wall.

Manu was one of the unskilled labourers from Montefrio who worked as a helping hand during the olive picking season in the winter. In the summer and early autumn, he helped out on building sites by mixing cement, cleaning, and doing a little bit of everything. So, on the advice of a man from Birmingham who lived in the village and never had to worry about his tap running dry and a young man, a boy really, who lived with his mother and pregnant girlfriend and did not seem to have any responsibilities in life, we ordered ten thousand litres to pour into our drying well.

When the water truck arrived, both Robert and I were grinning like two Cheshire cats who had found the fountain of youth. I handed Santiago a hundred euros, and he set up the pipes to transport the liquid from the tank on the back of the truck. It did not take very long for it to flow from the truck into the well. We waved Santiago goodbye and congratulated ourselves on a job well done.

'I don't understand what everyone here is complaining about,' I observed. Previously, we had to purchase a trailer and a plastic cube to bring it to the building site almost daily.

'Why don't they just order it? It's not that expensive,' I said smugly.

As the water delivery truck disappeared around the corner, I saw Pepe come down the driveway towards us. He was in a hurry and somewhat breathless.

'What was the truck doing here?' he asked.

You missed the action, I thought to myself, knowing how much Andalusian men like to watch work being done. I thought he was curious about the truck and explained to him what we had been doing just a few minutes earlier.

'But the water is just going to disappear,' he looked at us as if we were the thickest creatures on earth.

'How so?' I could see in his eyes that his estimation of us was dropping rapidly.

'The earth is dry,' he was now explaining basic geology to primary school kids. 'It is so dry; it will suck it all up.' He made some slurping sounds in case we could not understand the Spanish word for *sucking*. 'It will be gone before the morning.'

I was not impressed by this Andalusian Cassandra and shook my head sceptically. Robert, on the other hand, was getting a little frustrated — he had just literally thrown his money into the mud. We thanked Pepe for his concern and explained that our builders had suggested that we dump the water into the well.

'Yes,' Pepe was speaking to little children again. 'If your well is sealed in some way. If it's an underground tank, yes. But yours is a basic well in the ground. The water will be gone soon.'

Not convinced by his pessimistic outlook, I opened the lid on the top of the well, looked in, and saw that the well was full.

'He's talking rubbish,' I told Robert as we strolled back home. 'It will be fine.'

By the morning, all the liquid that Santiago had put in the well had disappeared. The parched soil had absorbed it, and the water level was as low as it was before the delivery. Since then, I had almost forgotten that Santiago existed. We had no use for his services because we had no place to store the water he could deliver. But now, with a newly built eighty-thousand-litre tank behind the house, we were playing a different game. I called him and ordered two truckloads.

It was evident from the speed and conviction with which Santiago set up the pipes and his small petrol water pump that it was not the first time he had done this job. While we waited in the shade of the fig tree for the truck to empty, he told me how busy he had been for the last two years. With the drought worsening every year, he was expecting a hectic summer. I was happy for him — a borehole and a water truck were significant investments, and his business relied on unpredictable weather. Once the first ten thousand litres had been pumped up into the tank, he went home for another load. A few hours later, I had enough of the precious stuff for another month, if not two.

'Could you bring one more load to top up the pool?' I realised that, instead of me transferring water from the tank to the pool, I could have him drop ten thousand litres directly into the pool to top it up, which he did.

After his third trip, I arranged with him to come once a month with two loads. As I watched the back of his truck, I was again grinning like a conniving Cheshire cat, but this time I had good reason to feel smug. I felt that our worries were over. It gave me a deep sense of relief. We'd struggled with not having any water in the well since the first year we moved in. It had been a constant worry. It is one thing to have only a little water for yourself — we can all make adjustments and change our habits — but we could not run a guest house without it.

As soon as Santiago left, George and Helen came down from their apartment with their leg of lamb all prepped for a barbecue dinner. I got a bottle of *Syrah* out and put George's favourite potatoes in the oven — smothered in our olive oil and homegrown rosemary and garlic.

It had been a very long year for me. The previous September, when Robert left for Oman, I used to sit alone on the patio, drying grapes and trying to fill the void by making lists of things to do. Now the lists were gone. I didn't need them. On any given day, there were twenty or so jobs to do inside and outside the house. I had suffered my first-ever fracture and made my first-ever visit to the hospital as an emergency patient. These could count as personal milestones.

I had made new friends and managed to calm the inner voices of doubt that often distracted me. I had even got my driving licence — it finally arrived at the post office, and the postman had even sent me a private WhatsApp message to celebrate. I did not have to ask friends and neighbours for favours anymore, but it was good to know that there was a safety net — people whom I could rely on.

When you start your life from scratch in a new place, it is easy to focus on the material things: getting the house done, fixing your garden, and buying a car. But what are they worth if there are no people around you to share them with? Being a freshly-minted immigrant can be a lonely time. And while I loved all the new people I had met, and some of the guests were quite entertaining, I started feeling isolated again. I owned a nice house, but it was not a home, not yet.

FOUR
BACK HOME

'Why is Bobby so fat?' were the first words Robert uttered when he exited Keith's car on his return home. Unaware of the rude comment, Bobby was jumping up and down like a circus dog, not believing his luck that his favourite master was home.

'Now that you're back, you can take him for long walks,' I suggested.

One might imagine that after being away from home for over six months, Robert would want to sit down and relax and absorb the view of the olive trees and the peace and quiet of the surroundings. Instead, he set off on an inspection tour — being the headmaster must have clearly gone to his head. He checked the new outbuilding behind the house, the replastered tool room, the new gutters, the water level in both tanks, the new pipe connections on the tanks, the swimming pool, and the vegetable garden. Nothing seemed to have been done to his imaginary high standards, so I decided it was time for a brief separation before we got into a heated debate. I left him and Bobby alone in the garden, digging potatoes for lunch.

A few hours later, after he had leisurely consumed a plate of baby potatoes with dill, some barbecued pork chops, and a cold beer, his outlook on life changed a little, and we were able to discuss a plan for the summer months in a civilised way. Neither of us felt like doing any house renovations in July and August. Besides the heat, such work would have been tricky to manage between guest bookings. I suggested that we focus on getting an automatic car for me so that I could cruise around stress-free when Robert returned to Oman in September. In theory, it was a perfect task for Robert, who is a bit of a petrolhead and considers watching videos about cars to be both a hobby and valuable research. I expected him to take on the task with some degree of enthusiasm and find us a good vehicle soon. But was I wrong?

It became evident that watching an endless stream of videos of strangers driving unattainable supercars on YouTube had not adequately prepared Robert for the time when he had to decide which car to buy for his own family. At first, I hoped I would be able to leave finding a car to him and would only have to give my input just before the purchase. But I was wrong. After the first three days of scouring the internet, he came up with a twenty-year-old Toyota Corolla in Barcelona, an ancient Mercedes station wagon in Santander, and another ancient Toyota outside Madrid.

'How are you going to inspect these cars?' was my first question after he presented me with his findings. 'It's a grand tour of Spain. Are there no second-hand cars in Granada or Malaga?'

'Why don't *you* try and find a car?' he was indignant.

I shook my head vigorously, subtly indicating *Do I have to do everything myself?* And sat down to work. After two hours of frantic internet research, my head was spinning. Coincidentally, I found the same old station wagon Merc that he did. I couldn't even find the Toyotas.

'I think they've sold the Toyotas already,' I told him as I went to the fridge to get a beer.

'Get me one too, please,' he was searching car-selling websites on another laptop.

A few days later, we were running out of ideas. We visited all the second-hand car dealers in Granada and nearby. But no matter how long we searched and how many cold beers we consumed in the process, it seemed that no reasonable second-hand cars were available in our mediocre price range. Robert even made a trip with our builder, Dani, to Ciudad Real to view an old four-by-four, which proved to be a complete waste of time.

'I wish we had grabbed that Corolla that was for sale in Barcelona,' Robert was getting desperate.

'We should have, but I don't understand how a twenty-year-old Corolla can cost eight thousand euros. That's too much. It's a student car.'

I could not apprehend why no decent second-hand cars were available for less than ten or eight thousand euros.

'It's because you want an automatic.'

This strict selection criterion had narrowed our search results significantly.

'Look at this,' Robert was showing me a website. 'BJ Cars imports cars from Belgium and Germany.'

A week or so into our search, he came across a website with second-hand cars that seemed priced within our range.

'They're in Malaga.'

The next day, we set off to Malaga to find a car for me. I hoped that after all the hours we had spent online visiting various local garages and dealers, our luck would be bound to change for the better.

When we arrived at the address listed on the website, BJ Cars was closed. The shutters and doors were locked down, and we could not even see inside the showroom. I called the number on the sign and was told that someone would arrive soon to assist us. I emphasised the fact that we had travelled from another province to view their cars. We had a couple of vehicles shortlisted, and while we waited for someone to open the shop, we sat in our car in the empty parking lot and discussed the pros and cons of each car on the list.

Twenty or so minutes later, two young men in tatty jeans and T-shirts arrived and began the somewhat complicated procedure of opening up the shop for us. They were certainly not in charge of the establishment because — unlike every other second-hand car salesperson we had previously met — they had nothing to say to us. So, we waited in silence for the grand reveal. Once all the shutters had been raised and the lights switched on, we were confronted with a motley collection of vehicles.

I know first-hand from my experience of staging photos for our guest house that photography can be deceptive. A clever angle, good lighting, and some delicate touches can suggest things to the viewer that are not actually in the photo. It's because our mind works by association rather than cold facts. We tend to focus on implied connotations based on our ideas and beliefs about the world while failing to see hard reality. Our attention focuses on what we wish was there. That, in short, was exactly what had happened to Robert and me when we visited BJ Cars.

The lights switched on, and *ta-dah!* We were presented with a pile of broken clunkers, most of which seemed to have been involved in a terrible accident on the autobahn somewhere between Berlin and Antwerp. The random way in which all the vehicles were arranged inside the 'showroom' suggested that some twisted mind had tried to reconstruct the horrific accident in which they were all involved, minus the bodies, thankfully. This was a case for the FBI's Serious Traffic Crimes Unit. But since we had insisted that the showroom be opened for us, it was only polite that we inspected the automobiles we had identified online.

I showed one of the men the photo of the first car that we had driven for two hours to inspect. He sighed loudly. The car in question was in the middle of the massive automotive Jenga tower they had created inside. We watched both men gently manoeuvre several cars to the side to make a narrow pathway between the collection of wrecks for us to access the specific vehicles that we had come to 'inspect'.

There was no mention of the near impossibility of taking any of these cars for a test drive. To do that, all the drivable vehicles would have to be taken out onto the street.

Even though I already knew we would not make an offer on any of the cars in this showroom, I thought it was only polite to at least quickly sit in two or three of them and pretend that we were discussing a potential purchase. Since the cars we saw online had lost their allure once we saw them in real life, the charade of pretending to be interested in them took all our acting skills. Robert opened the driver's side door, peeked inside, saw how utterly filthy the interior was and turned to me with a wry smile.

'Why don't you sit inside?' he invited me. 'You will be driving it most of the time.'

I gave him a look that promised him a great deal of pain and suffering once we were done 'inspecting' these clunkers. As I sat behind the sticky wheel, all I could think of was the dead skin, stale sweat, and piles of boogers that were inevitably hiding in the seat covers and the dashboard. The car's interior was rank with old sweat and cigarettes that had penetrated the scuffed and faded leather inside the car. I was never going to buy it. It would not be difficult for me to identify a list of this car's failings, all of which suggested to me the image of a down-on-his-luck mafia boss who had lost his place in the hierarchy and was doomed to drive this shambolic car, a symbol of his long-lost strength.

'This is a bully car,' I informed Robert.

'What do you mean?'

'It's a black Merc with black leather seats,' I thought I was being obvious. 'Someone bought it when it was new to show off. It has a terrible vibe.'

While I sat in the driver's seat, Robert leaned in from the other side of the car.

'Check the compartments.'

I opened the storage box between the seats and almost fainted. There was an abandoned lip balm and a small black, greasy hair comb. I felt that I was going to gag and exited the car immediately. There is a thing about personal possessions: once orphaned by their owners, they lose their original importance and merely bring forth feelings of disgust. A lipstick in a loved one's handbag is adorable. Your grandmother's hairbrush resting on her mirror stand is full of affection and intimacy. But once the people are gone, the personal objects they leave behind become revolting.

An abandoned ChapStick in a second-hand car is just as horrifying as seeing your grandmother's make-up set after her funeral. It's the absence of the *signified* that is so terrifying. Once the essence is gone, what's left is an empty shell, words with no *signifiers*, objects without meaning. I had felt this sense of utter revulsion once before when my grandmother's coffin was open for display in front of her mourners to kiss her thick make-up and say goodbye. I never got up from my pew, even though I was the favourite grandchild.

Once we left BJ Cars, I felt too upset to view any more second-hand car shops. The whole project was looking relatively futile. It appeared that in September, when Robert would return to Oman to work, I'd be doomed to continue driving the manual four-by-four and be forced to plan each trip according to the number of hills on the way and the time of day. It was Stefan and Emma who saved the day.

Not long after our trip to Malaga, we arranged a big party for Robert's birthday. As a product of a boarding school education where things were pretty much as depicted in Pink Floyd's famous video clip — little boarding-school boys going, one-by-one, through a giant mincer to create agreeable members of society — Robert demands a huge party be organised in his honour every year. Whether it's on a balcony of a Warsaw flat, in the middle of a Småland forest, or in a yurt on the Mongolian steppes, we start planning months in advance. He has enough decency not to ask me about his party in January; that's when my birthday is — an event usually forgotten and never celebrated, but come February, he starts nagging me about who's coming to his birthday. While he was away, I started planning in April and told all his friends to reserve the date in their summer calendars.

At that party, I entertained our Belgian and Dutch friends with our stories from BJ Cars and our efforts to find a second-hand car.

'Why don't you buy a car in Germany,' Emma looked at me matter-of-factly.

'It would cost a lot of money to import it, wouldn't it?' I was intrigued by her suggestion.

'No,' Emma was a Dutch-Belgian and had a maths teacher's mode of delivery. That is, she would tell you the solution as concisely as possible and just stare at you from behind her glasses, patiently waiting for you to do the equation correctly in your head.

'It's because it's the European Union?' I guessed.

'Yeah,' she said with a sigh that suggested I should have come up with this answer sooner.

Thankfully, she soon gave up on the Socratic method of trying to elicit the correct answers from me and went back to the blackboard to explain how buying a car in one EU country and bringing it to another worked.

The next day, while we were cleaning up after the party, I conveyed all this new information to Robert. It piqued his interest, and by the time the evening was over, he was browsing German second-hand car websites as if they were written in his native language. Three days later, we had a car reserved for us in Aachen, Germany. It felt like we had swum through the dirty swamp of Spanish second-hand car dealers and entered a blue lagoon of German dealers. All the cars in the photos looked spotless — they depicted all the tiny details of each car, so there was no question of one being misled by the photos. The cars also came with customer protection guarantees issued by the government.

'It says here that if we find out after the purchase that the car has been involved in an accident, the dealer will be fined twenty thousand euros and will lose their licence,' Robert read one of the assurances to me.

'That sounds fine. Let's book the ticket,' there was no doubt in my mind that we were doing the right thing.

While I looked after the guests and the dog, Robert flew to Cologne, took a train to Aachen, and drove back to Spain in our new automatic car. It was for the best that I didn't accompany him. To start with, I'm a terrible negotiator. I would not have brought the price down like he did when he was face-to-face with the dealer. Secondly, I would have made it into a mini-holiday. I'd have stayed in nice hotels, visited Paris on the way back, and maybe even stayed there for a few nights. Robert chose the way of the Spartans.

We booked him into the cheapest hotel he could find by the train station in Aachen. It had a shared bathroom and a tiny sink in the room. I was certain men use that bedroom sink at night for other purposes than brushing their teeth. He ate some hearty meals cooked by the matron of the German hotel and spent his time in the company of some travelling salesmen.

Once the paperwork for the car was ready, Robert was on his way back to Spain but somehow lost his way and went around the Arc de Triomphe several times before finding his way towards Bordeaux. This is according to his account. For all I know, he might have been in Saint-Tropez when he realised he was going in the wrong direction. It took him two days to drive home, during which he ate once — one should never underestimate the Scottish gene. He stopped for a cup of coffee in the Basque region, where he was served a piece of pork belly crackling with a cup of coffee. It lasted him for the next twenty-four hours. He slept for five hours in an 'Ass Hotel' — he obviously mispronounced a French name — and left said establishment at three am to continue his epic journey.

'Why didn't you eat something after the Basque country?' I asked while listening to his tales of self-inflicted suffering.

'I thought I was close to Madrid, and from there, I'd be home very soon.'

'It's a nine-hour drive from the Basque Country to our house,' I had little patience for this martyrdom. I'd need Dr Freud himself to help me understand the reason and the rationale of such behaviour. But I was grateful that I finally had a vehicle I could comfortably drive up and down our Andalusian towns' steep and narrow streets, so I suggested we go on a little holiday.

'Why don't we register the car and then visit Mini-Hollywood?' I felt it was the right place to go after the events of the previous year.

FIVE
SEASIDE HOLIDAYS

'Why is there never any fresh fish on the coast?' I was huffing and puffing in annoyance.

'It was supposed to be a fishing village! Where is the fish?' I was arguing with myself while Robert was trailing behind. He had lost his will to live an hour earlier and was now non-responsive.

By that point in time, we had been walking the streets of Mojácar for two hours in search of fresh fish to eat. My private obsession has spoiled many a holiday evening, but when I go on a beach holiday, I insist on eating fresh fish.

'Where's the fish?' I was talking to myself while striding the narrow pavements of the holiday village. 'I really don't understand how difficult it is to get up in the morning, go to the harbour, buy fish from the fishermen, and then cook it in your restaurant.'

My uninformed opinion of how to run a seaside fish restaurant did not seem to interest my husband.

'Who wants to eat hamburgers and pizza by the sea?' I was asking rhetorical questions. Robert wasn't even listening.

Just an hour earlier, already defeated by the hunt for the elusive fresh fish, he had suggested we have pizza at a touristy fast-food restaurant instead. Families and couples of various nationalities, mostly European from the languages I could discern, were seated on white plastic chairs in front of wobbly tables covered by red checkered PVC tablecloths. The place was lively and busy, but I refused to go in.

'No, I didn't come to the coast to eat frozen pizza from a microwave,' I was adamant. I gave the establishment's patrons a dirty look from the sidewalk, and we continued our quest. I was purposefully disparaging the place. I had no idea if the pizza was frozen and reheated in a microwave oven. From what I knew, it could have been the best pizza outside of Florence. But it wasn't what I was after.

The year before, we had gone with my sister and her family to Calahonda — a small fishing village, now a modest tourist resort, not far from Motril. I chose the place because of the low price of the beach hotel. I noticed that when you travel as seven people, the price often dictates your destination. I set up the booking inquiry on the booking website within a price range that allowed us to stay at a beach hotel but also prevented us from returning home with massive debt. Because it was the end of September, the hotel where we stayed was already winding down for the winter, when it would be closed to guests. The price was perfect. It included breakfast, and the hotel was right on the beach. One thing that might explain the low price was that, unlike the beaches outside Malaga or Fuengirola, the beach at Calahonda consists of pebbles and stones.

For me, it was an advantage because it meant less sand in the hotel room. But my niece, who was three, and my nephew, who was four, could not comprehend such an abomination. They stood at the entrance to the 'beach' with their colourful buckets and spades, ready to make cakes and build sand castles, unable to grasp what was in front of their eyes. I could empathise with their disappointment. In one of my adolescent hitchhiking escapades through Europe, my two girlfriends and I ended up in Rome. After a day of admiring various feats of architecture and art, we were ready for a day at the beach. We consulted a map, found a place by the sea, and took a train there. Our time on the train flew by in excitement about a day by the Mediterranean Sea, but all our enthusiasm left us as soon as we saw the black sand that confronted us. It was like a cruel joke set up for three Eastern European girls whose expectations of a beach holiday on the Med were informed by glossy travel brochures. We kept brave faces and made the most of the day, but in all honesty, I did not enjoy myself.

Twenty years later, in Calahonda, I had a more mature perspective on life and calmly accepted the pebbled beach. Because of all the rocks and stones, the snorkelling there was great. Even though it was late September, the water was still warm and crystal clear, and there was a good variety of marine life to observe underwater. In anticipation of how mental I might get in the evening looking for the catch of the day to eat, Robert went out on his own during the day and scouted the nearby restaurants vis-á-vis his requirement — low price for the fish; and mine — that it be fresh from the sea.

As luck would have it, our hotel had a beach restaurant serving the catch of the day at a non-exorbitant price. To make sure that there was fish ready for us, Robert made a reservation, and all we had to do was walk downstairs from our room into a restaurant decorated with orchids and other tropical flowers and be served perfectly cooked cod with a bottle of wine. It did remind me a lot of Thailand, which might be why I was so fervently searching for the same experience a year later in Mojácar.

But after another hour of walking, I was a broken person too. I wished we had stayed at the touristy pizzeria. At least we wouldn't have been hungry and exhausted, and we would have had stories to discuss by eavesdropping on the other patrons' private conversations and judging their misbehaving children. One of the joys of being a childless couple is that on holiday, you can spend hours criticising other people's poor parenting skills with a great sense of superiority. No matter how tempting it was to return to the pizzeria, I would not surrender. We kept on walking. That is the power of being on holiday; you spoil your current one by trying to replicate the good times you had in the past.

I can't explain what made me think Mojácar was a small fishing village. It might have been the fact that it was our first time on the coast of Almería — one of the favourite summer destinations for Spaniards from inland Andalusia. My neighbour, Rafa, had told me stories of the incredible beauty of Cabo de Gata, a wild nature reserve on the coast between Almería city and Mojácar. Based on these stories, I imagined the whole Almería coast to be untouched by tourism and consumerism. I expected the villages near the pristine nature reserve to be genuine and unspoilt. But it was quite the opposite.

Instead of an idyllic fishing village, Mojácar — at least the part of the village that is located by the sea, not the other side which is in the mountains and looks very much like Montefrio or any other white village with a castle stuck on top of it — turned out to be full of hideous tourist resorts. I was struck by the endless rows of identical balconies, one on top of the other facing the sea. On our very long hike through the village, we saw hundreds of them — or at least it felt like it. They were cramped little spaces where one would have neighbours all around and be forced to listen to their inane conversations from neighbouring balconies; because when people partake in a seaside holiday, they often fail to modulate the volume of their voice. It must be the constant susurrus of the waves that prompts people to yell at each other all day long.

I knew this type of resort holiday all too well. I had been there before, searching for the elusive Mediterranean holiday experience with sandy beaches, palm trees, and cocktails. As soon as you unpack your suitcase after a long flight and decide to sit down on the terrace with a crime novel and a glass of wine, you are confronted by your neighbours. On the right, a bargain-loving Brit in the sun — stuck for hours in her deckchair, drinking conspicuously transparent sparkling drinks and doing sudokus. On the left, a couple of German sun-worshippers, now the colour of overcooked caramel, are lying on their sun loungers as if mummified and developing third-degree sunburn. You sigh at the company and enter your room to get a fresh drink. There, you discover that right above your bedroom, there is a family with two or more kids; it's difficult to estimate from the level of noise they make. They all seem to have been in some terrible accident at some stage in their lives because their wooden prosthetic legs hammer against the ceiling above you all day and late into the night.

'Never mind. I'll sit on the terrace anyway,' you try to convince yourself that the thumping does not bother you at all.

That's when you hear the emerging ruckus underneath your terrace. There, oblivious to everyone in the world and enjoying the communal pool as if it were part of a private villa, you find the staple of any Spanish coastal resort, the stag or hen party. During the course of the day, you learn a lot about the individual members of the gang because they shout joking insults at each other from the swimming pool on the ground floor to the terrace of their holiday apartment on the fourth. This way, everyone in that hotel wing is kept up to date on their comings and goings. You are regularly informed about their physical and mental well-being: who is wasted, who is about to pass out, and who is taking the mickey. It's enchanting.

'At least we're not staying in one of these places,' I pointed to Robert as we passed yet another resort hotel.

It was true. Ours was a small hotel run by a Spanish family. I booked it because their primary advertisement photo featured a sea view with the beach framed by lush pink bougainvillaea. There are but a few things in life that won't sell if you put a pink bougainvillaea next to it. As soon as I saw the delicate flowers against the backdrop of the blue sky, I was hooked and lured in. Living a thousand metres above sea level and surrounded by hills and mountains, I needed a change of scenery. Especially because the Andalusian countryside can look quite desolate in the summer — the landscape takes on various shades of yellow ochre. The once colourful wildflowers and tall green grasses become desiccated and serve as a reminder of how dry it is.

From the photo provided on the booking site, I imagined us walking out of the hotel directly onto the beach. And indeed, I could walk from the hotel to the beach. But to do so, I had to become a human Frogger to cross a very busy main road and then walk down a narrow street for another 200 metres. How the photographer had managed to capture the tiny sliver of the beach seen from the hotel car park was a mystery that I set out to solve as soon as we had finished checking in. I poured myself a glass of Sauvignon Blanc from our portable fridge and went outside to investigate. Like a female Columbo, I walked between cars and motorbikes for half an hour, bending over, kneeling and squinting my eyes, trying to find the exact angle from which the misleading photo was taken.

'I think they photoshopped it,' I informed Robert of my findings as I stepped on top of our portable fridge to access my side of the bed where my mobile phone was charging on a miniature bedside table.

The room itself was another triumph of photo editing. I had stayed in my share of tiny rooms, but this one was made for dolls. Once we had placed our luggage on the floor, there was no more space to walk inside the room. If someone were watching us from outside — which would have been impossible because the only window in the room faced a brick wall two feet away — they might have thought we were playing *the floor is lava*. The room was perfectly designed for this game.

I could easily retrieve my clothes from the wardrobe without getting out of bed. From there, I could hop on one of the suitcases and step directly onto the bathroom mat. From the bathroom, I was but a step away from leaving the room entirely and finding myself in the hotel lobby, which was carpeted. I'm lying when I say I could take my clothes out of the wardrobe without getting out of bed since the suitcases on the floor prevented the dinky wardrobe doors from opening.

Considering ourselves fully-grown hoteliers by now, we decided to while away the rest of the afternoon by reading the hotel's reviews online. If you're staying at a miserable place, like we were, perusing the reviews of fellow sufferers will quickly cheer you up. Nothing makes me feel better than reading other people's righteous indignation. Skimming through negative hotel reviews is even better if you're staying at a lovely place where you can't fault anything. I highly recommend going online and reading *their* bad reviews. You will be provided with hours of free entertainment and might even gain some insight into the petty side of humanity.

Once we finished reading all the negative comments about our hotel, we felt better and almost vindicated. We were not the only ones duped by the photo of the beach and the spacious-looking rooms with sea views. We then began to compare our own guest rooms to the one where we were staying.

'We're charging too little for our rooms,' Robert stated the obvious after seeing the prices of other tiny rooms advertised online in Mojácar.

'Yes, but we don't have a beach on our doorstep,' I explained.

'We could photoshop it.'

'Hmm...we could also photoshop Niagara Falls in the background whilst we were at it and the Taj Mahal in the front garden.'

After we had exchanged several more creative ideas on how to make the location of our guesthouse more appealing to international tourists, it was time to set off to find a place to eat. We never managed to find a fish restaurant that satisfied our expectations. We ended up eating nuts and chips and drinking wine on the beach. We both felt satisfied with the meal — me with the fact that we were not sitting in a fast-food eatery, and Robert was happy to be saving money by not eating overpriced fresh fish in the only place we found that served it. The restaurant in question provided white tablecloths but charged a small fortune for a bottle of wine that usually costs two euros fifty. The next day, we went to Mini Hollywood, which was only an hour's drive from the coast and the main reason we had come to this part of Almería.

Consider the feeling of *déjà vu* and being trapped inside a *simulacrum*. At Mini Hollywood, we experienced both such states of mind. While most of us experience *déjà vu* now and again, being immersed within a *simulacrum* is a common enough event but may be challenging to spot. This is the case because the idea of a simulacrum is not easy to absorb, or at least it took *me* a few years to do so. If you're a student of literature or art, you would have learnt of *simulacra* and the roles they play. A *simulacrum* can be succinctly defined as a 'bad imitation'. But this definition does not capture the full extent of the fantastic effect simulacra may have on the observer. A *simulacrum* is a copy that does not claim to be sourced from the original that we might believe it to be putatively imitating. It's better than the original. It's more polished, prettier, and redesigned so that everyone can enjoy it without thinking of the reality it transcends.

Mini Hollywood was built in the 1960s as a set for Spaghetti Western movies, called such because most of the actors and film crews were Italian. Their voices were dubbed into English for American audiences. As we drove across the desert and the dry mountains of Almería, it was clear why Sergio Leone had chosen this area to film. We could have been in Arizona or Colorado. The landscape seemed strangely familiar because we knew it from the Westerns we had seen as children. The odd giant cactus, strange rock formations, dry river beds — they all made us feel at home.

Once inside the theme park, the feeling of familiarity did not leave us. Wherever we looked, we felt as if we had been there before: inside the cold, dusty prison cell, behind the sheriff's desk, in an old pharmacy, by the gallows in the main square, and inside the saloon. A shootout broke out at midday, and we watched it as if it was an entirely normal thing to happen. A common-day occurrence. Jesse James and some other bandits jumped off second-floor balconies onto conveniently placed hay bales. Once on the ground, they stole the sheriff's horses and disappeared in a cloud of dust with their revolvers raucously shooting bullets into the air. Everyone was mesmerised by the show.

'Let's go to the saloon,' I suggested once the dust had settled and it was evident that the actors had gone off on their lunch break.

The saloon was complete with a swing door, flowery red wallpaper, plush curtains, chandeliers, a piano, and a row of can-can dancers. Sitting at a table and drinking beer, I could observe the balustrade of the second floor where the 'girls' would live and 'work'. I loved every minute inside this strange, unreal world. It was better than the real Wild West. To start with, I was confident it was cleaner, and it even had presentable toilets and running water. As a woman, I could sit comfortably in the saloon, drink cold beer and not worry about the possibility of getting raped or shot, or both. No orphans or poor children were begging outside the grocer's or doing physical labour for a loaf of bread. The kids ran around with plastic pistols and pretended to be shooting each other. Unlike their antecedents from the previous centuries, they had not a care in the world.

The world is a better place now than ever before. I thought to myself while enjoying this nostalgic rendition of the good old Wild West.

'I'd definitely come back,' I told Robert. 'There's so much more to see here.'

SIX
OREGANO OIL

The rest of our summer went by quickly, with me constantly venting and rolling my eyes about the guests' comments and their outlandish requests and Robert mentally preparing himself for another stint in Oman. In the last week of August, I dropped him off at Malaga airport and drove myself home to an empty house once again. Saying goodbye to a loved one for an extended period of time is never easy, especially if you are the one who is to stay behind. It's a void that brings heartache. However, unlike the previous year, this time, I felt prepared. I didn't have to make a list of things to do; I didn't have to bury rubbish in the field or ask a neighbour to bring me groceries. In some sense, it was a good experience. Once again, I was an independent woman, and more importantly, I was taking notes for a time when I might be alone for good.

In the first week of September, my friend Keith came by for coffee and asked me whether I'd mind helping him out. He had to go to the UK for a month or so, but his house-sitter didn't have a car. He asked if I'd mind giving her a lift to Alcalá to grocery shop once a week or help her if she needed anything from the shops. I agreed instantly as I did not think it would be a problem. I could stop by their house in Venta Valero on my way to town, pick her up, and then drop her off on the way back. I was happy to return the favour since Keith had kindly chauffeured me to the shops when I didn't have my licence.

'You'll really like her,' he breathlessly informed me once we had made arrangements for his house-sitter. 'She's a writer, very well-educated, and has travelled all over the world.'

'Oh, yeah?' I couldn't understand why this would make me like her, but I didn't argue.

'Her name is Chila or something like it. She's Hungarian. She's almost eighty, but you wouldn't know,' Keith continued.

Now the pieces of the puzzle fell into place. *Of course, since we were both from the Eastern Bloc, we would be instant friends*, I thought, but I kept a poker face; the one you have when a friend insults you deeply with their general ignorance, but you don't want to make a fuss.

It was not the first time in my life that an Anglophone expat had assumed that we Slavs are the same. Before moving to Spain, I had worked with American, British, Australian, and Canadian expats in the UAE for many years. While the Commonwealth and ex-British colonies were well-represented at the universities there, continental Europeans were a rarity. I had met the odd Spanish nurse, a German professor of anatomy, a French linguist, and there was me, a Polish teacher of English. The Europeans could be counted on the fingers of one hand. Being a minority among English-speaking expats meant that they were always trying to find me a friend. If another Polish teacher arrived at another department or another school, my American friends would go out of their way to introduce us to each other.

'This is Magda,' they'd drag a pale and apprehensive blonde girl to my lunch table and introduce the poor victim to me. 'Magda, this is Sabina. She's also from Poland.'

We'd both nod and exchange formal 'Nice-to-meet-yous', but then the inevitable silence would fall. The 'matchmaker' would stand by, pleased with her rare find and probably expecting us to shower each other with excited chit-chat in our native tongue and shout *Thank you!* to the person who introduced us to each other. But that wasn't going to happen.

'Imagine the roles were reversed,' I once explained to an American friend. 'And I dragged you to Costa café to meet a random stranger from the States and expected you to be instant friends with her just because you're from the same country.' When you switch the roles around, the idea sounds insane, yet, they never ceased in their match-making efforts.

Another issue with being from a country of no global political importance, like Poland, is that expats assume that the whole country is like a small village where everyone knows each other. I was sitting in my garden once in Al Ain, chatting to one of Robert's American friends. Jim seemed to be a somewhat worldly man. He was a musician from New York and had played sets with Sting and Alanis Morissette, or so he said. I wasn't quite listening since his stories of past fame and fortune were usually long-winded and quite improbable, but since he was Robert's friend, I feigned interest. That's when he caught me off guard.

'So, do you know them?' Jim asked.

'Do I know whom?' I had been planning something in my head while pretending to be listening, so I had no idea what he was talking about.

'The two Polish cyclists who crossed the Gobi Desert.'

'I haven't heard of them,' I admitted.

'So, you don't know them,' Jim kept on using the word *know*, which was puzzling.

'No, I don't *know* them.'

Hearing that, he seemed disappointed. I suspected he was planning to add his knowing someone who knew the famous cyclists to his repertoire of party fables.

'Actually, Jim,' I was tired of his ignorance. 'There are almost forty million people in Poland. It's unlikely that I would know these two men you speak of.'

There was really nothing much to add to this, and I was relieved when Robert appeared in the garden, and they both wandered off.

The truth is that, in my time living with expats, I'd heard of every Polish stereotype, from Stanley Kowalski to Sophie from *Sophie's Choice*. For many, Stanley Kowalski would be the only famous Pole they'd know by their full name. Some might even have thought he was a real person. Never mind Nicolaus Copernicus, Joseph Conrad, Marie Curie, Frederic Chopin, Alfred Tarski, or even the disgraced Roman Polanski. I leaned back in my sun lounger, closed my eyes, and wanted to scream, 'Stella!'.

As I sat on my patio in Spain, looking at the empty coffee cup and my friend Keith across the table, I died a little inside.

Really? I thought to myself. *In his mind, I have much in common with an octogenarian Hungarian.*

'You know,' I decided to educate Keith. 'Hungarians are not Slavic. Their language is fundamentally different from Polish, Slovakian, or even Czech. And they don't get along well with their Slavic neighbours.'

'Oh, really?' I could see Keith struggled to compute the claim that nations that existed in the same general area of Europe did not automatically share the same traditions or values. Imagine I'd told him to be friends with a stranger from Copenhagen – it's not that far from the UK, and their languages have the same Germanic origins. But I left it at that. Hungarian, as it stands, is an impossible language. And while I can travel to Prague or Bratislava and understand more or less what's going on without having to study the languages spoken there at length, Hungarian is often the butt of a joke among most Slavic-speaking Eastern Europeans. It sounds pretty funny to our ears, and it makes absolutely no sense.

'Can you come by this week to meet her before I leave?' Keith asked.

'Yes, I'll come on Thursday morning.'

As promised, the following Thursday, I parked my car outside

Keith's cottage in Venta and shouted 'Hello' until I saw him come down from the patio on the other side of the house. I intended to introduce myself and exchange numbers with Chila so we could schedule her pick-ups once Keith had gone to the UK. As it turned out, Chila – or whatever her name was – wasn't even Hungarian. She was one of those Canadians who are so hungry for ancestry that they give themselves the nationality of their long-gone grandparents. She was as Hungarian as I was German.

The infatuation that people whose ancestors fled Europe for a better life in North America have with the Old World has always been a mystery to me. *You're identifying with the country that persecuted, mistreated, or actively discriminated against your family?* I always think when confronted with Canadians who claim to be 'Irish', Israelis who are 'Polish', or Americans who are 'Dutch'. All of these claims smack of insincerity, especially when these people can't actually speak the language of the country that they purport to be from.

For this reason, I was distrustful of 'Canadian-Hungarian' Chila as soon as I met her. I didn't want to stay long, so I only asked for a glass of water. But as we sat in the shade of the patio, Chila started to narrate a very long story from the time when she was a student at the Sorbonne. People who struggle with their identity also tend to embellish their own past. So, I listened to this modern-day Gertrude Stein with great scepticism. For some reason, the punchline of her anecdote was presented to Keith and me in French. I don't know what gave her the impression that I was so 'cultured'. Between Keith and I, we could just about order *café au lait* and a croissant in a Parisian bistro. To my surprise, he started to laugh hysterically and, to follow suit in this game of charades, I smiled in appreciation of her tale, whatever ending she had attached to it.

'Isn't she great?' he asked me, still enjoying the story I knew very well he did not understand.

'Yes, she is something,' I smiled. 'So, what do you write about?' I asked Chila, who was sitting in front of her tiny laptop. I had clearly disturbed her creative hour.

'I write stories for children.'

'Where do you publish them?'

'I have a WordPress blog, but I haven't been able to access it for the last few months because I've lost my password. So it's a bit outdated now.'

I did not need to hear more. I decided to keep a close but discreet eye on her while Keith was away.

That September, Chila grew on my brain like an incurable tumour. Every encounter was painful, communicatively awkward, and generally disturbing. On the days when I drove her to Alcalá, I had to go home, open a bottle of wine and spend half-an-hour venting with Robert on Skype. If I didn't, her words would just play in my head repeatedly, accompanied by my own inane background commentary.

One day, she showed up at my house uninvited. She had hitched a ride with her neighbours and my friends Lucas and Arie, who sometimes came over for evening drinks. I could not believe my eyes when I saw her.

'I thought I'd come over with the guys. It's more social this way,' she said. I could not understand what made her think I wanted to socialise with her. Was it the deadpan face I gave her whenever she told one of her incredible fables, each time from a different world capital? Was it my general lack of enthusiasm whenever I saw her? As I promised Keith, I was determined to be a good chauffeur, but I was not prepared to be her friend.

She got out of the car and came to the patio.

'Do you have any oregano oil?' I looked at her, not correctly computing her solicitation, given its impromptu nature and the context in which it was asked.

'I have oregano. What are you cooking?'

'I cut my finger in the car,' she said as if this answered my question.

'What do you want oregano oil for?'

'I cut my finger.' I was used to going around like this in circles during our trips to the supermarket, so her inability to communicate simple matters in a straightforward manner came as no surprise. I assumed one put this ointment on cuts.

'I don't have oregano oil,' I said harshly. *I'm not a freaking shaman.* I wanted to add.

I think the reason I used to lose my patience with Chila in a matter of seconds was that I feared I was staring into my future self. Look, my subconscious would whisper, one day you too will become a dotty old lady, starved of human company, forcing yourself onto others and confusing them with your obscure references.

'Do you have caraway seeds?' Chila interrupted my introspective trip into the future.

'I don't know. What's that?'

She seemed shocked by my ignorance of Eastern European herbs and spices. While she tried to explain to me what this spice was, I Googled it on my phone. I realised I knew what it was.

'I don't have any. They don't sell them in Mercadona. The Spanish don't use them very often.' I used my robot delivery.

'But you're Polish. Don't you use caraway seeds in your kitchen?'

'No, I don't.' *I'm not a babushka from Lublin circa 1880s.* I wanted to say, but instead, I politely inquired about the supposed medicinal properties of said caraway seeds since it followed hot on the heels of her petition for oregano oil.

'It's not for my finger. I'm making a Hungarian dish for Lucas and Arie. They've been so nice to me,' the implication being that if I were nicer to her, I might also be treated to her prized cuisine.

As I went to the kitchen to get a bottle of chilled cava and some glasses – Lucas and I were both partial to a glass of cava on a lovely summer evening – Lucas followed me to the kitchen while Chila held Arie captive with another one of her tales of international travel and intrigue.

'I'm sorry,' Lucas apologised. 'It feels like she's by the gate each time I drive by. She waved us down and invited herself to join us. She's a menace.'

Lucas and I had already exchanged our first impressions of Chila, and neither of us was a fan. While my *cortijo* was a little too far for her to walk by and pester me, poor Lucas was the victim of frequent pop-ins and spontaneous requests to run errands.

'I have guests. I have a lot of work, cleaning and cooking, but she won't leave. Yesterday, she popped in at noon and left after five.' He was desperate.

'Next time, I'll tell her that I'm busy.' These were hard words for someone as kind and warm-hearted as Lucas. 'I can't do it anymore. I told Keith I could help her if she needed anything....' He stopped short because we heard Chila approaching the kitchen.

'Would you like some cava?' I asked, and we all went out to the patio.

SEVEN
STARRY NIGHT

The following week, Chila organised a dinner party for Lucas, Arie, their two American Workaways, and me. Since I felt lonely and spent most of my days talking to myself, the two cats, and Bobby, I agreed to go, thus confirming my reputation as the biggest hypocrite in the world.

I'm usually apprehensive about attending dinner parties with people I have just met. A set dinner party means that you are trapped next to someone you don't know or, worse still, don't like, and you are forced to explore topics of conversation that do not offend or bore your conversation partner. Alternatively, you're left sitting alone at the table while the hosts spend most of the evening banging pots and pans in the kitchen. I arrived shortly after seven, as invited, and was informed that the rest of the party was coming after eight because they had had some kind of home emergency.

How convenient for them. I wish I had thought of that and also delayed my arrival.

'Would you like some cava?' she asked. Yes, of course, I would.

As she leisurely wandered off to the kitchen, I sat down on a patio chair, and a dreadful thought started to cloud my mind. I looked at the clock on my mobile phone and saw it was only seven-fifteen. How was I supposed to sit here for another hour in the company of this lunatic? Because I had to drive home through the dark country roads, I couldn't drink more than that one glass of cava.

Well, this glass would have to get me through the next hour with Chila and then some more. I was entertaining myself on Keith's patio.

As it transpired, I needn't have worried. Chila was one of those hosts who disappears into the kitchen for hours on end, comes out occasionally red-faced from the stove with a meagre plate of food, puts it on the table, and goes back to cooking. Or perhaps she didn't want to talk to me. I whiled away the hour with my glass of cava, soaking in the views of the olive hills and playing with Keith's dog Eddie.

As soon as Lucas and Arie arrived with their Workaways, the party started. I was happy to be there with people who could make jokes and have fun. Chila was out of sight for most of the time, and it felt like we were guests at a private restaurant. First, she served an aperitif, a hot spinach dip with crackers. This went down well with the assembled guests. Then came the starter, her version of gazpacho – the famous cold tomato, cucumber, and pepper soup. The gazpacho was already on shaky ground as it was, according to our chef, a Portuguese rendition of the famous Andalusian dish. Things started to rapidly fall apart after the soup was served.

For the main course, Chila was going to serve us roast chicken. After she collected the gazpacho cups and listened quizzically to the Americans excuse themselves from not eating it, she went on for a long time informing us in minute detail about the main course and all the thinking and decision-making involved in cooking it. I looked at my phone clock. It was already nine thirty and getting dark. I didn't want to drive home in complete darkness in the middle of the night. While it's not a problem when you have company in the car, driving alone in the countryside at night is scary. I decided I'd give her party another hour and go home. I thought it'd be best to inform her of my intention in a polite way. However, once she heard that I could not stay indefinitely, she acquired a certain speed to her movements but kept calling Lucas into the kitchen for advice and moral support. Why roasting a chicken with some vegetables needed two people was beyond my power of understanding. Unless they were both kneeling in front of the oven and praying to it, there was nothing to do while the bird was in the oven.

As soon as Lucas left to help Chila, the party became quiet. While Arie was funny and entertaining when he was in the company of Lucas, without him, he enjoyed educating his listeners about holistic healing, spiritualism and shamanic massage therapies. This time, he decided to talk about his crystals and how he would re-energise them under the next full moon. He started off on this fascinating topic by addressing the female Workaway and went on to explore the riveting subject of the spiritual cleaning of crystals. Since I was lost in my own thoughts, I couldn't make any sense of what they were talking about. However, not understanding what someone is talking about has never prevented me from joining in on a conversation.

'What crystals?'

I thought they were talking about house cleaning, as this was one of the chores assigned to their Workaways, but I couldn't recall seeing any crystal vases or glasses in their house.

It soon came to light that while his minions from across the pond were cleaning the house for paying guests, gardening, and reorganising the storage room, Arie had spent the day arranging his energy crystals in strategic places around the garden in anticipation of a full moon bath, thereby cleansing them and re-vitalising their magical healing powers. *No wonder they needed Workaways*, I thought. I wish I could have him retell his analysis of crystal powers in detail to showcase its absurdity, but I was interrupted by Chila's announcement that the chicken was ready.

She came onto the patio and placed a gently roasted chicken in the middle of the table. The chicken was definitely on the small side. While Chila returned to the kitchen to get the vegetables and potatoes, Arie and I exchanged puzzled glances across the table. We were both calculating how she planned to feed six adults with one underfed, anaemic chicken.

'Are you vegetarians?' I asked the visiting couple.

'No, we love meat,' the boy declared.

No one else was a vegetarian at the table, so unless the chicken was going to multiply itself *à la* Bethsaida-style, someone was going to go home hungry. As soon as Chila brought the veg to the table and told us to help ourselves, I strategically snatched a chicken leg. Arie followed suit and snagged a breast. Being a good husband, he also appropriated a leg and thigh for Lucas, who was stuck in the kitchen making Chila's gravy. The young American man quickly realised what was happening and secured the last good piece of meat, the other breast. His girlfriend, obviously better educated and more courteous than the rest of us, was served a chicken wing. Once Chila and Lucas had returned from the kitchen and sat down, we were served the roasted vegetables. Chila salvaged for herself the other pitiful wing from the now stripped-down chicken carcass and looked mildly confused.

'Oh, I thought there would be enough for all of us,' she said. 'Help yourselves to the roast vegetables. It's zucchini and eggplant. What I normally do is...' she started a long diatribe on the details of the technique which she had implemented to roast the vegetables and the health-cum-flavour merits of some spice or other that she had so thoughtfully sprinkled over the said veg.

I find it so interesting when people explain to me how they have cooked something when it's clear from the dish's look and consistency how it was prepared. Despite the long monologue on the topic of roasting vegetables, I was curious how she had managed to serve raw aubergine after it had spent at least two hours in the oven. It was now past ten, and I was on borrowed time, so I didn't say anything untoward. I discreetly moved the raw aubergine aside, ate the soggy courgettes, and finished my shrivelled chicken leg. Once everyone had finished eating and our hostess had begun to clean the table, I quietly announced that I had to leave. I explained that I didn't want to drive in complete darkness, and so on. I didn't mention that I was also worried that I might have to listen to more nonsensical talk about magic crystals.

'But I was just about to serve the salad,' Chila said.

'The salad?' the American girl seemed confused, as we were all, in fact.

'Yes, it's a French dinner party. In France, you eat salad after the main course. Then they have a cheese course, followed by a dessert. You'll miss out if you leave now.'

The Americans picked up on her explication of what a French menu was and asked her to elaborate on the topic in a manner typical of blue-eyed Americans. Based on the speed with which the food had been served thus far during the evening's proceedings, I'd have to stay until the early morning before the final curtain would be called on this one-act play. I thanked her for her hospitality and bid everyone a fond farewell.

The drive home was exactly as grim as I expected. It was pitch black, and on the narrow roads surrounded by olives and some forest, I constantly spotted fluorescent pairs of eyes peeping out from the side of the road. The unblinking eyes belonged to the multitude of rabbits, foxes, stray cats, and village dogs who had decided to take a nocturnal prowl. I didn't want to run over any of these poor animals, so I drove very carefully, scanning the road ahead.

It was just 11 pm at the time, and I hoped that all the drunks at the San Miguel Bar in Venta were still busy drinking and hadn't taken to the roads just yet. I did not want to be hit by a drunk driver. Drink-driving is a significant problem in rural Andalusia. Many small family-run bars and restaurants are scattered amid the olive groves, far away from the main roads. Most of them are not even pinned on Google Maps. You need to have local knowledge to find them. From the police's perspective, they are notoriously tricky to patrol adequately because there are always so many dirt tracks that lead to and from these establishments.

Fortunately, I arrived home safe and sound, without encountering any other cars on the road. Once I exited my car, I looked at the starry night. The Milky Way was wending its way above my head, and the Big Dipper was hiding behind the roof of the house. I heard Bobby barking inside. I was home, but again, it felt empty. I let Bobby out and poured myself a well-deserved glass of red wine. I sat on the patio alone, looking at the stars and feeling a little disheartened that there was no one to talk to. No one to share the evening's absurdities and annoyances with. I knew Robert would love to hear the story about Chila's spectacularly underwhelming dinner party, but I had to wait until the next day to tell him all about it during our scheduled Skype call. I saw a glimpse of myself in forty years, all by myself. I was only thirty-nine, but I didn't think it was too early to prepare for the inevitable loneliness.

Was it the accident I had suffered that year or the months I had spent alone? I was slowly getting ready. Only a fool lives day after day and does not think about the inexorable end. I didn't know if I was ready, but my time alone had strengthened me. If I could move a ton of wood with one hand, run a rural B&B without water or a driving licence, and make friends in the middle of nowhere, I would survive.

But I did not have to wait another forty years to see death, illness, and loneliness in my house. If I had a crystal ball, I would have seen the lively village of Montefrio turn into a post-apocalyptic ghost town occupied by strange creatures in hazmat suits patrolling the streets and spraying bleach onto every surface. Who could have foreseen empty supermarket shelves, normally outgoing Spaniards keeping their distance and checking each other for the signs of the zombie infection, and me sitting alone on the patio, isolated and very, very worried? But that story was yet to come and was quite unimaginable on that September night.

I looked up at the night sky and desisted from my melancholic pondering of death and loneliness. Van Gogh's *The Starry Night* was displayed in front of me in all its splendour. I had learned a great deal by living alone, but I had also become somewhat mean of spirit and frightfully facetious. I should have been kinder and more tolerant of Chila and her antics. I should have been more patient with the Workaways. I should not have made fun of the guests and turned their little mishaps into my private entertainment. It was time to break free from the confines of the mental prison I had constructed for myself, get a job, and bring my husband back home.

'And you need to stop rolling your eyes at everything, missy!' I recalled this excellent advice from an old friend. With this admonishment in mind, I refreshed my wine glass.

EIGHT
TRUSTWORTHY HOUSE-SITTERS

To say that I embarked on a full-blown job hunt the next day would be a blatant lie. My approach did not include scouring the internet for teaching positions, polishing and updating my CV, and sending it out to dozens of educational institutions every day. I postponed my job search until the job came to me. One October morning, while I was drinking my morning coffee and browsing my Facebook posts, I saw that a local expat woman advertised a job vacancy at a local language school. This was a very rare opportunity.

There were about half a dozen language schools in Alcalá at the time. Each school employed one or two native English speakers as so-called 'teaching assistants' with whom the students could practise listening and speaking. Consequently, the number of available teaching positions in the nearest town was very limited, and those lucky few who had a position would hold on to it for many years. I knew how tight the teaching job market was because, during the second year of our house remodelling, we both tried to get teaching jobs to make ends meet when we ran out of money. Even though we were invited for an interview by one of the *academies* (the Spanish name given to such language schools), the job location was in Valdepeñas de Jaén, an hour's drive from our house. We declined the job offer because it did not make sense for us to drive for almost two hours to make just 30-45 euros.

The other academies in Alcalá had their tried-and-trusted teaching staff who did not seem to wish to leave their jobs. That's why, as soon as I saw the news that there was an opening in Alcalá, I sent the British woman my latest CV. I had updated it the previous year when I considered returning to the Middle East to rebuild our budget. I had not even managed to scroll down to the next Facebook post before she replied to my response. Her name was Lucy. She had been a teaching assistant at the language school for a few years until she decided, in an apparent bout of 'mid-life crisis', to pursue her life-long dream of opening a mindfulness studio.

'Can you start next week?' her voice had a definite sense of urgency.

I figured out that the Spanish owner had put her in charge of finding her replacement, and as soon as she had done so, she would be free to follow her dream.

'I'm so sorry,' I had to level with her. 'I did not expect to be hired so soon. I have already got flight tickets to Oman for November.'

It was true. Desperate to chase away my loneliness, I had booked a return flight to Oman to stay with Robert in Sur. We would return home together at the end of November.

The accommodation is free, so it's only the flight. I convinced myself that travelling across the continents was the only logical thing to do. *It would be silly not to go.*

It was partially true. Robert's apartment was already paid for, and

Sur is a charming small fishing town on the Indian Ocean, which I had visited several times when we lived in the UEA. Snorkelling in the Indian Ocean was one of the things that I missed the most after we moved to Andalusia. On some particularly dreadful days during our renovation years, I would go out onto the dirty patio, look at the horrible cement mixer and think back to the days when we spent almost every winter wild-camping on Masirah Island in Oman.

You'll never swim in the Indian Ocean again, a mean-spirited troll would whisper in my ear. *You've spent all your money on this house. How do you think you'll ever save enough money to travel to the Indian Ocean again?*

The troll in my head was right. I had no clue how I would ever save enough to travel back to the Indian Ocean and enjoy the warm spectacle of the rugged coral, the colourful fish, the dolphins, and the turtles.

But then, I argued with the troll. *When I was twenty, I couldn't imagine I would ever earn enough money to buy my own laptop. And look at me now! I go through laptops like socks.*

The troll remained sceptical of my exaggeration.

Needless to say, I found the idea of a return visit to the Indian Ocean irresistible, and on one of my lonelier nights, and with some encouragement from a bottle of Syrah, I booked myself a flight.

'I could start teaching in December,' I tried to negotiate with Lucy.

'I'll talk to the owner, but we need someone to start as soon as possible. I don't think we can wait until December.'

She was very nice about it, but neither of us wanted to make a compromise. I didn't want to give up my last opportunity to swim in the Indian Ocean, and she was determined to start her new life venture as soon as possible. We parted ways on amicable terms, but I didn't think I'd ever hear from the school again. Once I let this opportunity for steady employment pass me by, it was time to find someone to look after Bobby and the cats while I was gallivanting in Oman. Even though I got burnt by the Workaway website before, I decided to start my search there.

Once again, like the year before, I was bombarded by stories of human misfortune, alternative lifestyles, midlife crises, millennial pipedreams, and just downright weird proposals. I could not find anyone with whom I could leave the house and the pets and sleep peacefully at night. That's when Trish suggested *trustworthy house-sitters*. I instantly took to the site's name, a very clever marketing ploy on the side of its creators. I was also charmed by the profiles of the prospective house-sitters. It was almost the opposite of the Workaway site.

Men in tweed jackets and women dressed in their Sunday best posed with well-groomed pets next to immaculately polished kitchen counters. To demonstrate the range of their 'hobbies', the wives presented their sponge cakes, and the husbands showed off their brawn by repairing boilers and trimming hedges. They all looked very normal, a little *too normal*. *A Wisteria Lane 'normal'*, I would say to anyone who used to binge-watch *Desperate Housewives* in the late noughties. Notwithstanding the obvious exaggeration of their aspirant house-sitters' skills, the *trustworthy house-sitter* website beat the mixed bag of candidates found on the Workaway site. Thus informed, I began my auditions. I narrowed down my choices to three couples and set up online interviews.

I chose couples over singles because I felt that a lonely country house in the middle of nowhere would probably wear a single person down. It drove *me* to madness occasionally, and I lived there by conscious design. I didn't want to return home after a month in Oman and be welcomed by a Robinson Crusoe character who had been reduced to talking to a volleyball with a crude face painted on it.

A good question one might ask was why I had bothered to set up these online interviews. In my past life, the one in which I would wear a nice suit, clean shoes, and brush my hair every morning, I served on many interview panels. To be honest, most of the teachers I had recommended for employment turned out to be wackadoodles. In my defence, I was not the only person responsible for these recommendations. We were all part of the university's collegial recruitment and interview team. We'd often pass each other in the corridor, months after we had hired a new shining star of educational professionalism, and look at each other in horror.

'This guy is a maniac,' the same person who had liked the

candidate's quirkiness during the interview would comment six months later.

'She's a raving lunatic,' a manager would observe about another one of our recommendations when it was too late to send her back home. 'Who hired her?'

'You did,' I'd remind him.

'We all did,' he'd correct me.

The majority of the strangers whom we hired to join the teaching faculty would start strong with a fantastic interview. George, Julie, Christine, Claudia, or whoever was sitting at the video-conferencing equipment would finish an interview and could not believe their luck. Why would this extraordinarily qualified and successful person want to work for us?

Perfect!

We've got them.

We would stand up and congratulate each other on the successful interview.

The new teachers would arrive at the university and coast for the first three months. They'd exchange pleasantries, keep their desk tidy, ensure their students were happy and learning, come in on time, do their work, and so on. But as soon as the probation period was over, the 'crazy' would emerge. Usually, the transformation wasn't slow and gradual. The metamorphosis was like a jack-in-the-box, sudden and drastic. One day, their office desk would be occupied with nothing but neatly organised stacks of student essays and a couple of books. The next, old clippings of newspaper articles that mentioned the teacher's name would appear.

'Esteemed Shaikh Al-Speare of Outer Coriolanustan meets the Faculty of National Professionally Vibrant University' or 'Dr Tee Chalotabull, Senior Lecturer at South Harmon Institute of Technology, provides training for TESOL Teachers in Madagascar'

Such self-congratulatory clippings and photos would decorate their desk, revealing far too much about our co-workers' simultaneous low self-esteem and implicit smugness. Now that they had their foot firmly in the door, they'd stop preparing for any of their classes, come late, leave early, and snub everyone who did not please them.

With this experience in mind, I should have known better than to trust what little I could learn from a fifteen-minute Skype interview. But still, I had made more effort than I did when I hired two Polish 'chefs' the year before to look after my house and the pets for a month while I went to a teachers' conference in Dubai and visited Robert in Oman. Back then, I just read through their profiles, exchanged a few emails, and let them take over my life without background checks. All I had was a vague text message from someone they said was their character reference.

The interviews for my new house-sitters went well. But what else would one expect? They weren't going to show up drunk and incoherent or start gibbering about their magic crystals during this short first encounter. So, after the initial Skype call, I was really none the wiser. There was a very dignified couple in their 60s from London who used the house-sitting site to holiday in Spain. Another was a lovely middle-aged couple from Birmingham who had recently experienced a health scare, some sort of cancer. Once the beast had become manageable, they decided to live their lives to the full and travel the world while house-sitting. Finally, there were a couple of digital nomads from New Zealand in their 40s who used the house-sitting scheme to travel Europe.

While I pondered the pros and cons of each of my candidates, I began to think that house-sitting was an excellent gig for anyone who wanted to travel the world.

Why didn't I think of it before? I asked myself.

We could travel across South America and not pay a penny for our accommodation. I thought I was onto something.

Out of curiosity, I re-opened the website and searched for house-sitting jobs in South America. There weren't that many listed, so I narrowed my search to specific countries until I found a remote cottage in the Colombian rainforest. The place looked ideal for us. The house was made of wood and seemed very cosy. It also had a huge veranda overlooking the mountains. I imagined us sitting on the wooden porch, drinking wine, and gazing at the misty vapour clouds over a verdant rainforest with the sounds of benign creatures as a soundtrack.

While, in my mind's eye, I was sipping wine and taking in magnificent views, I forgot one detail that was mentioned in the listing.

The house-sitters for this property were expected to look after four cats, each with a different dietary requirement. Two of them needed life-saving medicine. The profile of the house owner primarily consisted of very detailed instructions of what quantities of food each feline consumed, how these meals were to be prepared, and the doses of medication that had to be administered at a precise time every day. I looked at my two cats, who were, I had to admit, a bit scruffy from chasing mice and rabbits in the field all night and fighting with other country cats. They enjoyed unrestricted access to a bowl of water and a continuously full bowl of dry food so that they could help themselves to the buffet whenever they wanted. Whitey was an especially shifty character, and in the summer, days would go by when he would absent himself from the house. Sometimes, I would wake up at night and hear him crunching on his dry food, only to disappear into the dark as soon as his belly was full.

After reading through the requirements listed on the posting, I realised I lacked the constitution to be a house-sitter. The house owners on this website would never accept my pet ownership ethos. I was confident that if we were to reside in the Colombian cottage I had found, the four cats would disappear into the forest forever or be eaten by a jaguar as soon as I took charge of the place. So, I put aside my plans of travelling the world without paying for accommodation and decided to focus on the job at hand, namely, to select a couple of suitable house-sitters for my own pets.

I had a strong feeling that whomever I chose to house-sit for me would turn out to be either a trickster or a fruitcake. I hoped to find out before they arrived on my doorstep. So, I re-read their internet profiles, looking for any statements that would reveal their character flaws, but I could not find any. Then I re-read their references. But I soon realised that their friends could have written them, so there was no point in calling the listed referees to verify. I applied a forensic linguistic approach to search for signs of mental deficiency but found none. When I ran out of ideas, I went with an old-and-trusted method of selection, otherwise known as 'Eeny, meeny, miny, moe'. It fell on the New Zealanders.

I called them to inform them of my decision. In response, they cheered and thanked me profusely, as if they had just won the lottery. They made further inquiries about Bobby, Twiggy, and Whitey and seemed unreasonably enchanted and excited by my descriptions. A stranger overhearing this conversation might have thought that we were talking about my darling prodigies performing one of Beethoven's trios — Bobby on the piano, Twiggy on the cello, and Whitey playing the violin.

I didn't trust their optimism, but then I had had a previous bad experience with house-sitters, so my extra caution was not unwarranted. I still had a month before I travelled to Oman. We had some guests booked throughout October, but not in such numbers that they'd take up all of my attention. To keep busy and expand my social network, I re-joined my Spanish classes in Alcalá la Real.

NINE
ALL THE COUSINS OF ANNE BOLEYN

'Qué tal, guapa!' I heard Blanca's enthusiastic voice as I entered the language school where she was conducting her 'Spanish for foreigners' classes. She was walking down the corridor when I entered.

I smiled. I had to give it to her; no one else I knew could beat her passion for work and general *joie de vivre*. She hadn't seen me for a year because I had had to abandon my classes due to a lack of transport. Yet she acted as if we were two bridesmaids going out for a hen party. She made me feel very welcome. This particular feature of hers made her an excellent teacher, especially since many of her students were retired expats who had last sat in a classroom forty or fifty years earlier. No matter how poor our Spanish pronunciation, how weak our Spanish grammar was, or how misguided our choice of vocabulary was, she stood patiently in front of the whiteboard, seemingly engrossed in our stories. Her slender build, short, well-trimmed blonde hair, and intense brown eyes gave her the appearance of an elf whose sole purpose in this world was to listen and relish in our tales, which centred all too frequently around our never-ending house renovations, and friends and family coming to visit.

Watching her listen with genuine eagerness to one of us retelling her a ponderous story about a weekend visit to Leroy Merlin in Granada to buy a new tap or faucet for the kitchen sink, I used to think she had the patience of a saint.

'We bought our kitchen taps in the UK, but they don't fit. Our Spanish plumber told us that here they are…whereas in the UK, they are…and so now we have to…and then…. You see…' they'd drone on about the kitchen sink and then move on to bathroom fittings, shower heads, and pipe fittings. The stories were never told in one smooth delivery. Instead, they contained 'dramatic' pauses allowing the orator to fumble with his or her phone in search of the missing vocabulary in their online translator.

The problem with stories about house renovations is that they have a lot in common with pet stories. They are usually incredibly riveting for the speaker and his or her spouse but bear very little interest for the audience, who will tend to drift off after the first sentence. Even though we all were renovating our houses, we didn't want to listen to someone else's long narrative about searching for the right taps. We had our own tediously mundane stories to share, given the opportunity. And while the rest of the class dozed off, Blanca had nothing but encouragement for the presenter. Because of this attitude, she became my teaching role model.

Inside her classroom, the desks were arranged in a boardroom style, so the students sat facing each other. I saw some familiar faces present. Amy and Roy were sitting in front. Céline was also in attendance, opposite Roy. The four of us had studied Spanish together in the past and had subsequently become friends. Roy and Amy were early retirees from the UK and had a small guesthouse in a village outside Alcalá. Céline and her husband Leon were Belgian and had decided to dedicate their retirement to rescuing *galgos*, Spanish greyhounds. Leon didn't attend these classes, so I swiftly occupied the empty seat next to Céline.

I didn't know the others, but we were soon introduced to each other. There were two other couples in the class, one from Ireland and the other from the Midlands, and two bohemian-looking women from Castillo with matching dangling earrings and an assembly of colourful shawls. Finally, there was a Slovakian girl, who was immediately introduced to me by Blanca as if we were long-lost siblings. Her name was Magda, and to my great relief, she was just as put off by the insinuation that we should be best friends just because of the geographical and cultural proximity of our home countries as I was. This attitude made me like her instantly. No sooner had we finished our introductions than my archenemy and her pompous husband arrived. Gwen and Max were back in my life. In typical fashion, they walked in hunched down and looking apologetic for being late while shoving around the chairs and rearranging them to their suiting. For some reason, Max decided to sit next to me while his wife took the seat next to Amy.

'Long time no see,' Max whispered to me while the rest of the class was talking about their week in Spanish. 'How's the bed and breakfast?'

'Very good. Thank you. And yours?'

'We've decided to open it for the next season.'

That was surprising because he and Gwen had been renovating their rental cottages when we had first met two years earlier.

'We're not in a rush,' he waved off my confusion about the long delay in opening their business. 'Anyway, how's Robert? Is he still in Yemen?'

I love it when people purposefully misremember details of my life in an attempt to put me down. It's very droll.

'No, he isn't in Yemen,' I said, choosing not to clarify any further. I then gestured to indicate that we should listen to the others and not chat between ourselves.

'People in my village put water bottles in their doorway. Do you know why?' Magda asked in Spanish. Note that it was Blanca's routine to start each class by asking: '*Do you have any questions about anything?*'

It'd been a year since I last participated in a Spanish language class, and apart from my hospitality vocabulary, my lexis remained somewhat limited. I was sure I had misunderstood her. Because I lived in the countryside, I hardly ever spent time strolling the streets of the local villages and looking at their doorways. I could not understand or imagine what she was talking about, but the others lapped the topic up. They all had examples and possible explanations for this curious practice of placing a water bottle in front of a doorway. While the details and rationales varied, they all seemed to agree that the bottles deterred dogs from doing their business on the doorstep. Because I walked Bobby among the olive groves and never kept track of this canine behaviour, I found the whole discussion a bit surreal and difficult to relate to.

'Does anyone else have any questions?' Blanca asked once we had exhausted the topic of water bottles as a canine urinary defence. I assumed that her question was designed to prompt any queries related to the Spanish language, but the others interpreted it differently. It seemed that the language class had morphed into a support-group meeting where the participants shared all and every personal interaction with Spanish people or culture during the previous week.

'A *jabalí* killed my neighbour's dog,' an elderly Irishman with grey hair and a skinny physique informed us.

I realised that while my Spanish was reasonably fluent when chatting to local guests about what to see and do around Montefrio or when showing them around the house, it had stagnated at an intermediate level. Everyone else in the room seemed to know what *jabalí* referred to because they were nodding their heads and showing sympathy for the dog. I could no longer pretend that I understood all these new words.

'What is a *jabalí*?' I asked in Spanish.

Because we were supposed to be an upper-intermediate class, or 'advanced' as some of us claimed, Blanca proceeded to explain it to me in Spanish. Amy saw the confusion on my face. In my mind, I saw a prehistoric creature with grey or brown hair, sharp teeth, and a murderous appetite for dogs.

'It's a wild boar,' she cut a long story short by translating the word for me.

'Ahh, a wild boar. I see these on the road near my house, maybe seven or eight, the whole family.' In my eagerness to share my story, I couldn't remember the past form of the verb *see*, but I decided to speak anyway, even if what I was saying was barely intelligible.

My little story and poor command of Spanish grammar inspired the others to share their encounters with the wild boar near their own homes. In full disclosure, most of these chance meetings were retold second-hand. But from their reports, it would appear that the *jabalí* were quite a troublemaker, and they were almost overrun by them. As I listened, I remembered Old Gabi, the previous owner of our cottage, telling me that he had had to put a fence around the property because hungry wild boars would come close to the house to eat the acorns from the oak trees. I was feeling very grateful for his foresight. Perhaps the fence made me so ignorant of the hordes of vicious brutes lurking outside. I reflected on my morning walks when Bobby usually abandoned me and disappeared into the underbrush in the forest on the top of the hill opposite the house, searching for rabbits and foxes, only to reappear at the gate on my way back.

That's where they must live, I thought in horror.

'Well, they are not normally dangerous,' claimed one of the bohemian women from Castillo in defence of the poor creatures whose character was being assassinated with great enthusiasm. 'Unless it's a female protecting her babies. Then she can kill a man.'

I didn't see how this titbit of information improved the *jabalí's* tarnished image. Once everyone had shared their stories about wild boars, we moved on with the lesson, which, as in the past, consisted of endlessly translating sentences that had little use to anyone in the room and writing out neat rows of verb conjugations.

'Next week, we'll have the Speaking Club,' Blanca announced at the end. It was her idea to jazz up her classes, and even though the Speaking Club hardly ever produced the results she hoped for, she was unwilling to let it go.

'The topic is 'ancestry'. I'd like you to talk about your family and your origins. You can talk about where your name and surname come from,' she explained.

Little did she know that she had just unleashed an absolute monster of a topic — I knew that unchecked feelings of self-importance and pretentiousness were going to fly high in next week's class. I braced myself in bemused anticipation.

The upside of this assignment was that I didn't need much time to prepare. I wasn't going to share the actual details of my family history with this group of strangers. I didn't feel like it was the right place or time. Also, I'd have to navigate several past forms at once, and I wasn't ready to do that spontaneously. Instead, I opted to talk about the meaning of my name and surname, a task which took me a minute to prepare some notes for. My name derives from a Roman or Etruscan tribe, and my surname is the name of the place where my great-great-grandfather lived centuries ago. Hundreds of places are based on some form or other of *Ostrów*, so it remains impossible to identify a particular ancestral village with any degree of certainty. That was it. My name means nothing, and my surname means very little.

Did I wish my name meant something more significant, like *graceful, joyful,* or *the Gift of God*? As a young teen, I did. I was jealous of my sister's name, *Beata*, which means *blessed*. Or my friend Marta, *the lady*, or Kasia, who was *pure*. Even my mother's name, *Kamila*, or *a helper to the priest*, means something. And my grandmother's name, *Honorata, the woman of honour*, beat all these other names by a country mile. When I was a teenager hungry for identity affirmation, I searched my name in an onomatological dictionary. I was confronted with the prosaic description: *Sabina* — 'a woman of the Sabine tribe'. It was disappointing that my name was just a name, but it freed me from any suggestion of nominalistic determinism. Names are arbitrary, a random collection of phonemes that we have chosen to assign a reference to. I also liked the fact that my name wasn't constrained by association with a random adjective. I wasn't sure I could live up to being *graceful, joyful,* or *the Gift of God*.

But some of my classmates had different opinions on this topic. Thus, the following week, I had to endure a series of tedious lectures with pages of detailed notes on the meaning and origin of everyone's name being read out to the class as if these names were of mystical significance. After we took a deep dive into the Celtic roots of *Brian* and examined the Roman glory of *Max*, a Leicester woman with short grey hair took over the portentous job of enthralling the class with an analysis of her name. It was Carol Smith or something similarly momentous, so I didn't think she'd have much to say about it. And neither did she. Instead of explaining the origins of her name, she told us about the astonishing findings she had made on an ancestry website. As she was explaining her obsession with the ancestry website and outlined her lineage, I was going over a shopping list in my head when I heard Roy exclaim excitedly:

'So, you're related to the Tudors?'

Carol perused her notes.

'Well, only to Henry VIII through marriage to Anne Boleyn,' she clarified while pointing at something in her notebook that only the people on her side of the table could see.

She took a regal sip of tepid water from the plastic cup in front of her and looked down upon the paupers who sat around her. To her annoyance, Roy did not seem to immediately understand the relationship between her and Henry VIII. In his defence, it was tangential at best.

'Wasn't Elizabeth I Anne's daughter?' Roy asked.

Carol nodded.

'But Elizabeth didn't have any children, so how can you be related to Ann Boleyn?' he asked naively.

'It's through a 'bloodlike', Carol put down her notebook containing a succession of elaborate drawings of the various lineages of distant cousins, decided to ignore Roy's challenge of her imperial origins and continued to dwell on her ancestors.

'Some of my relatives were Danish, and some went to America. I also have a dash of Norwegian and French in me,' she told us as if this explained her noble past.

'Can anyone find a relation on the ancestry website?' Gwen asked in an effort to change the topic, which was getting confusing and difficult to follow for anyone who had not spent every minute of their free time on the website during the last five years. 'Can you find my relatives?'

While Carol explained the ins and outs of the ancestry website, Gwen's eyes lit up. Perhaps she, too, had a similarly majestic past. Might not she be a distant relative of Mary, Queen of Scots? I was never to find out. I attended three more classes that month and then flew to Oman. I promised Blanca that I would do my homework while I was away and rejoin the class in December, but as it happened, I never returned to my Spanish classes. When we returned from Oman in December, we decided to take advantage of the house-sitters' availability, who were already *in situ* and went off to explore Lisbon. Then Christmas came and went, and by Epiphany, my life was on a new trajectory. We would finally start putting down roots in our beautiful adopted country.

We'd make new friends over the next few years, but the Spanish classes always left me with a warm and fuzzy feeling — the same I have for my primary school classmates. We were all in it together, unaware of what life would bring us. I sometimes fondly recall my *compadres*. Would I have listened more attentively to their stories had I known that not four years would pass before one of them would die from a malignant brain tumour, another would get divorced after twenty years of marriage, and another would be diagnosed with an incapacitating genetic illness? Such are the unexpected vagaries and randomness of life.

TEN

MASIRAH DAYS

I n the usual Baader-Meinhof fashion, once I'd learned the word *jabalí*, these wild beasts seemed everywhere. In October, a *jabalí* killed Lucas' sweet little dog, Chiquita. She had gone out for her morning walk by herself and never came back. Poor Lucas spent the whole day searching the hills around his house until he found her. It was evident from the wounds what had killed her and how.

Then, two days after I'd travelled to Oman, I received a message from my Kiwi house-sitters.

First of all, I just want to let you know that Bobby is fine, so don't be alarmed. We had a bit of an adventure this morning.

We went for a morning walk with Bobby to the old hacienda. He was off the lead, running up and down the hills. As we were walking back, we heard Bobby barking at something incessantly. He sounded very angry. Oli ran into the olives to see what was going on, and there was a huge wild boar right in front of Bobby. When I saw it, I climbed up an olive tree in case it wanted to attack us, and Oli grabbed a stick from the ground and tried to protect Bobby while he kept his eye on the nearest tree for a quick escape. It must have been all the screaming and barking because the wild boar looked at us, turned around and ran away. Bobby looked quite relieved when the wild boar left because he didn't even chase after it. We put him back on his lead and walked home. We won't be going for walks in that direction anymore. Anyway, we are all fine, albeit a bit shaken.
The cats are good, sunning themselves on the terrace all day.
Hope you're enjoying your holiday.
Best,
Kate

I read the email on my laptop. I was sitting on a dilapidated chair in a small apartment in Sur while all the local mosques were calling the faithful to the *Zuhr* prayer. It was noon. As luck would have it, a week before my departure from Spain, I had been commissioned to develop a set of educational materials for an online course, so instead of being free to traipse along the beach while Robert was at school, I was trapped in front of my laptop. The work was a bit monotonous and not extremely inspiring, thus prompting my frequent mental breaks, which entailed diving down the rabbit hole of my social media and email accounts. I looked out the apartment window — the orange plastic tint that had been stuck to the glass gave the landscape outside a definite post-apocalyptic feel. It wasn't helped by the fact that the apartment was just on the outskirts of Sur, overlooking the main Muscat-Sur highway. I was surrounded by large expanses of sand and rubble, highlighted by a roundabout and a busy KFC drive-thru. It was a far cry from the idyllic Indian Ocean holiday I had signed up for. I wrote back to

Kate and assured her that should a wild pig gnaw on Bobby, I wouldn't blame them.

We can't control these things, was my stoic stance on this potential danger to my precious dog.

Also, the cats might get eaten by foxes. They love hunting for cats and rabbits, so don't worry if they disappear. There's nothing we can do about it, I wanted to add, but I realised that this would have the reverse effect to my intention of putting the house-sitters at ease, so I deleted the comment about local foxes killing cats.

The most important is that both you and Oli escaped unharmed. I wrote instead.

I concluded my email with a few more positive sentences. Kate's family were Welsh farmers who had emigrated to New Zealand in the 1950s. Because she grew up on a sheep farm in the middle of nowhere, I was confident in her ability to handle challenging situations should anything adverse happen. She didn't need to worry in advance about foxes, snakes, ticks, uncovered boreholes hidden in the grassland, or speeding drivers running over dogs, cats, rabbits, frogs, and even little birds.

When you live in the countryside or close to nature, thinking about the things that can go wrong can be overwhelming at times. At any given moment, one of your limbs might be chopped off or sawed off by accident. A heavy object might fall on your head, that's given. Tripping over a random stick, stepping on a rusty nail, tumbling down a ladder, burning your hands in the fire, injuring your eye with a sharp object — that's all the bread-and-butter of rural living. Once I had contemplated the list of possible mundane accidents, I became a little more creative. What if one of the cats fell into José's giant cacti plantation or if Bobby ran into the combine harvester as it was cutting the wheat in the neighbouring field? I was getting delirious with worry because it was November, and the wheat harvest had concluded in July. It was time to clear my head. Instead of staring at the orange moonscape outside, I decided to take a short walk along the beach which was on the other side of the road, behind a row of old-fashioned villas.

As soon as I left the air-conditioned building, the tremendous humidity in the air outside hit me in the face. The air carried a distinct odour of dead algae and rotting rubbish bins. Because it was the hottest time of the day, there weren't many people on the streets. Most men were at the mosque, and local women did not normally stroll the streets in the direct sun. In desperate hope for a private swim in the ocean, I wore my bathing suit under a loose dress and a towel under my arm. There was a gap in the row of houses which allowed me access to the beach. I knew the way because we had had a small barbecue on the beach the night before. In the daylight, the beach itself wasn't particularly pleasant — it was covered in plastic bags and other rubbish brought to the shore with the tide.

The previous night, as we sat on our plastic camel mats, we grilled some steaks and drank duty-free vodka premixed in the apartment with orange juice. We also spotted several groups of young men — young Omanis and migrant workers from Bangladesh and Pakistan — cruising the beach in search of a date. Next to us, there was an Omani family having a picnic in the back of their Land Cruiser. I couldn't see their faces because there were no lights near the beach, and the moon had not yet risen. We only heard their children running around and screaming in joy because they were out on the beach at night. Hiding in coves and behind the various rock formations that dotted the beach, unmarried couples exploited the freedom afforded by the darkness and secrecy that surrounded us all.

This was a far cry from the Omani beach experience that I remembered from our holidays on Masirah Island, where we would have the whole beach to ourselves. As far as the eye could see, white sand and turquoise water would stretch before us. In the evening, as the tide ebbed, we would hear the ghost crabs exit their holes in their search for food along the shoreline. It was on Masirah Island where we discovered that crabs love barbecued chicken. After our evening meal, I'd leave the leftover bones and other scraps for a feral cat that used to sit on a rock behind our tent, waiting for us to go to bed before he would stealthily search through our belongings, looking for food. But one evening, the cat wasn't there. Admittedly, he didn't visit us every night. I assumed that on some days, he was fed by the local fishermen who went out on calm nights in their fishing dinghies.

Anyway, one night, the crabs got to the chicken leftovers that I had placed some short distance from our camp. As soon as their little heads and antennae-like eyestalks emerged from their burrows, a massive free-for-all, all-inclusive, all-you-can-eat buffet extravaganza ensued. In a matter of minutes, bones and scraps of meat were being dragged off in all directions across the wet sand. Each creature scavenged voraciously for himself or herself. Some crafty individuals dragged some pieces of food to their burrow, hiding them there before setting off again to collect more scraps. We watched as this feeding frenzy unfolded. We made small discoveries every day we spent on the island as we observed the marine and coastal flora and fauna go about their day, blissfully unaware of (or deeply disinterested in) what we humans were up to. Perhaps, because the animals in that area hardly ever interacted with or saw humans, they did not seem to be scared of us.

Masirah Island itself has a population of a few thousand people, the majority of whom live mainly in the small town of Hilf, in the north of the island. The town was an organic by-product of the former RAF base established in the early 1930s and subsequently used by the Royal Air Force of Oman. As one heads away from the town, the shoreline is sparsely populated by occasional fishing 'villages' which consist of a dozen or so shacks made of driftwood and coconut palm-tree fronds and covered with corrugated iron roofs to protect them from seasonal monsoons and cyclones.

It was never difficult to find a secluded spot on the beach near the town, but we preferred to camp far to the south on the island, so we'd drive for an hour before looking for a place to set up our camp. In this part of the island, there were no buildings or people as far as the eye could see. We were spoilt by having a long stretch of beach to the front of us and an arid mountain range behind us. The nights on the beach were often pitch black until the moon rose. On some nights, if we were lucky, the bioluminescence would delineate ghostly outlines of the gently breaking waves at our feet. In the morning, as we prepared for some shallow-water snorkelling action, we would often spot pods of dolphins swimming past our camp just offshore. Discarded plastic bags and the debris from passing ships made their presence on these beaches, too, I am sad to report. They seem to be an inevitable part of the Indian Ocean experience, a disheartening sign of our times.

The southern part of the island, where we camped, was quite deserted and very Robinson Crusoesque, except, perhaps, for the regular flight of fighter jets that flew low-level sorties back to their base each morning after their practise bomb runs at a target area in the mountains about five kilometres inland from our camp. For some reason, I didn't mind the raucous noise that the jets made. I'd sit in my camping chair, drink coffee, and curiously gaze at them over the top of whatever book I was reading. I found them strangely charming and a reminder of the island's martial history and Oman's strong ties with the UK. Because of the island's historical connection with the RAF, many of the local people who we met and chatted to on the ferry from the mainland of Oman spoke excellent English, the British variety, of course.

Once disembarked from the ferry, we'd see ubiquitous short-wheelbase Land Rover Defenders in bright blue, yellow, and pink colours. These were not factory colours for the model. I assumed that the locals painted these ex-military vehicles with cheap house paint to cover up the RAF camouflage markings. Nostalgia for the old military connection with the UK was quite palatable on this small, mostly uninhabited island. At the time of our first visit, Sultan Qaboos, Oman's ruler, had reigned the country for thirty-six years. He remained in this position for another fourteen years until his sad death in 2020.

While many of the Omani locals had fallen for the charms of old Blighty, we fell in love with the desert island experience. We made Masirah our regular winter destination and visited there almost every year during our nine-year stay in the Emirates. Each winter that we went on our camping expedition to Masirah, we brought an increasing number of 'creature comforts' to make our stay more pleasurable. The first time we visited the island, we slept in a cramped supermarket tent, which, on the second day of our sojourn, was twisted into bits by the wind and almost flew away. We also had a small gas cooker, like the one hikers take with them into the mountains. We had a basic cool box made from cheap plastic, which, after an eight-hour drive from home, barely kept our food at room temperature. And we had a woven plastic camel mat to sit on. We called it a 'camel mat' because it was great for sitting on the sand. It was a big reversible mat gaudily decorated with colourful Arabic and Indian patterns. Most local families used them on picnics in the desert or on the beach. I presume that in the olden days, the original Bedouin inhabitants would fabricate similar mats from goat or camel hair with strips of skin as an edge-binding. Or, if they lived by the ocean, mats would be woven from green palm tree leaves and coconut coir. The modern version of these mats, which most inhabitants of the Gulf Peninsula sit on every weekend to enjoy the great outdoors with family and friends, is made of polypropylene.

On our second trip to the island, we came better prepared. We bought a bigger but sturdier tent which we set up in a sheltered spot so that the afternoon winds would not rip it apart. On the backseat of the car was a sizeable Waeco fridge-freezer which we would connect to the car's battery each time we went for a little drive to explore the island. Another sand mat extended our living space, and we had a basic canopy for shade, which we stretched from the top of the tent to the car. This extra shade provided a welcome respite from the midday sun. In the evenings, after a leisurely day of snorkelling and reading, I'd go to the back of the car, pick up a 'special' bottle of water which we filled at home with gin or vodka, retrieve some ice cubes from the freezer, and retire to my lounger. Examining the gentle sunset over the ocean with a cool drink in hand, we always felt quite self-congratulatory.

'People pay a lot of money to sit on a beach like this,' Robert would observe.

Because nothing brings my husband as much joy as saving money, or rather, not spending any, I chose not to point out the cost of the fridge freezer, the fancy tent, the awning, and the dozen other gadgets that we had hauled all the way from our home in Al Ain to make our beach holiday a little bit more comfortable.

The fridge freezer was still a novelty on our camping escapades, and its virtues were a regular topic of discussion. It brought a genuine smile to my face each time I stood up to refresh my drink and scooped up a couple of ice cubes for my G and T. I'm not a huge fan of spirits.

However, because alcohol was extremely difficult to get hold of in Oman, especially for non-residents like us who didn't have the special permit to buy booze at the off-licence in Muscat, we used to fill disposable bottles of water with transparent spirits like vodka or gin and mix these 'special' bottles with other bottles that we took with us to the island. In one of the more enlightened moments in my life, I realised, after filling a few 'special' bottles, that we were going to (a) struggle to find the booze among the real bottles of water and (b) mistake the vodka or gin for Adam's ale and drink some strong spirits in one gulp by mistake. To avoid this, I placed tiny secret marks on the bottles with a permanent marker. Sometimes, I had difficulties identifying these marks. That's why, once we arrived on the island — an eight-hour drive from the Emirate's border and a good hour on the ferry — I'd pull out my secret bottles from the cases of regular water and place them in a dedicated spot in the car.

'If we were at a resort, you'd pay a lot of money for a cocktail,' Robert used to like to elaborate on exactly how much money he was 'saving'.

'It's not a cocktail,' I'd point at my vodka and orange. I couldn't understand by what stretch of imagination he called it a 'cocktail'.

'Yes, it's a screwdriver. Thus, it is a cocktail.'

I looked at the stainless steel cup from which I was drinking my 'cocktail'. It had a handle like an English tea mug.

'I think we have very different definitions of what constitutes a cocktail,' I replied.

'A cocktail is at least one spirit mixed with fruit juice,' my linguist husband, who I often use as a walking dictionary when I don't have access to Google, informed me.

'Maybe in your world,' I begged to differ. 'The ingredients themselves don't make a cocktail. You're missing the preparation of the drink and how it's presented.'

'No, the essence lies in its spirit and juice.'

'OK,' I took another sip and became somewhat passionate about this topic. It's one of the reasons I don't drink spirits. 'Next time I serve you some eggs with sugar, cocoa powder, and flour, we can call it a cake.'

I could see him searching his tiny little mind for a witty retort.

'If it does not have the required shape or form and is divorced from its teleological purpose, then there is no cake. You can't call a crumb that has fallen onto a napkin a 'cake'. The crumb may represent the substance of a cake, but not its essence.'

At this stage of the proceedings, we moved on to semiotics and pondered several other things that could or could not keep their essence if presented in a novel form. We discovered that we both had very strong and very different opinions about 'substance', 'essence', and 'meaning'.

These were happy times. We really must have had very little to worry about if we had time to spend our evenings on the beach binge-reading crime novels, discussing the importance of ice cubes, and elaborating on the essence of a 'cocktail'.

In those days, even if we wanted to stay at a nice beach resort, there wasn't one on the island. We knew this from experience because, during our first trip, when the ocean winds destroyed our tent, we drove around the island in search of accommodation. The island is about a hundred kilometres long, which is about sixty-two miles. Once we reached the southernmost point, we were enchanted by the wilderness, the rock formations, and the deserted beach. We took a long walk and found all sorts of treasures: a massive conglomeration of sun-bleached oyster shells that had detached itself from a rock, a giant leatherback turtle shell, including a pristine example of a turtle skull. The skull was spotlessly clean and dry. I picked it up and found the jaw close by. Putting these two pieces together, I fancied myself a female Hamlet. I looked to the horizon with the skull in one hand and the dead oyster shells in the other. Deep thoughts about life and our impermanent bodies swirled across my mind.

'Can we take the turtle shell home?' I didn't think we could because the inside had not dried out completely. But I hoped that Robert would know how to transport the leatherback shell to our house in Al Ain.

'It's going to stink up the car, and we don't know what's inside,' it was the occasional voice of reason, and so I dropped the topic.

We returned to the car and left my treasures in the boot. I still have the oyster shells, but I gave the turtle skull to a friend, a professor of anatomy in Al Ain. I thought it would look very becoming on his desk or a bookshelf. As for me, the skull was quite hypnotic. If I had kept it on my own desk, I might have gone through the whole Shakespearean rigmarole in my head, to ultimately lose my mind. The turtle head spoke directly to me and my sense of whimsy, so it was best left with someone who used logic and science on a daily basis and was immune to its mesmerising power.

'Let's have a swim here before we continue back to town,' I suggested once the skull was wrapped in some towels for safe transport.

While Robert was an excellent swimmer, I was mediocre at best. Until I got my first set of flippers, my only claim to glory was that I was very good at not drowning. But my cheap Carrefour flippers, or swimming fins, transformed my aquatic experience. I became very confident, even a bit too confident, considering how little ocean experience I had. I had bought the snorkelling equipment just before our first trip to Masirah. I was browsing the supermarket shelves for ideas and activities to do on the beach when I spotted a simple snorkelling set in a plastic box. I might have seen people snorkelling before, but I had never given the activity a lot of thought. Because I grew up in the north of Poland by the Baltic Sea, which, even in the summer, is so cold that it's only good for jumping ankle-deep in the waves, my understanding of sea sports was minimal. Despite my limited experience, I took to snorkelling like a fish to water.

Once we arrived on the island, it took me ten minutes to figure everything out. Soon I was cruising around the underwater rock formations like a human shark taking in the spectacular coral growths and dozens of varieties of colourful, tropical fish. Robert, on the other hand, who as a young man used to kayak and do other water sports in East London in South Africa, had a hard time putting his face underwater and taking deep breaths through the snorkel hose. To compound his hesitation towards sub-aquatic breathing, his facemask kept on falling off, his fins got stuck in the sand, or his snorkel got flooded. Because of all this drama, I took on the role of the leader during our snorkelling expeditions. This particular time it wasn't different. I had swum out quite far, and when I turned around to see where Robert was, I noticed that he was still sitting on the beach, fighting with his flippers, as they were being washed away with the waves and splashing his poor face with sea water as he tried to fit his face-mask. I continued swimming, as it was best not to watch him struggle so pitifully. I calmed my nerves by watching a small school of anemone fish pass underneath me. A few minutes later, Robert caught up with me, and we followed the edge of the coral reef without realising that we were swimming quite far out from the shore.

The problem with snorkelling in a location where the water is crystal clear and the coral and varieties of fish are so beautiful is that you can lose track of time. When we finally took a rest to get some fresh air and clear our masks, we saw that we were quite far from the shore.

'We need to go back,' I declared, being the weaker swimmer.

No sooner had I finished speaking when I spotted a shark swimming directly towards us. The shark then disappeared under the water about a metre from us. It was clear that Robert had seen it, too, because he did not waste any time in deliberations. A rock protruded from the surface about ten metres away from us, towards which we both swam as quickly as we could. We scrabbled on top of the rock with our flippers still in the ocean. The rock's surface was covered in sharp barnacles and oyster shells, and as we scrambled on top of this refuge, we both painfully scratched our legs on their sharp edges. Blood ran from our legs into the water around us. We were now sitting on a lonely rock surrounded by the ocean, about 70 metres from the beach. As is always the case in life, we had a choice. We could either enter the ocean and lose one or two limbs to the shark or have our backsides reconfigured by the razor-sharp barnacles. We wisely chose the latter. The scratches didn't hurt because of the adrenaline rushing through us. It took us ten or more minutes on the rock to regain our normal breathing pattern, slow down our heart rate, and assess the situation. I was rather put off by the amount of blood dripping from a cut on my shin. Robert's legs were similarly scratched, and he was also bleeding gently.

I don't think the writers of Steven Spielberg's *Jaws* could have come up with a better scenario for two fools who were about to get chewed up by a shark. We were the perfect sacrificial characters for the beginning of a horror movie; two innocents in the wilderness with no experience and little idea of the dangers that lurk beneath the waves. My mind was filled with scenes from *Jaws* because the film constituted the sole source of my knowledge about sharks. It seemed that Robert's scholarship on the topic was just as limited. We compared notes and agreed that a single drop of blood in the water would attract the great white. Considering that we had dripped significantly more than a cupful of blood into the water at this point, I was a bit surprised that there wasn't already a whole feeding frenzy of sharks circling the miniature island on which we sought refuge. We expected imminent demise. An appalling silence fell between us as we mentally recalculated our chances of swimming back to the shore faster than a shark.

I don't know how long we were transfixed on the rock. However, the afternoon sun was definitely getting to our heads, and we were dehydrated and delirious. Any hope that someone might pass by our beach to rescue us from the rock came and went. On the positive side, the anticipated feeding frenzy of blood-hungry sharks had not taken place.

'It wasn't a full-grown shark,' I ventured a suggestion. 'He was about your size.'

I had no idea about shark sizes, but I imagined, based on *Jaws*, that a shark of just under two metres in length could not be an adult shark with an adult shark's appetite.

'Maybe he was just as scared of us as we were of him?' I was planting a seed for our escape.

'Shall we just swim to the shore as quickly as we can?' Robert felt it was time for action before we became too weak to swim.

We decided that he would swim off the rock first, and once he was on shore, I would follow. There was no real point in both of us getting eaten by the shark.

ELEVEN
LET'S GO FISHING

O nce we were both back on shore, we sat silently on the sand in the shade of the car, contemplating what we had just been through.

'Let's go back to town and find a hotel or somewhere to sleep,' I suggested.

When the wind ripped apart our tent, we had considered sleeping in the back of the SUV. But now, suffering from a mild dose of heat stroke and exhausted by the emotions that a near-death experience brings, I just wanted to lie down on a mattress in a dark room. Robert silently agreed, and we drove north to the town. On the outskirts of Hilf, we stopped at the petrol station, and Robert got out to ask where we might be able to find a place to stay. While Oman is relatively liberal, it would not have been appropriate for a woman to approach and talk with a strange man in public. I watched from the passenger window as Robert spoke to one of the customers at the petrol station. The man was dressed in a neat brown *dishdasha*, and on his head was a type of colourful and intricately decorated scarf wrapped like a turban. With the usual Omani hospitality, the man insisted on taking us to the island's only hotel. We followed him through a couple of streets, and there, at the end of town, tucked between the town's desalination plant and the airbase, was a small, lonely hotel.

We said goodbye to our impromptu guide and walked into the reception office. The aroma of burnt frankincense was so dense in the air that I could taste it. Several small charcoal incense burners were placed in various corners of the reception and near the staircase to the rooms, and clouds of incense billowed across the tiled reception area. It was perhaps for the best because we did not smell too fresh ourselves after spending a night in a tent and a day on the beach. Once we had ascended a narrow flight of stairs to our room, it became apparent why the young Omani receptionist was fumigating the place with *al-luban* or frankincense. The hotel was permeated with the mouldy smell that many a seaside hotel is blessed with, especially if it is not ventilated properly. It was not a pleasant odour, but we tolerated it out of necessity. The bathroom was basic. It had a squat-down toilet and a shower inhabited by the customary family of shiny cockroaches, who, on sensing our intrusion into their natural domain, scrambled frantically to collect their belongings and scuttle off to hide in the shower drain. The bed was adorned with a thick, coarse woollen blanket, which was a peculiar choice of hotel bedding since it was 30 degrees Celsius, or 86 Fahrenheit, outside. With the heat and humidity swirling around us, inside and out, I struggled to imagine who on earth would want to wrap themselves in a thick blanket. Another problem with the blanket was that it had no cover, thus suggesting to me that it had been in direct contact with the previous guests' sweaty skin. Like a CSI detective collecting samples from a crime scene, I picked up the offending item between my thumb and index finger and placed it on a jauntily tilted shelf inside a musty wardrobe. I gently closed the door on 'Exhibit A'.

If we had arrived at this hotel at the beginning of our trip, I would have immediately turned around and looked for other options. But, since we were exhausted from our ocean adventure earlier that morning, we needed to rest in a dark room, away from the scorching sun and aeonian wind. After a short siesta, we turned the room into a campsite. With our camping gear set out all around the room, we settled in as if we were occupying a tent on the beach, just minus the elements or the view. Since the hotel was situated right on the beach, one would expect great sea views. But the genius architect who designed this sorry establishment had located the entrance door to each room facing the sea. As a result, the bedroom windows overlooked the car park, a side wall of the desalination plant, and the main road. The constant thrum of the plant's massive diesel engines did not contribute positively to the general ambience. After a non-exotic meal of Chinese noodles cooked on a portable gas stove, we spent a few fruitful hours discussing the various failings of the hotel and how they could be fixed. But after a while, our cramped, putrid-smelling, cockroach-infested cell began to suffocate us. We had had enough and so headed back to the beach for a barbecue and drinks.

On the way there, we purchased some meat and vegetables for the evening meal. It was a relief to be back next to the sea. Again, we were sitting on clean sand and could breathe the air without gagging. The moon had not yet risen, and the beach was pitch black. In the distance, I saw a lonely wavering light heading towards us.

'What's that?' I asked.

'A boat?'

Several fishing dinghies were out, each with a small light in front to guide them.

'No, it's not on the water. It's moving along the shore,' I pointed at the light moving in our direction.

'I think it's a motorbike,' Robert hesitated.

And indeed, we soon heard the purring of a small-capacity motor, and a tall Omani man arrived before us, a dignified visitor to our temporary set-up of two well-used camping chairs, a battered cool box, and a portable barbecue. From the handles of his motorbike hung two large fish.

'Good evening,' the man spoke English with a slightly-forced British accent. 'I saw the fire from my house,' he pointed into the darkness from whence he had emerged. 'And I thought that you might enjoy some fish.'

He unhooked the fish from the handlebar and showed it to us. They were beautiful specimens and clearly very fresh. I felt terrible because we had already eaten and didn't have a proper fridge to store these very large fish. It was, in fact, far too much food for two people to eat in one sitting. I explained all this to the stranger. He did not seem particularly bothered by our refusal of his generous offer since there was no change in his friendly demeanour. He put the fish away, and we continued to chat amicably.

'What kind of fish is it?' Robert asked.

'It's kingfish,' the man explained. 'There's a great deal of kingfish and tuna in these waters.'

Robert, a very keen but extremely unlucky fisherman, was all ears. We didn't mention to Ali, for that was his name, that we had spent the first day on the island sitting on the rocks with rods in the water and dreaming of pulling out a fish.

There were many lovely coves around the island with rock formations, some extending far into the ocean. The island's location and the fact that we saw an abundance of fish while snorkelling off the beach led us to believe we were in an angler's paradise. I was confident that we would eat fresh fish from the sea daily. But hours spent standing and crouching on the sharp rocks had not yielded any results. False alarms would be triggered line after line. After jerking hard on the line, we would inevitably discover that, instead of striking a fish, the hook had attached itself to the bottom of the ocean. The waves crashing against the rocks were too strong and prevented us from diving down to salvage our hooks. We had to cut them off the line and attach a new one.

But this was not the first time we had failed to reel in any fish. Given his meagre record, Robert's perseverance at fishing was puzzling. For a large number of hours and locations where he had tried fishing in the past, I could count his catch on the fingers of one hand. For me, the indomitable fisherman's loyal companion, it seemed like a pointless endeavour. Far too many afternoons of our life had been idled away at the side of a Swedish lake and on the banks of various rivers and canals in the Netherlands. Only once, while camping by a fjord in Norway, did he get lucky. It was an extremely secluded spot not far from Nordkapp. On this particular fishing expedition, each time Robert cast his line, it would start pulling against him almost immediately, and in minutes he would be holding a beautiful sea cod in his hand. Within half an hour, we had caught enough for a generous fish supper and the next day's breakfast. Even though the good fortune that we had experienced while fishing in the pristine Norwegian waters eventually turned out to be quite elusive and impossible to emulate, it hadn't stopped Robert from accumulating more and more elaborate fishing equipment; further motivating him to angle each time he saw a large body of water.

'If you like fishing, I can organise a fishing trip for you,' Ali suggested. 'You can charter my boat, and I'll bring two crew to assist us.'

This sounded fantastic. We agreed on the price and discussed some more details about the trip. Ali was going to collect us the following day with his boat from the beach outside our hotel. We parted ways. He had to arrange the impromptu fishing trip for two clueless tourists, and we had to get some sleep before an early morning rise.

The sky was still a cool pink-orange, and the sun had not yet risen when we emerged from our room. I was carrying a canvas bag with copious supplies of sunblock cream, caps, sun hats, sunglasses, and potable water for the boat trip. Robert was holding on to his faithful fishing box and foldable rod. From the beach, we could see the little harbour where the car ferries and bigger fishing boats would be moored. There weren't any fancy speedboats or luxury yachts in sight. The harbour contained only industrial vessels, and many were in quite a dilapidated state, covered in rust and inhabited by generations of seagulls. An old-fashioned wooden *dhow* lay somewhat forlornly on its side at the entrance to the harbour. While we discussed the state of the boats, Ali arrived, piloting a small fibreglass fishing dinghy.

We used a short rickety pier to embark on his humble vessel. For some reason, he ceremoniously handed us two pairs of brand-new white cotton gloves. While he confidently told us about his best fishing location and explained what type of fish we were after, his two Omani companions, who appeared to be in their late twenties, arrived. They were carrying a large Styrofoam box filled with ice to store all the fish we would catch. They had also very thoughtfully brought along several shopping bags of bottled water and juice for everyone to drink.

While the *dishdasha*, a long ankle-length robe with long sleeves, is the customary attire of Omani men, it's neither comfortable nor practical when partaking in the physical labour of any kind, especially fishing. Our crew wore white cotton shirts with short sleeves and open necks. The shirts were quite long and loose-fitting. The crew's apparel was completed by pyjama-style trousers displaying various checked patterns and colours. Ali and one of his crew, Mansoor, wore traditional Omani caps, round and flat at the top. However, the third crew member Abdul Rahman sported a New York Yankees cap he had purchased while visiting his brother in Dubai. All of the men spoke perfect English and seemed strangely worldly and cosmopolitan. I found their demeanour and manners fascinating because they all hailed from a small, isolated fishing island with no direct road connection to the capital city of Oman, Muscat.

Masirah was very different to the fishing villages found along the coast of the mainland. There, children would often stare at me in bewilderment as if they were seeing a Western woman in jeans and a T-shirt for the first time in their lives. In some of the more remote villages, the inhabitants spoke dying languages, many of which had only a few hundred speakers left. The people of Masirah, to whom we chatted on the ferry and in the shops, were familiar with foreigners. They came across as sophisticated, well-spoken, and confident in themselves. I felt they'd feel at home whether they went to Dubai, New York, or London. Our fishing crew was the same. While Mansoor steered the boat and Ali stood alert on the prow, looking out for rocks and guiding Mansoor's navigation, Abdul Rahman regaled us with stories of his time at Muscat University, where he had studied engineering.

We learned that none of the crew on our impromptu charter was a full-time fisherman. They just loved fishing. They did it on the weekends and in the evenings, if they had time, to get fresh fish for their families. But they all had jobs either at the RAFO air base or in the town of Hilf. As Abdul Rahman eloquently told us more about life on his home island, a dark thought crossed my mind. *Have we been duped again?* I wondered. I couldn't believe that we had ventured out into the ocean with three strange men and were willing to pay them money for this escapade. But then, they all looked so sincere and honest. I could not tell if they were grifters or genuine people, so I decided to relax and enjoy my boat ride. While Robert was after his elusive fish, I merely wanted to be out on the open water for a few hours. At that time, we lived by the edge of the Empty Quarter in Al Ain, where the red dunes stretched as far as one could see. And so, the endless waves and the turquoise water constituted a welcome respite from the dry landscape of our home at the time.

Soon, Ali indicated to Mansoor that he had found a good fishing spot. They switched off the motor and started preparing the fishing gear. There was a definite mismatch between their fishing gear and ours. Robert's fishing box had been bought in Sweden a few years earlier and contained an extensive collection of hooks, sinkers, snaps, and swivels. He also had a variety of silicon lures of various colours and sizes. While Robert unfolded and prepared his European-style fishing rod, Ali handed me a coil of transparent line wrapped around a circular piece of plastic. At the end of the line, he attached a hook and took a sliver of sardine flesh they had brought in a small plastic bag. He asked me to put on the gloves he had given me earlier. I was still quite puzzled about how to fish with this contraption, so I watched Mansoor and Abdul Rahman prepare similar systems for themselves and start fishing. They simply threw the line overboard and waited for the fish to take the bait.

I did the same and watched the men for clues on what to do next. While the four of us were sitting in our spots with lines in the water, Robert was still assembling his Swedish rod. From our past fishing trips, I knew that preparing the thin nylon line he uses was fiddly, and the tiny parts that had to go together could make the most patient of saints lose their composure. For this reason, I didn't ask him any questions. The other men on the boat sensed that the Scandinavian rod might soon end up in the water and thus chose to focus on their own lines.

After just a few minutes, Abdul Rahman pulled in his line with a lovely *hammour* at the end. I was gobsmacked. Never in my life did I expect us to see a fish so quickly. But Abdul Rahman was not happy with the size of the fish. He thought it was too small and tossed it back into the briny blue. Soon our boat became a real-life version of *Let's Go Fishing!*, a game I enjoyed as a child. From either side of the boat, the Omani men were eagerly reeling in fish, unhooking each one with a professional twist of the wrist, and then, based on its size, placing the fish into the Styrofoam container or releasing it back into the sea. Of course, the Omani men's success attracted a flock of seagulls to our location. The gulls circled the boat and flew over our heads in anticipation of securing one of the fish that would be thrown overboard.

At that moment, I felt a sudden pull, and as I wrapped the line back around the plastic wheel with my gloved hand, I was pleased to see a good-sized *hammour* emerge from the surface. I looked at Robert, who had just finished setting up his fishing rod.

'You should try this,' I suggested since the Omani method seemed highly productive.

'No. I want to use my rod.'

That's fine. I thought while I attached a small piece of fresh squid to my hook and threw the line overboard.

Every few minutes, someone on the boat would bring up a fish. Everyone, that is, except Robert, who sat morosely with his hi-tech Scandinavian equipment, waiting for the fish to be tempted by a gaudy pink lump of silicon onto his hook.

'Why don't you try some real bait,' Ali suggested a new approach.

Encouraged by Ali, Robert switched out the imitation silicon fish that fooled no one for a juicy piece of sardine. A difference between the local fishing technique and using a fishing rod was that Robert felt he had to cast his bait out from the boat. With the local contraption, the Omanis merely dropped their lines directly over the side of the boat.

As Robert cast out, a crafty seagull chased the sardine at the end of the line and caught it mid-air. However, the hook became entangled in the poor bird's wing. When I saw what had happened, I almost fainted. The distressed and unbalanced bird crash-landed onto the water, now paddling around and squawking like a demented beast. All the blood drained from Robert's face as if he had downed the Ancient Mariner's albatross. I realised he was as well-equipped to handle this avian-marine drama as I was. We sat in silence, wondering what we were supposed to do.

It was patently clear that we could not abandon the poor animal with the line wrapped around his wing. Even if we cut the line from the rod, the unfortunate creature would forever be left with a small hook stuck in its wing. It would be very cruel. But as a consequence of my severe fear of birds (acquired as a child when a giant rooster attacked me), I was not mentally prepared to hold an adult seagull in my arms with its sharp beak next to my face while someone removed the hook.

Fortunately for *me*, Oman was a traditional Muslim country, and the men on the boat didn't even contemplate involving me, a mere woman, in the wildlife rescue that unfolded. The Omanis kept calm and gently pulled the gull to the side of the boat. It was, after all, still attached to Robert's line. The bird stopped panicking once it was near us and yielded to Mansoor's calm and matter-of-fact attitude. He slowly leaned over the boat's edge to pull the bird up and held it on the plank that traversed our craft amidship. The two other crew members restricted the bird's movement while Robert pulled the unfortunate hook out. It wasn't a large hook, so the operation went smoothly and with little drama. As soon as we were done, the gull soared away, up into the deep blue sky, and, without looking back, towards the safety of the fishing harbour. Both parties had had the adventure of their lifetime, it seemed.

After his disastrous attempt at using the Swedish fishing rod, Robert abandoned it and used my handline. By then, I had caught two decent-sized fish, more than I had ever caught. I was happy sitting on the boat's prow, enjoying the sea view. As I watched my hapless husband for another hour, I began to suspect that the sea gods had cursed him. Granted, he caught a lot of marine life during the remainder of the trip, but each time he pulled a creature of the deep up onboard, we were informed that what he had caught was either inedible or dangerous. While the other men on the boat pulled up grouper, kingfish, and mackerel, Robert's fish were all relatives of Leviathan. Even Ali looked at some of the specimens that Robert caught with eyes wild in disbelief. They were all quickly thrown back into the ocean, with a short prayer muttered in Arabic to disperse the evil presence from our vessel.

But their heartfelt prayers didn't dispel the bad omen that Robert had cast upon our trip because, in the next moment, all hell broke loose onboard. Even the previously calm and collected Monsoor began to scream and jump about. He was pointing at the two-foot moray eel that Robert had, with ignorant insouciance, reeled in on deck. The eel had firmly attached itself to the plank that went across the boat by twisting its body around it in muscular convulsive curls. It took me a few seconds to realise what the commotion was about. The three crewmen suddenly turned into a bomb disposal squad. Ali approached the eel as if it was some kind of a marine explosive device about to explode in our faces. He moved in slow motion and spoke gently in Arabic to the other men while keeping a fixed eye on the moray eel. His voice was as calm as if he were a yoga instructor during a particularly relaxing mindfulness session. Under his direction, they mercifully dispatched and removed the unwelcome passenger.

It was the first time I had seen a moray eel, and I was deeply unaware of its vices. The eels I am familiar with come from the Baltic Sea and are usually served smoked or as part of a delicious fish paste. The eel that had landed on our boat looked very attractive and not harmful at all. It was covered in hundreds of tiny spots that were quite becoming. Were we alone on the boat, there is no doubt that either Robert or I would have touched it as soon as it landed on deck. According to Ali, we would then have suffered excruciating pain and lost a copious number of red blood cells. We might even have had to be helicoptered to the hospital in Muscat. Reportedly, the moray eel inhabiting the seas around Masirah Island tends to attach itself to human skin and never let go.

In hindsight, some of the dangers posed by the moray eel might have been exaggerated by Monsoor. I assumed that making a living from the ocean and spending so much of their lives on the water, Omani children were warned never to touch the moray eel. As is always the case with such cautionary tales, they become somewhat embellished by our elders to ensure that no harm comes our way.

After our encounter with the eel, we changed our fishing spot for good measure. Robert and the Omanis continued fishing for another hour, and then we made our way back to the shore. We disembarked, and Ali's helpers heaved the Styrofoam box out from the deck floor. They opened it up with proud smiles on their faces. It was a great catch. We had kingfish, *hammour*, and a few other species I could not identify. There was enough fish in the container for a small fishmonger's stand, and all the fish were of a good size and healthy-looking. As I leaned forward to select the few specimens that Robert and I had caught, there appeared to be a huge misunderstanding. Apparently, *all the fish was for us.* I looked at Ali in disbelief.

'But we just need a few for the barbecue.' I explained that we couldn't take it all with us to Al Ain.

'But it's your fish', Ali insisted.

'What am I supposed to do with it?' I said in a friendly tone. 'We can't eat it all, and we can't keep it in the hotel room. Can you take it, please?'

After a few more minutes of going back and forth, the Omanis agreed to take the rest of the fish. They were, after all, incredibly honest and assumed that all of the fish they caught was for us since we had chartered the boat. We parted in good spirits. They had been paid in cash *and* had a load of fresh fish to take home, and we had had a fantastic day on a fishing boat. We went to the reception and asked if the hotel's chef could clean the fish for us. That evening, we enjoyed some delicious fresh fish on our portable barbecue on the beach. These were good times. We were young and had very little to worry about. It felt like new experiences were waiting for us around every corner.

As I sat contemplating on the beach in Sur years later, I recalled these memories of our past life, unsure whether I should go for a swim or remain in safety on the sand. Why did we leave this life of seemingly constant adventure and move to Andalusia, where, for the last four years, we had been under constant financial and emotional pressure? When we left the Middle East in 2014, I had very little to show for my life. We had a shipping container full of things and some memories of our sometimes bizarre escapades, but not much more. Nothing of substance, one might say. If we had died out there on that Masirah rock by either starving to death or by being eaten by a shark, what would our obituaries read?

> *To commemorate a foolish couple*
> *Who, whilst camping, had some trouble.*
> *They succumbed to a struggle.*
> *But no light they saw at the end of the tunnel.*
> *By a well-fed shark, their days were darkened;*
> *A dirge to Masirah Island.*

On our long journeys to Masirah Island, we would listen to a series of philosophy lectures that I had burned onto a collection of CDs. We enjoyed listening to the lecturer's ideas and arguments repeatedly. Some of the philosophers, like Kant, I already knew well. Others, like Nietzsche, came in one ear and went out the other. Some, like Hegel, went over my head. But it was Jean-Paul Sartre, the philosopher whose ideas I associated with during my teenage years (mostly by wearing black outfits and being miserable), that stayed with me. When I contemplated his radical substantialism as an adult, I realised I had previously misunderstood his central message. I was responsible for making my own life into a fundamental project that would give rise to my essence. I didn't think renovating a house was substantial enough to call it a fundamental life project.

There must be something for me, I thought. *I can't remain an empty shell.*

I had to keep on looking.

TWELVE
A DRY SPELL

'I've booked us a room at a nice resort outside Muscat,' I told Robert as soon as he returned from work to his dingy Sur apartment.

Because Robert is cautious with spending money, I usually just go ahead and book our holidays and tell him afterwards.

'But I thought we were supposed to be saving money,' he made an excellent point.

'Yes, but I will lose my mind in this tiny apartment. I can't even swim in the ocean because there're people everywhere looking at me.'

I didn't know if there were people *everywhere*, but the row of villas with blacked-out windows overlooking the nearest beach was not conducive to a relaxing swim. Especially if you were a Western woman in a bathing suit in a very traditional Muslim town. I felt as if I was being watched all the time.

'Also, I need to have some wine. *Please!*' I was building my case for a relaxing weekend somewhere private near the Indian Ocean.

By then, I had been visiting Robert in Sur for two weeks, and we had finished off the duty-free bottle of vodka I had bought at the airport. The last time I had tasted wine was in Andalusia. There was no booze shop in Sur. If you were desperate and had contacts in the Indian expat community, you might be able to score some moonshine from a secret hole-in-the-wall booze dispensary, but I wasn't keen on taking that route.

I had purchased a bottle of the stuff the previous year when I visited Robert in February. It was always a bit of a gamble. We would order a couple of bottles and wait anxiously to see what was delivered. The transaction had to be quick, so we took whatever the fixer could get. What we received was always a very strong spirit of an unknown brand. The spartan label stated matter-of-factly what the contents were; in this case, it read 'Dark Rum'. We savoured it for a few weeks by concocting various juice and soft drink mixes to make it somewhat palatable. In hindsight, I came very close to re-inventing *toddy*, a traditional Indian concoction made of alcohol, hot water, and sugar. But no matter how much I was tempted to have a warming nightcap, I could not take any more of these dark rum 'cocktails'.

Another place in Sur where one could legally purchase a pint of lager or a glass of wine was the bar in the Sur Resort Hotel. But, desperate as I was, I would never venture into that circle of hell. The bar was adjacent to the 'beach resort', supposedly accommodating tourists who visited Sur to observe the sea turtles hatch on the local beaches. However, over the decades, the bar had become the primary watering hole for the local Omani alcoholics, Sur's wretched disgrace. The lives of these men had gone so amiss that they could not even organise an Indian fixer to get them a bottle to drink in the privacy of their homes. Or perhaps their families prohibited such a transgression of Islamic law at home? These poor Omani men from the town and the surrounding mountain villages had spent their families' fortunes buying glass after glass of liquor in the hope that their lives would be different. I could see them outside the bar's car park in their Land Cruisers first thing in the morning and then late at night, tottering around the crowded car park, looking for the vehicle they had parked ten hours earlier.

Samira's brother told Robert that the men at the bar brought shame to their families. It was a small town, and everyone knew whose father, brother, husband, or uncle had dedicated their life to alcohol consumption. I couldn't help but wonder about the gender injustice associated with this vice. If Omani women had brought this type of dishonour to their families in broad daylight, their behaviour would have been dealt with without hesitation. They'd be locked up in a small room inside the walled compound. Being men, however, they continued to disgrace their loved ones until their wives had nothing to put in the pot and the children had nothing decent to wear. But I shouldn't judge. I had only been there for two weeks and had an urge to drink a glass of wine. If I were condemned to live in Sur for the rest of my life, I, too, might have made the bar my main port of call.

Given that I had not had a drink for the longest period of my adult life, I felt that the world had lost its vibrancy and joy.

What was the point of working all day if there was no reward at the end of it?

At night, we sat like two schmucks in front of the laptop, watching programs with nothing to lubricate the conversation.

I entertained many a thought on the topic of wine and life *à la* the Rubaiyat. *Is this how people live their lives?* I thought. *Stone-cold sober? It must be hard. Day after day, facing a pointless existence with nothing to lift their spirits.*

Obviously, my mind was free to wonder and speculate. *Imagine a world in which there was no wine at all.* Omar Khayyam's thesis of seizing the day definitely appealed to me in my present circumstance.

'I'm going to lose my mind if I don't get a glass of wine,' I rested my case about going to Muscat.

The following Thursday, we were on the highway to Muscat. On the right was the endless Indian Ocean, and on the left, arid mountains and *wadis* delineated the narrow coastal strip. We found our resort easily enough, but once we checked in, one thing became apparent. It was a dry hotel.

'How can a tourist hotel in a capital city be dry?' I asked in disbelief. 'Who comes here?'

Based on our past life in the Emirates, I erroneously assumed that all hotels sold alcohol. Man, I was really looking forward to a cocktail by the pool and some wine in the evening. This was my worst nightmare.

'We can find a booze shop in town. I'm sure,' Robert could see I was about to snap.

As we walked past the reception area, I sensed that the receptionist was reading my mind. He had seen the expression on my face when he informed me that there was no alcohol for sale on the premises. We went to the nearest taxi stop and made inquiries. An Omani taxi driver called Suroor knew the location of two alcohol shops. He tried to explain to us where they were, but since we didn't know the layout of Muscat, his references to various landmarks made no sense to us.

A common feature of the Emirates and Oman is that secondary streets have no name, only numbers. Only the main roads have a proper name and may serve as a reference point. But these names can be very confusing. The names of various important sheikhs in the state's history (who were usually members of the same royal family) are often confusingly similar, so it is not uncommon to find names such as *Mohamed Hamad Sultan Abdullah Street, Hamad Mohamed Sultan Abdullah Street, Sultan Mohamed Hamad Abdullah Street,* and *Abdullah Mohamed Hamad Sultan Street* in the same town. Suppose you are the designated navigator in a car. In that case, you have to be a quick reader and have an excellent short-term memory to be sure that you are on *Sultan Hamad Mohamed Abdullah Street* and not *Sultan Mohamed Abdullah Hamad Street.*

Because most of the street names in the Emirates and Oman are very long, impossible to remember, and prone to change if the name-holder falls out of grace with the ruling family, most people use significant landmarks to navigate the cities and towns. For example, a Carrefour store is usually a good point of reference, or a Lulu

Hypermarket, the Indian version of Carrefour. After referring to hypermarkets and malls as landmarks, the desperate inhabitants of these towns who wish to provide a visitor with directions might mention local international hotels and hospitals as reference points. Notwithstanding this, the most commonly referred to landmarks in the Gulf are the ubiquitous roundabouts.

True to the ostentatious taste of many Arabs, the roundabouts of the Emirates and Oman are often adorned with the most bizarre of structures, including a treasure box the size of a small house, a giant pearl, a falcon in flight, an hour-glass frozen in time, massive fake incense burners, water jugs, coffee pots, a herd of Bambi (no acknowledgement to Disney), and anything else, really, that may have brought a gormless grin to the local ruler-cum-city-planner's face. All these 'monuments' are of humongous proportions. Consider a pearl the size of a hot air balloon, a coffee pot the dimensions of a double-decker bus, and incense burners the size of industrial chimneys. There is even the Clock Tower roundabout in central downtown Al Ain, which is neither a roundabout nor a tower. I never saw the clock show the right time, either.

During my time in Al Ain, whenever a courier called to ask for directions, I would recite from memory:

Go to Al Jimi Mall. From Carrefour, continue to the Clock Tower Roundabout, turn right at Al Ain Hospital, and then turn right by the Sheikh's Palace. The compound is on the left. Call me when you are outside the gate. I'll come out.

Of course, this system of navigating around a city requires intimate prior knowledge of said landmarks. Otherwise, whatever directions you might give to a visitor will be complete gibberish. I had frustratedly wasted many an afternoon in the Middle East on the phone with deliverymen who were new to Al Ain and were hopelessly lost. Now, I was on the other end of the navigation challenge in Muscat. The taxi driver gave us directions that made a lot of sense to him but were complete gobbledygook to us.

Go to Lulu and then take the first right towards the Coffee Pot roundabout. From the Coffee Pot roundabout, turn right before the

Hilton. Then turn left towards the mall. You will see a fountain. Go there, and the shop is just before the fountain on your right.

We listened to his polite instructions twice and realised we would never find the shop in question.

'Can we follow you in our car? Would that be OK?' Robert suggested.

It was obvious that it was not the first time that visitors to Muscat had to follow the taxi driver to their destination because the driver did not hesitate.

'Of course. I'll wait here for you. We go together.'

The liquor store was but a short ten-minute drive from our hotel. On the way, I made a conscious effort to memorise the order of the relevant landmarks since we had to be able to return to our accommodation without the assistance of the taxi driver. One problem at the time was that the navigation app on our 'smart' phones did not work in Oman. Either there was a problem with the roaming service, or Google Maps was unavailable in Oman. Or a combination of both. Skype and several social media apps were banned, so I assumed that was why Google Maps might not have been accessible. But then it could have been my Spanish network's lack of collaboration with the Omani network. Whatever the reason we couldn't use the navigation app, I felt it was a big adjustment to regress to the traditional way of providing directions. A little over a year earlier, Robert and I had roamed the narrow and twisty streets of Ronda with no idea where we were going but for the little robotic voice that emanated from my phone. Here, on Muscat's high-speed, four-lane highways, we had to rely on our inherent sense of direction and memory.

I thus used several clever mnemonics to recall our way back to the hotel. We paid our taxi fare and dismissed the kind Omani driver, who seemed uncomfortable being stationary outside the booze shop for too long. Inside the establishment, I felt back at home. During our life in Al Ain, we frequented a small Indian-run establishment conveniently close to our house. When we started to patronise his shop, Robert informed the shopkeeper that our alcohol licences were being processed, and the manager sold us as much wine as we wanted. After a few months, he stopped asking for our licences.

In those days in the Gulf, expats were required to have an alcohol licence to be able to make any purchases at a licensed booze shop. In all honesty, we had good intentions in applying for the licences and would have secured them without any problems. However, because our local Indian-run business kept supplying us with booze without questions, we spent nine years in the Middle East, never worrying about the legality of our purchases.

By our second year in Al Ain, we knew the names of the manager and all the shop assistants. They could have set their watches by my appearance in the shop. Every Thursday at five-thirty, I was ready for my weekend's purchase. They must have assumed we held a valid licence, and we thought having one was unnecessary. We approached the Muscat off-licence with the same level of arrogant ignorance. Little did we know.

With a trolley full of Cabernet Sauvignon and some bottles of gin for Robert, we headed towards the checkout till. But soon, the error of our ways became apparent. The clerk totalled our purchases while we were chatting about some inconsequential topic.

'Can I see your licence, please?' a friendly voice interrupted our chit-chat.

'We're just visiting,' I explained. 'We don't have a licence.' I assumed in my naivety that this would end the conversation.

'I'm sorry, but we can only sell to residents of Oman with the licence.'

'But we're just visiting.' Like most people who refuse to admit to being wrong, I repeated the same phrase and failed to listen properly to what I was being told.

'I'm sorry,' you must put these back on the shelves.

'That was humiliating,' Robert muttered in disappointment as we piloted our small trolley back to the shelves lined with wine, beer, and spirits.

I wasn't having it. I went back to the till.

'Look,' I tried to appeal to his humanity. 'By mistake, I've booked a weekend in a dry hotel. Is there any way you can sell us the wine?' I was begging in a whisper since I was insinuating that the clerk might break the rules for me.

'I'm sorry. Maybe someone in the shop can add it to their licence,' he suggested.

'What do you mean?'

'Everyone has a monthly allowance. They can add your purchase to their licence if they don't mind using up their allowance. You need to ask,' he explained in a hushed tone since this solution was illegal too.

I turned around and looked at the customers browsing the shelves. While they were scanning the bottles looking for their favourite tipple, I was trying to evaluate how likely they would be to share their monthly allowance of liquor with a complete stranger and simultaneously commit a misdemeanour.

First, I approached an Indian man in a suit. He had kind eyes, and I had high hopes that I could procure a box of Cabernet Sauvignon without any fuss. He was not at all interested in my proposal. From the look he gave me, he must have assumed that I had run out of my own allotment and was now pestering law-abiding licence-holders for more.

I realised that I needed to share my story with my next potential Good Samaritan if I were to gain any credibility and pity. The next person I spoke with turned out to be a family doctor. He seemed very sympathetic to my plight of booking into an alcohol-free hotel and assured me that if it were not for his wife's birthday party that weekend, he would have shared his quota with me. I was deeply suspicious that he had just invented the story, but I had no proof. *Was the wife even real?* Internally, I questioned the veracity of his claim, but I could see his point. Were I allotted a strictly limited amount of wine per month, I don't think there would be much left to share. I thanked him for his understanding and returned to where Robert was standing. He was also busy pestering legitimate customers for help.

He seemed to have had better luck with a group of young American EFL teachers loading their trolleys in preparation for a Thanksgiving party. There were four of them, and they all held licences. So, between them, they could accommodate a few litres for our purchase.

'I haven't used my allowance this month,' a young Californian woman informed us. 'So, if it's just a box of wine, you're welcome. Happy Thanksgiving!'

Her friends approved of her generous offer. But as I looked at the trolley they had loaded to the brim with beers and spirits, I noted that my humble box of wine was but a drop in the ocean. We agreed to meet the young Americans outside the shop to avoid getting the shop assistant into trouble. Once outside, I discretely handed over the money and received a plastic bag with the wine. We thanked them profusely but did not want to linger in the car park in case an undercover officer was stationed outside the shop.

Once we returned to our hotel room, things started to look up again.

'We should go on a trip to see the turtles,' I proposed.

'What kind of boat would we go on?' Robert seemed interested.

I was on my laptop reading up on a tour of the marine reserve near Muscat. The advertised adventure combined several activities that we both enjoyed; snorkelling with marine creatures for me and imagining that he owned a boat and was sailing across the world for Robert.

'It's an hour's trip on the boat, then we snorkel and watch some turtles and look at the coral, have snacks and drinks on the beach on a desert island, and then return to the harbour,' I summarised the itinerary.

I booked it for the next day because the trip wasn't too expensive, and there were still two spots left on tomorrow's tour.

'How do we get to the marina,' Robert asked.

'It's straightforward. We just keep the ocean to our right, and we'll be there in twenty minutes,' were my famous last words.

THIRTEEN
PRINCESS LATIFA

Few things in life test the strength of your marriage as thoroughly as being lost in a foreign country. We'd been driving at a good pace for over half an hour, and there was no sign of the marina from which we were supposed to set off to Daymaniyat Islands outside Muscat to swim with the turtles.

'You're driving away from the ocean. We need to get off this highway,' I was shouting. 'We were supposed to be on the boat five minutes ago. The captain said to be on the boat at least half an hour before departure.'

'Where am I supposed to get off? You tell me.'

I had no answer to this. Tensions were high. We were driving on the Muscat highway at over a 120 kilometres an hour, just about keeping up with the morning traffic. There didn't appear to be any signs indicating a turn-off.

'Maybe we can just drive all the way to Nizwa and look for a boat there,' I turned to sarcasm as another exit sign for Nizwa passed over our heads.

The brand-new highway, albeit beautifully surfaced, was bereft of any helpful road signs, apart from some random signs that indicated a route in the very general direction of Nizwa, a city over 150 kilometres inland at the foot of the Al Hajar Mountains.

I was irate about the situation we were in. I had been dreaming of snorkelling in the marine reserve for a long time. It used to be my favourite holiday pastime when we lived in the Emirates, but since we had moved to the mountains of Andalusia, there were no opportunities for such marine exploration. I was so disappointed with myself for not accurately writing down the directions or not taking a taxi to the marina. We were going to miss this amazing trip because of the poor internet connection on our phones.

'You need to stop looking at your phone and tell me where to go,' I heard an irritated voice.

'I've no idea. I've never been here before. Your guess is as good as mine. We should have kept the ocean to the right.'

'But the highway didn't keep the ocean to the right. It heads inland.'

Suddenly, we spotted a small exit sign in Arabic and mistransliterated English. I had never heard of the area's name before, but at least we would be off the highway.

'Let's go off here,' I demanded. 'We need to stop somewhere and look at a map.'

Even though I had no clue where we were, I felt we should try our luck on the minor roads that followed the coastline. After a few minutes, we found ourselves in a small town or suburb of Muscat. I could not tell. At this stage, we had been driving for over forty minutes away from the city centre and might as well have been outside Muscat. As we entered the town, my phone rang.

'Is this Sapeena Ostiska?' I heard a male voice enquire.

'Yes.'

'It's Captain Ahmed from the turtle tour. We are waiting for you and Mr Robert. Are you coming?'

'We're lost,' there was no point concealing the truth from the man.

'Where are you?'

Why people insist on asking you where you are when you are lost is hard to comprehend. I wouldn't have been lost if I had known where I was.

'I have no idea.'

'Are you near the marina?'

He was really not getting the point that we were lost.

'Maybe,' I guessed, unaware of how wrong I was.

'Can you ask someone?' that was the first good idea.

'I'll ask a taxi driver,' I told him and started to manically gesticulate to Robert to pull over as I spotted a taxi parked near a small shopping centre.

I exited the car and sprinted over to the lonesome taxi. The driver rolled down the window of his banged-up Toyota Corolla, and I handed him my mobile.

'Can you tell this man where we are?' I pleaded, somewhat out of breath.

The men exchanged greetings in Arabic and discussed our predicament for a few minutes. The driver handed my mobile back to me.

'He says that you are in ...' To this day, I have no idea where we were on that stressful morning. The captain continued: 'It's about thirty minutes from the marina. Do you want us to wait for you? I can explain to the other passengers.'

'Yes, please. That would be wonderful.'

'But you must follow the taxi driver. Give him your phone please, and I will tell him where to go. He has no idea where the marina is.'

I handed my phone back to the taxi driver, and he listened to the captain's instructions. In the meantime, I returned to our rental car and explained the Captain's plan to Robert.

'Good, but you must go with the driver and tell him to slow down if he starts to lose me.'

Robert feared that, inspired by 'the need for speed', we'd lose the taxi driver after the first roundabout. This was a valid point. Omani taxi drivers like to break land speed records just on regular journeys.

'OK,' I agreed. 'Follow us.'

I got into the taxi, and our little magical mystery tour through the coastal villages outside Muscat began. In my misguided sense of direction, I had a feeling that the ocean would appear around the next corner. Still, we seemed to be driving through various fishing settlements, past malls and desalination plants, back on the highway, and again through several other small villages.

Every few minutes, the driver would call the captain on his phone to check if he was going in the right direction. I'd already had a morning imbued with stress and adrenaline. I didn't need the extra aggravation of watching the driver dial the captain's number while going over a hundred kilometres an hour along a twisty narrow road. I questioned my judgment of hiring this taxi and wondered whether the pleasure of turtle-watching was worth dying for. At that moment, I put my hand in my pocket and realised I had both my phone and Robert's phone. I placed the two phones on my lap.

Super, I told myself, looking back to see if Robert was still following us.

'Slow down, please.' Now I was apprehensive that we would lose Robert. *How would we find each other? He does not know my number or his phone number.*

'My husband drives slowly, *shway shway*,' I tried to explain the situation with the little Arabic I had picked up over the years.

After another emotionally exhausting fifteen minutes, I finally saw the sign for the marina. I don't think I had ever been so happy to see a bunch of bobbing boats in my whole life. From the back seat, I cheered and applauded the driver's good sense of navigation. He must have thought I was the loopiest lady he had ever driven. I knew we had no time to spare, so as soon as the car stopped, I gratefully handed the driver his fare plus a generous tip. Robert pulled up, locked the car, and quickly joined me as we walked down a ramp to the water. Captain Ahmed was waiting for us with a friendly smile. Like so many Omani small business owners, he was Mr Congeniality himself.

Notwithstanding that we had arrived fifty minutes late, he could not have been more welcoming and understanding. This, of course, could not be said of our fellow passengers, who gave us cold stares as we boarded, uttering heartfelt apologies. Since all the other passengers were British, I had an opportunity to experience being sent to Coventry. It was not a pleasant experience.

Had our fellow travellers been Spanish, French, or American, we would have been barraged with a series of questions about the reason for our tardiness. A few expletives might have been thrown our way, and jokes would have been made at our expense. Perhaps we would have been chided for our complete lack of respect for other people's time. But then we would have embarked on our marine adventure with the air cleared. New friendships would be formed, and maybe one or two other passengers would have mentioned the time when they, too, had delayed the departure of a pleasure trip.

However, being British and, by default, non-confrontational in such a social situation, our fellow passengers maintained an uncomfortable silence. No one mentioned the fact that we were horrendously late and had wasted an hour of everyone's time. They merely looked out across the harbour and pretended that everything was fine. The jovial captain directed us to two seats at the back of the boat, the only two seats left. Since no one wanted to talk to us, we eavesdropped on their conversations. At the same time, the captain manoeuvred the motorboat past several luxury yachts, out of the busy marina and into the ocean.

'We have exactly the same boat,' we heard a woman in her fifties announce. 'It's in the marina in the centre of town.'

I couldn't see her face because our seats were in the stern facing out to the sea while hers was behind us, facing forward on the boat's starboard side. I looked around and appraised the vessel. It was a sturdy modern fibreglass vessel that could accommodate ten to twelve passengers. There was a generous shaded area and plenty of storage space on the deck for snorkelling equipment and refreshments.

'Why don't you take *your* boat to the Daymaniyat Islands?' a stranger beside her enquired.

Yes, w*hy don't you?* I wondered, too.

We were both similarly puzzled by the incongruity of her statement. *Why was she paying for a boat trip if she owned a boat that was exactly the same as this one? Robert's facial expression asked.* Thankfully, she explained her reasoning to us all in a thunderous voice that could be heard over the drone of the engines.

'Well, there is a lot of maintenance involved...' she pontificated on with a list of details regarding the upkeep of her craft. 'That's why we timeshare it. Two other families own shares in the boat. We use it once a month for the weekend and have drinks and picnics in the marina.'

It sounded to me that she had bought herself a very expensive table at a restaurant with a sea view, but unlike a real restaurant, she had to make her own food and serve her own drinks.

'To take it out...' she sighed. 'It's so much work. It's much easier to go on a trip like this one.'

I tossed Robert a knowing smile. *Are you listening to this?* The woman brilliantly made my point against Robert's dream of owning a small boat. While she presented an excellent argument against buying a boat, the sea gods reinforced this point.

At first, we thought that we had the best seats on the boat. The cityscape of Muscat and the shore receded over the horizon as we were gently moved by the waves and the irresistible thrust of the four powerful motors that propelled us forward. But as soon as Captain Ahmed hit the gas, we were in for another experience. To say it was a choppy morning would be an understatement. It was like being in a front seat at a Water World show with a frantic giant orca that was intent on drowning us. In five minutes, we were thoroughly soaked through by the splashing waves and engine spray.

'We'll dry up later,' I shouted at Robert over the noise of the breaking waves and the motors.

The soaking we received was inconvenient, but what really disabused Robert from his boat-ownership aspirations was the constant motion of the boat as we rose on the crest of the waves and then dropped down from a great height.

'I have to break through the waves,' the captain yelled out an apology as some passengers were getting visibly green. 'The sea is very bad today. Many boats didn't go out, but I hate disappointing my customers.'

I've been on less vomit-inducing roller-coasters, I thought to myself but did not say the *v*-word in case it would trigger a physical response from other passengers.

'There's nothing like taking a boat trip to put you off buying one,' Robert seemed quite proud of his witticism as he wiped the streaming seawater from his face with his towel.

It took us a good hour to get to the marine reserve, where we were supposed to swim with the turtles. The trip was torturous, to say the least, and by the time we arrived at the islands, I wished we had missed the boat's departure altogether. Now *I* kept silent while the other passengers let rip with a series of complaints about Mother Nature. Fortunately, the captain moored in a picturesque bay between two rocky islands, and the violent bucking of the boat subsided to a gentle swaying that had an immediate calming effect on the passengers. Everyone regained their natural colour, and smiles reappeared on previously tense countenances.

Captain Ahmed called for our attention and told us about the marine life in the reserve and what types of coral, turtles, and fish species we could expect to see on our snorkelling adventure. He gave us friendly but firm instructions on what not to do. We were moored somewhat away from the reef on a sandy seafloor to preserve the coral. It was a protected area in that the number of people visiting it was limited, and their behaviour was strictly controlled. Once we were told where we could swim to observe the marine life, we donned our snorkelling gear and, one by one, jumped into the sea from the small platform at the stern of the boat.

I find swimming underwater and gazing at the sealife a most relaxing experience. I have tried meditation in the past, but I always feel more irritated after a session than before. I'd get my yoga mat in place and arrange my legs and hands in the prescribed manner. I'd close my eyes to help me get into the 'zen zone' and become 'mindful'. Then, after ten seconds, I'd feel an itch. I'd adjust my sock, scratch my ankle, and start over. I would just about close my eyes again when I might spot a misplaced book resting on a chair. Something had to be done about it. I'd sigh, get up, and put it back on the bookshelf.

OK, OK. Now, I'm ready. I'd reassure myself before settling down for the third time to meditate.

As soon as I'd get into the required meditative pose, an uninvited fly would sit on my arm and buzz around my head. I'd try to stay calm and channel my inner Dalai Lama by contemplating the fly's inalienable right to live. Thirty seconds might pass before I'd get up, go to the kitchen, fetch a can of fly spray and terminate the pesky insect with extreme prejudice in the most unmindful of ways.

Now you're ready. I'd try to convince myself that I was capable of remaining stationary in one spot for more than a few minutes in a state of introspection. I never succeeded.

But what I might have failed to achieve motionless on my yoga mat I perfected when snorkelling. I was aided by the absolute and all-encompassing silence that I experienced each time I dove below the ocean's surface. The auditory deprivation, combined with the gentle movement, instilled a feeling of peaceful serenity. The fish and other sea creatures would just go about their everyday activities oblivious of my presence. Their aquatic antics presented me with a spectacle that could never bore me. I could stay there for hours on end in the warm tropical water, swimming along the reef and admiring the wonderful shapes and colours of a world usually hidden from us.

We had swum up and down the reef's edge a few times when Captain Ahmed joined our group. He was equipped with a professional underwater photography camera. As Robert and I resurfaced to breathe and exchange experiences, he invited us to follow him. He wanted to take a photo of Princess Latifa.

'It's lunchtime, and she always dines in the same spot,' he explained and then disappeared underwater.

We followed his lead but kept our distance, not wanting to scare the turtles or the fish. As promised, Princess Latifa was at the bottom of the seafloor, grazing on a salad of algae and seaweed filaments. She was a beautiful, medium-sized green sea turtle. We watched her in awe for some time and followed Captain Ahmed to another spot to meet 'Sultan' and then 'Nouf'. I forgot to ask how he knew which turtles were male and which were female. They all looked very similar to my untrained eye. Whether it was a mere party trick or a genuine love of the marine environment, I was impressed by his effort in giving all the local turtles names and reporting on their personalities and habits.

The green sea turtle travels great distances between nesting sites and foraging grounds. The turtles we met that day would soon travel across the Indian Ocean to the beaches of Bangladesh and India, where they would eat their fill. Subsequently, I often thought of Princess Latifa, alone in the ocean, her small flippers pushing through rough seas, dodging fishing nets and plastic bags. I hope she made it.

FOURTEEN
GOODBYE OMAN

'Samira has asked me whether we could meet her at her father's farm on Saturday,' Robert informed me once we were back in Sur.

It was a somewhat strange invitation, so I asked why.

'She wants our advice about building a spa there.'

I sighed.

Samira was the reason why we were back in Oman. A year earlier, when we were stuck trying to decide whether we should tutor the children of Chinese overachievers online or go back to teaching in the Middle East, she emailed Robert out of nowhere and asked if he could come over to Sur to help her start a private school. Samira had been his student back in Al Ain, where he taught teacher-trainees for many years. She was originally from Sur but had been living in Al-Buraimi, a small border town next to Al Ain. In those days, many young people in Al-Buraimi attended school and university across the border in the UAE.

She was already a mature student when we first met her in 2010. Back then, there was no highway to Sur, and a four-by-four vehicle would be needed to make the twelve-hour trip from Sur to Al Ain. At the time, I didn't know that there was a personal reason why she lived so far from her family home. I found out years later that Samira was a young divorcee with a baby boy whose father refused to acknowledge his existence. Embarrassed by the predicament that the strict Omani patriarchy had placed her in, her brothers had sent her across the country to live with her eldest sister and study in Al Ain.

But once young Samira had overcome the shame and humiliation of being a young divorcee, very little could stop her in her tracks. Over the years, she grew from strength to strength with a little help from her family. She earned her Master's Degree in teaching English and owned and ran a small grocery shop near her sister's house. Once her confidence was fully restored, she decided to return to her home town with a bang. She wasn't going to be a teacher — that would have been too easy. She was going to open a private school.

In Sur at that time, there were only a handful of small private schools. Most of these were run by Indian and Pakistani educators and catered to local expats from India, Pakistan, Sudan, and some Arab countries, such as Jordan and Syria. Samira's school would be the first private school run by an Omani that would cater for Omani students, many of whom didn't even live in Sur but were scattered across the several mountain villages around the town. I admired her moxie and resilience.

'It's just so hard on Faris,' she told me over an informal lunch. Faris was now ten years old. 'His father lives 300 metres from us, and he hasn't visited him once. He's told everyone that Faris is not his son. The children at the school know about it and mock him.'

I looked down at my Subway sandwich — a novelty food in this part of the world and hence considered a somewhat fancy lunch option. At a loss as to how to diplomatically respond to her story, I resorted to clichés.

'It's not your fault.'

'You should focus on the positive.'

'Things will get better.'

I hated myself for regurgitating these trite truisms in the face of someone's heartbreak. I should have kept silent.

'Why do you live so close to him?' I asked the first rational question that came to my mind.

'I don't have much choice. I'm not married, so I can't rent by myself. I had to move back with my parents, who live on the same street. It was an arranged marriage. Our families had been friends for many decades. But not anymore. The *jinn* is following me, you know.'

As a sucker for tales of the supernatural and dark magic, I am all ears if they are told to me first-hand by people I know. One of her theories was that a *jinn* had come to her wedding and placed an evil spell on her marriage. In the Gulf culture, a *jinn* is an evil creature whose sole aim is to destroy our plans and mess with our minds. It seemed to me that a *jinn* had attached itself to Samira long before her wedding day. Her misfortunes and strange experiences had started in her adolescence.

As a teenager, she was sent to a boarding school in the dry, hot mountains near Nizwa, far away from the cool breeze of the Indian Ocean. Unlike British boarding schools, which might be associated with privilege and money, in remote parts of Oman, they were merely convenient schools where students lived during the week because their homes were too far away to travel to every day.

Sixteen-year-old Samira, alone in Nizwa, soon became possessed. She would be locked up for days in her bedroom while a local shaman would be called in to exorcise the *jinn*. But she could not be rid of the ghosts of strangers strolling the corridors of her boarding school. One strange apparition, dressed in a black *abaya* and with long wild hair let loose, would wander into her locked room, sit at the foot of her bed, and cry most sorrowfully. Samira would scream out, night after night, until her father was called in to come and take her home.

After hearing Samira's stories, I assumed her family to be a bunch of uncaring monsters. But this image could not be reconciled with the family's beautiful farm in the middle of an oasis where Robert and I met her one afternoon to discuss her new business idea.

'What's this building? Is this your summer house?' I pointed to a tiled structure surrounded by mature date and banana trees.

'No, the house is over there,' she pointed to the left, but it was not immediately visible through the abundance of date palm trees. 'This is a *hammam*. There is a swimming pool inside and a barbecue. My father built it when we were children so that we could play in the water on hot days.'

We walked up the stairs to the *hammam*, and Samira found a key hidden under a flower pot near the entrance door. The space inside was beautifully tiled with colourful Arabic patterns. There was a large empty swimming pool in the middle of the generously-sized room and various other areas for entertainment. In the background, I spotted a kitchen area and a steel grid for a barbecue. It was plain to see that love for his family inspired these facilities. This wasn't a place created by a tyrant whose only wish in life was to deprive his daughters of their freedom.

'We used to come here all the time in the summer,' Samira explained as we snooped around. 'My brothers and sisters and I would play in the pool, and my father would barbecue a goat or chickens from the farm.'

It was clear in my mind that her parents had created this stunning private haven for their family so they could enjoy each other's company outside the constraints of the Muslim community in which they lived. I could see them all, twenty years younger, jumping into the pool and having the time of their lives. Their laughter still echoed throughout the spacious building, and I was impressed by her parents' outstanding achievement of creating a place that resonated with happiness even after it had fallen into disuse.

'So, you see, we already have a pool,' Samira started to outline her new venture for us. 'I'll show you the rest.'

We exited the pool building to explore the farmlands, surrounded by lush swathes of bamboo — there was evidently a lot of water around. As we traversed the narrow pathways around the expansive tomato and cucumber patches, we could neither see nor hear the city's traffic. Shaded by tall coconut trees and ancient mango trees, I felt that this was a place made of dreams.

'On this track, we could have a circular bicycle path for the ladies,' Samira continued. 'Many local women would like to do sports but can't cycle by the beach or in the city. But they could come here and cycle around the farm. We'd build a high wall all around the property for privacy.'

'There could be a spa where our summer house is. We would have to knock it down and build it again, but I think it can be ready in three months,' Samira was building her resort and spa empire right before my eyes.

'It would be like the resort clubs at Al Ain or Abu Dhabi hotels. The ladies would pay a monthly or annual subscription and come here any time.'

'Without their husbands or children?' I wondered how feasible her idea was.

'Exactly!'

Samira's spa idea started to resemble some sort of dystopian commune. I looked in the direction of the Bangladeshi workers who were busy cleaning the chicken coops about 50 metres from the proposed spa headquarters.

'Let's choose a goat?' Samira suddenly changed the subject.

'Choose a goat?' I asked.

'To eat,' Robert chimed in, giving me a knowing look. By now, he had been accustomed to the Omani tradition of killing a baby goat to cook for a party or an important celebration.

'We're going to have a party for you and Robert at the school before you travel home.'

It was the end of November, and we had decided that Robert would travel back home with me. He had agreed to return in the spring if Samira needed further help running the school.

Even though I refused to choose the goats that would be slaughtered, two were selected by the farmhands once we had left the farm and were served the next day at the school. All the teachers and Samira's family were in attendance to bid us farewell, so no one noticed that I did not eat any of the goat meat. In true Omani generosity, the tables were fully laden with ginormous platters of spicy *biryani* rice, dried fruit, and large chunks of goat meat. Various colourful macaroni dishes were also served to create a fusion of Eastern and Western plates. During my time as a primary school teacher in Al Ain, where most of my colleagues were from Jordan and Syria, I noticed that any dish consisting of macaroni and cheese, usually with very overcooked pasta and a generous helping of cheese and luminescent boiled vegetables, was the way to an Arab woman's heart.

'We're going to get some *karak*,' announced Farida, an Indian kindergarten teacher, as she turned to me. 'Do you want to come with us?'

In the inevitable absence of alcohol, guests at public events in Oman tend to compensate for this by overindulging in sugar and caffeine. *Karak* is a concoction combining a diabetes-inducing amount of sugar and a heart-exploding amount of caffeine. There are various recipes for *karak*. Many families add their own little tweaks to the traditional recipe and swear that theirs is the real *karak*. A sectarian conflict would rapidly escalate if one recipe were declared regnant over another.

The basic idea behind preparation of *karak* is the lengthy infusion of several handfuls of strong black tea leaves in boiling water until the resulting dark liquid looks like engine oil, a potion anecdotally drunk in prison. The only difference between the variant served to the incarcerated is the addition of cardamon seeds and other spices, depending on the region and personal preferences. To this black concoction, you add copious amounts of sugar and a generous amount of condensed milk to make it palatable. The end product is guaranteed to give the consumer a boost of sugary glucose and a strong caffeine kick. It is a good party stimulant, and the subsequent sugar-induced headache is not unlike a hangover.

While I don't count myself as a connoisseur of *karak*, I decided to seize the opportunity to take a break from the party. As always happens at such get-togethers in the Gulf, I was marooned at the women's table. Unfortunately, I did not know any of the women, but I did know some of Samira's numerous brothers. Samira was nowhere to be seen, and Robert and other men were chatting and laughing on the other side of the school lawn. Despite my desire to change tables, it would not be appropriate for me to join the men's table. I felt a bit stuck, surrounded by women from Sudan, Palestine, Iraq, and a few other places who spoke very little English or had no interest in chatting with a complete stranger who was about to fly off. No one noticed when Farida and I left the table.

A taxi was waiting for us outside the school's gate. Farida's friend, a fellow English teacher, Joyce, was waiting for us in the back seat. The windows were rolled down as she was finishing a cigarette.

'I didn't know you smoked?' I remarked. I'd met Joyce a few times at the school. She was a lively primary school teacher; for some reason, I never thought she was a smoker.

'I smoke on the weekends,' she said with a slight South-African accent.

We closed the doors, and soon all my memories of life in the Middle East washed over me. *How many times before have I lived this scenario?* I asked myself. Sitting on the grimy, sweat-stained, once cream-coloured velvet seat of a clunky Corolla infused with the driver's BO and the passengers' tobacco smoke brought back memories of many a night out in Al Ain and subsequent breakneck speed trips home in the back of similarly dilapidated Corollas. The drivers of these taxis had one speed, which was as fast as humanly possible, so it helped if you maintained a somewhat loose connection with reality and your sense of personal preservation.

Oftentimes, when taking a taxi during the daytime, I'd negotiate with the man behind the wheel and drop subtle hints suggesting that he slow down:

'I'm not really in a hurry,' I would inform the wannabe Verstappen.

'I think you need to slow down here; there's a speed camera ahead,' a lie that never worked.

'Watch out for the school crossing!' would fall on deaf ears.

It was only when comfortably inebriated that I would give in and give the taxi driver free rein to try to kill me.

I suppose I've had a good run at this life. I would reflect while watching the blurry lights of lampposts and other vehicles whizzing past.

This journey in Sur was no different. In a few seconds, the driver was going a hundred kilometres an hour even though we were still in a residential area with apartments, family houses, and shops on both sides of the street. Even though we were traversing the suburb faster than Carlos Sainz in his prime, I noticed we had driven past the tea shop.

'Aren't we getting *karak*?' I thought our mission was to fuel the ladies at the school with caffeine and sugar.

'We'll come back for it,' Farida informed me. 'Let's have a drink first.'

Since almost a week had passed since our expedition to Muscat, where we secured a box (now empty) of wine, I didn't challenge this proposed detour. The taxi dropped us off outside the Sur Beach Hotel, one of three city establishments boasting a bar. I wasn't sure what the plan was because I knew that the bar was full of drunk Omani men, and I couldn't imagine Farida or Joyce wanting to spend any time inside there. I held my tongue and followed them through the hotel reception area to the garden on the other side, where we found a small green lawn with a few tables set out for guests. Both teachers appeared to have become regulars at the hotel because the waiter merely confirmed our order and walked quickly away. Serving us drinks in the garden was not strictly legal, but sitting in the disgusting bar inside the hotel building was also impossible.

I looked over at the moon rising over the Indian Ocean. There was a lovely breeze coming in from the sea. Soon our cocktails were served, and the girls chatted about their lives in Sur, problems at the school, and what they did on the weekends. It was all too familiar. I had been there almost fifteen years earlier when I first arrived in the UAE and secured a last-minute job at a private American-curriculum primary school. I took a sip of my cocktail and looked up at the stars. It felt like fate was compressing all my Middle Eastern experiences into one. The smells and sounds were too familiar, the stories were predictable, and the feeling inside me was hollow. I was once again watching life through a window. It was time for us to go home.

FIFTEEN

VINHO VERDE

Almost a week later, I was standing on the Queen's Terrace in Sintra, Portugal, taking in the views of the vast Atlantic Ocean on the one side and the city of Lisbon peeking its head behind the forests on the other. It was early December, and the cold air created clouds of breathy condensation from our mouths each time we spoke. All the other tourists around us wore winter jackets topped with oversized woolly scarves. Men and women sat together, drinking hot chocolate and mulled wine bought from the palace's café. There was a Christmassy feeling in the air. We couldn't have been further away from Oman.

I hadn't planned to visit Portugal, but when our house-sitters asked if they could stay for another week after our arrival until their next assignment, I decided it was an excellent opportunity for us to go on a short holiday.

'They've already been in the house for a month and haven't complained about how remote it is and that they have to pump water into the tank every week. They haven't broken anything, and they know the pets,' I reasoned with Robert.

'It's not easy to find good house-sitters, and I have no idea when we can take another holiday,' I pleaded.

The latter was an accurate observation. With our new savings, we planned to finally renovate the first floor of our house, the living room and the kitchen. This meant we would spend the next few months on a building site. I hoped that we would be finished before the next tourist season.

This plan seemed to convince Robert. We returned home and were met by Bobby at the gate, who couldn't believe his luck that we were back. He thus spent the first hour after our arrival jumping up and down like a trained circus dog. I checked on the cats, who seemed indifferent and aloof; that is to say, they were their regular selves. Since everything seemed to be in good order at the house, we repacked our suitcases and, the next morning, bid everyone a fond farewell and drove off to Lisbon for a few days. It was only a seven-hour trip, and after passing the city of Cordoba, most of the drive was on a smooth highway with very little traffic.

I didn't have any great expectations of Lisbon. I had a vague idea of the old-fashioned trams that tourists can take in the old town, and I had seen some photos of some beautifully tiled façades. However, my first glimpse of the capital was quite breathtaking.

'It's beautiful,' I stated the obvious as we waited in a long line of cars to exit the highway and pay the toll fee.

Before us lay the mighty River Tagus and, on its banks, the most picturesque assembly of houses, churches, and stately buildings. All in different colours and styles, the buildings appeared to be hanging onto the cliff for their very lives. Should one building at the top tumble down, they would all collapse like domino pieces. Or at least, it seemed so from the other side of the river. I wasn't surprised the following day when I read a sign on a street art mural in the old town that the earthquake of 1755 had almost completely destroyed the city.

The apartment we rented for a few days was in a modern suburb on the flat outskirts of the city. There was no imminent threat of a Baroque cathedral or a Neoclassical palace toppling over onto the roof of the building where we slept. But more importantly, the place had free parking. In the days leading up to our getaway, I imagined us staying in a tiled townhouse in the old town with a terrace overlooking the river. I combed the booking sites for places in Lisbon's old quarters that met my criteria: a balcony with a view, a king-size bed, and a parking space. I soon dropped the large bed from my search and resigned myself to being uncomfortable at night. But even then, I couldn't find any properties that matched my requirements. I dropped the 'terrace' from the search filter and decided we could find a restaurant with a view. But still, there was nothing available. I might as well have searched for a villa with a pool on Mars. It became clear to me that there was no parking space in Lisbon's old town — short of leaving our car leaning vertically in the narrow space between two 18th-century townhouses, I had to change my priorities.

'We can use Uber to go to the city centre and back,' I explained my plan to Robert.

The Uber solution worked out perfectly. We left our car safe in the suburb, allowing us to spend a whole day wandering the streets of Lisbon without being forced to remember where we had left it or worrying whether it had been legally parked. When we were tired of sightseeing and wanted to go back, I'd simply press the button on my phone, and in a few minutes, a car would arrive wherever we were standing at that given moment. It was our first time using Uber, and we couldn't get enough of the magic trick.

In our previous experience as city tourists, we'd had to search for a taxi rank. We would then have had to negotiate a price beforehand (to avoid a nasty surprise at our destination) and explain to the driver where we wanted to go. But with the Uber app, all this hassle was gone. Our destination address in Lisbon was programmed in the app's memory, the computer estimated the price, and the driver came to fetch us wherever we happened to be waiting. One possible downside of Uber is that even after spending a week in the city, I have no idea of Lisbon's geography and only a vague understanding of the various *bairros* because we ended up traversing the neighbourhoods like a tumbleweed in our exploration of the city without giving the slightest thought about remembering where we were or where we were going.

Our days in Lisbon were filled with fantastic walks past colourful buildings, examining ingenious street art, and jumping on and off quaint yellow trams. At dusk, we explored several Christmas markets where we drank dozens of thimble-sized cups of a sweet, cherry-like liqueur called Ginja. We ate Portuguese pastries and watched families delight at the winter fairs, accompanied by children screaming in fear from the mini rollercoaster rides. Most of our visit to Lisbon was spent walking the city's streets as we revelled in our newly-regained sense of freedom after being confined by the benighted mores of the Middle East. While we couldn't get enough of the city's delicious food, drink, and atmosphere, one issue became apparent; there were no public toilets in the fancier parts of the capital.

The restaurants and cafés had toilets, of course, but after yet another *bica*, aka a Portuguese espresso, I would often be desperate to use an establishment's facilities soon after I had left it.

'I really need to use the toilet,' I informed Robert for the third time as we marched down the neoclassical avenues of Baixa, Lisbon's elegant downtown.

Being used to living in the countryside, where endless olive groves provide ample privacy in case of a toilet emergency, I had forgotten that, in the city, one can't just roam aimlessly without a pitstop in sight.

'Where is a McDonald's when you need one?' I asked a rhetorical question.

'Just go into one of the restaurants,' Robert thought it was that simple.

'There's a *maître d'* outside each of them,' I pointed at the upmarket Art Deco-decorated establishments that lined the streets. 'It'd be like going to the Louvre to buy some stationary. I'm not spending eight euros on a glass of wine just to use the toilet. You're out of your mind.'

As my issue was burning, I was getting more annoyed by the minute. Had we been in a less classy neighbourhood, I could have been creative with my problem. For example, in Belém, the gateway of the great explorers, an expansive park stretched along the river bank. In the Alfama, a medieval maze, there are hundreds of little shabby cafés and restaurants packed with tourists, where no one would notice an additional 'customer' sneaking in and out to use the bathroom. In the bohemian Bairro Alto, there were plenty of art galleries and museums where one could step in under the pretence of looking for some fine art to buy, feign interest in the work on display until the manager left you alone, and then take advantage of the bathroom facilities.

Baixa district, rebuilt after the great earthquake, was 'the pinnacle of urban planning'. That's what I read on one of the tourist websites on my phone. True to its neoclassical heritage, it represented a victory of concrete and stone over Nature. I could imagine how the neighbourhood had looked two hundred years earlier. The perfect white façades lined the generous pavements and squares so that the wealthy owners of these houses could parade up and down spacious avenues in their horse-drawn carriages. The real business of life was conducted in the back alleys, where housekeepers and maids dealt with tradesmen, beggars, stray dogs, and the waste generated by the city. And that's where I spotted a glimmer of hope. It was not a McDonald's but a Subway.

'Just pretend to browse the menu as if we're about to order while I pop into the bathroom,' I instructed my less city-savvy husband.

As someone who grew up in South Africa and spent most of his childhood either running barefoot in the African bush or at boarding school, Robert had little understanding of the nuances of using an establishment's bathrooms while not actually being a patron. On the other hand, as a graduate student in Poland's capital, I used to maintain a mental map of the university libraries, health clinics, museums, pubs, and art centres where one could use the ladies' room unnoticed. Unfortunately, this knowledge is not immediately transferable from city to city. In each new destination, one has to spend several weeks reconnoitring establishments where the manager and staff couldn't care less who frequented their lavatory.

The lonely Subway that we entered seemed to be one such place. The place wasn't crowded, but the young sandwich artists behind the counter did not even look up from their mobile phones when we entered the building. While Robert stood and read their menu, I went round the side of the counter and headed towards the bathrooms. My heart sank. The door to the stalls was locked. A prominent sign on the wall informed 'patrons' to ask for the key at the counter. Desperate, I pulled on the women's stall's handle to discover it was not locked. A good Samaritan had left the lock in the locked position, thus preventing the door from closing properly.

Thank you! I praised the forward-thinking genius who had just saved my day.

I didn't mind that the door was unlocked. I left the stall rejuvenated and ready to continue our exploration of the grand city of Lisbon.

'We should go on a food tour,' I suggested to Robert as we boldly left the Subway empty-handed.

I wouldn't have thought of it myself, but I kept receiving messages on my phone suggesting I partake in various Airbnb experiences. Since we still had some 'super-host' credit on the app, I thought we could put it to good use. On hearing that we would only pay half price for the tour, Robert didn't need any more convincing.

The following evening, I found myself in a harbour tavern looking at a slice of toasted, rustic-looking bread bedecked with some juicy, tinned sardines. It was not very different from an impromptu lunch that I might rustle up for myself at home if I had no time to cook. But I didn't point out this lack of culinary effort to anyone else at the restaurant table.

The two American couples sitting opposite me must have thought this 'open sandwich' represented the pinnacle of human culinary technique. They were *aww*-ing and *ooh*-ing over the little plates of tinned sardines as if they had been presented with the most delicate exotic tropical fish prepared by the emperor's private chef. But then again, maybe they were just feeling sorry for the poor Europeans who deem tinned fish on toast as something worthy of serving in a restaurant on a 'food tour'. Our food guide was positively excited about the dish. But she was Portuguese and was also paid to promote the food.

Notwithstanding the simplicity of some of the dishes served to us on our gastronomic tour, Ruthy was the perfect hostess with her vibrant smile and voluminous black hair. It became apparent that she had begun her *Treasures of Lisboa* tour by shocking the small group of tourists who had signed up with her. I couldn't have been the only person in our group thinking: *What the heck! This was supposed to be a gourmet tour?!* While looking doubtfully at the tinned sardines. With a charming degree of practised confidence, Ruthy addressed the elephant in the room.

She gently explained to us that canned sardines are synonymous with Lisbon. Sardines were introduced to the European diet by the Romans, who settled across the Iberian Peninsula and discovered that the Atlantic shores abounded in this delicious snack. As Ruthy explained, the best time to taste fresh sardines in Lisbon was in June —when the whole city of Lisbon goes nuts for the oily morsel and devotes all the nation's time and energy to grilling them.

Ruthy spoke passionately about Portugal's canning industry which, unsurprisingly, reached its peak during the First World War, when Europe was hungry for food that could be stored for a long time and easily transported from place to place. Portuguese appetite for the tinned fish hasn't slowed down since. Listening to Ruthy, I gave in. As someone who can't stand food blogging, food Instagraming, and any other self-aggrandising efforts published on social media under the guise of educating the masses about comestibles, I was positively enchanted by Ruthy's narrative.

She told us genuine stories about her search for the best local dishes and her dedication to her food tour business. As it transpired, Ruthy often travelled outside the capital to local farms to taste their produce. She would spend her time sampling a variety of olive oil, jams, cheeses, sausages, and baked goods. On one of her food expeditions, she discovered chocolate-coated olives, which she served to us under an ancient olive tree at the top of Alfama, overlooking the city's nightscape.

Over the next few hours, our small group of 'food tourists' climbed the narrow, medieval streets of Alfama from one gourmet pitstop to another. At each restaurant, we were introduced to a different Portuguese beverage to accompany each plate of food. As a result, by the third restaurant, the atmosphere in our randomly selected group of strangers was positively jovial. There were two American couples, two British couples, and us. After serving us various artisanal beers in the first two restaurants, Ruthy moved us on to the local wines.

'This is Vinho Verde,' she announced as the young, smartly-dressed waiter distributed several bottles of this wine across our farmhouse-style table.

'It's green wine,' Bill, a chunky Englishman in his late fifties, translated for the Americans at the table and me.

Bill was the type of person who had an inherent need to educate others, especially foreigners. Soon, large chunks of Ruthy's presentation were explained to me, the simpleton from Poland, and Bill's 'cousins' from across the pond. Fortunately, the Americans at the table and I were used to being patronised by boundlessly sagacious Bills of this world because none of us protested. We nodded in appreciation of the man's gratuitous lecture.

'It's like Beaujolais,' infected by Bill's pompousness, Robert, too, decided to educate us on the matter of Portuguese wine. The fact that at home, he drank his red plonk with sparkling lemon water did not prevent him from chiming in on the virtues of Portuguese wine and thus generously added some unnecessary fluff to the already god-awful vacuous discussion.

'We tasted real Beaujolais last year when we travelled across Burgundy,' Liz, Bill's wife whose white, medium-length hair was styled in honour of Albert Einstein, supported Robert's theory of Vinho Verde being a poor man's Beaujolais.

In a matter of seconds, all the self-appointed wine experts at the table started to debate what Vinho Verde might be and ignored the only authority who could have shed any light on the subject. Fortunately, Ruthy was again allowed to speak and clarified for the misguided oenophiles that Vinho Verde was not the same as a Beaujolais Nouveau. The restaurant's sommelier presented us with a few varieties of Vinho Verde, which we all tasted and made loud obtuse observations about each type.

The wine was slightly effervescent, fresh, and crispy. It instantly became my favourite wine. As our cheeks were glowing red, our banter became somewhat overfamiliar. Ruthy announced it was time for us to go to the next restaurant. It was a good call. Were we to demolish another bottle of Vinho Verde, the food tour would have come to a halt on the homemade *pastéis de bacalhau* or the cod croquettes that we were all gleefully scoffing down between the glasses of wine.

Another brisk walk up the Alfama steps helped sober us up a bit. At the next stop, we were welcomed by a slightly podgy, elderly man standing before a fire pit, roasting delicious-looking *chorizo* sausages, or as the Portuguese call them, *chouriço*. If you don't know how to read Portuguese, I can assure you that it sounds like the Spanish *chorizo*, but as if it were pronounced by a high-class person since there are some extra vowel sounds in the word that don't exist in the Spanish pronunciation.

As I sat down to my fire-grilled sausages, I thought that everything we had tasted thus far had an equivalent in the Spanish cuisine; the sardines, the *croquetas*, the sausages. Even the olive oil testing was vaguely familiar, though — as Robert and I agreed when going over the events later on in our Airbnb apartment — our olive oil from Montefrio was far superior to the Portuguese gold medal winner that Ruthy lectured to us.

I didn't want to be a party pooper, so I kept the idea to myself that Spanish and Portuguese food is strikingly similar. The sizzling hot sausages were paired with various winter liqueurs, including my good friend, Ginja. With this much alcohol consumed in a relatively short period of time, the group were all now laughing hysterically at each other's jokes as if we were lifelong friends.

'We should ask these people if they want to go for a drink later,' Robert surreptitiously whispered while we were all chatting.

Evidently, his judgment was severely affected by all the booze and food he had consumed.

'Let's see how we feel at the end of the tour,' I suggested prudence with our newly found friendships, especially since we were only halfway through the food tour.

When it comes to establishing new friendships, Robert and I display dramatically different approaches. While I would describe my style of making new acquaintances as feline-like, Robert takes on the Labrador approach. As soon as he manages to have an amicable chat with someone, he decides that from now on, they should become members of our small family. On the other hand, I like to sit on the fence for a while and scrutinise their every move and word. Neither tactic is healthy and seldom yields good results. But this time, my method turned out to be the better one. As we crawled from one restaurant to another, our previously ebullient group members began to tire of each other's company. Our once gay and joyful assembly of strangers became more solemn and introspective as our frenetic consumption of alcohol proceeded apace.

Bill's British self-importance was no longer quirky, Liz turned into an airhead, and the Americans' curious enthusiasm started to rub everyone up the wrong way. It was the story of many friendships in a nutshell. We started as total strangers, became inseparable at Vinho Verde, and learned more and more about each other. By the last course of our unduly familiar tour, which was black coffee with the iconic *pastéis de nata*, or custard tarts, only gently simmering contempt for one another remained.

As we stood outside the traditional pastry café, our last stop on the food tour, it was evident that we all wanted to go our separate ways and, preferably, never to see each other again. It was an awkward goodbye, and to fill the silence, Bill divulged some last-minute personal travel tips while the Americans told us of all the wonders of Europe they were scheduled to visit the following week. As for Robert and I, we couldn't wait to return to our little Airbnb apartment in the suburbs to sit down and digest the day's events.

'I think we should visit this castle in Sintra,' I suggested while reading a description of the place on my phone. By now, I was comfortably sprawled out on the sofa with a glass of red and fact-checking Bill's travel tips. Since Robert himself was not interested in doing any travel research, he agreed to my proposal. The following day, we drove out of Lisbon to the small town of Sintra.

A common feature of many world heritage sites is that they look much better in real life than in photos. What I referred to as 'Sintra Castle' is, in fact, called Pena Palace. It is a royal residence on top of a mountain in the town of Sintra. The distinction between a palace and a castle was justified in the case of Pena Palace since the creative king who designed it, Ferdinand II, styled parts of the building to resemble a Roman castle. My first impression of Pena Palace was not that of a medieval fort but rather an installation on the set of a Disney movie. My first glimpse of the monument was breathtaking. The intricate decorations, elegant style, and bright colours of the façade would kick anyone's imagination into overdrive.

Were Ferdinand II still alive, he could easily have joined Disney's Imagineering team. Two hundred years ago, he stood at the ruins of a sixteenth-century monastery in the Sintra Mountains. Enchanted by the location, he used his magic wand to raise one fantastic structure after another.

'I wish to have a Moorish fortress,' he would touch the ground and abracadabra! It appeared.
'I wish to have a Gothic palace.' Shazam!
'A Renaissance chapel with a dome.' Done!
'Some Islamic tiling.' Alakazam!
'A splash of the most vibrant colours money can buy.' Presto!
'An enormous park with trees and plants from the most exotic places in the world.' Voilà!
'A Swiss chalet surrounded by giant sequoias.' Here it is!

I don't know much about Ferdinand II, but one thing is sure, the artist-king had an imagination, and he didn't waste his talents. Like Disneyland, Pena Palace is a hotchpotch of creative ideas that bring people great joy. On the palace grounds, one finds expression of a deep nostalgia for the past, the spirit of the great explorations to the New World, a dash of romanticised Nature, and classical splendour. As we strolled the rooms of bygone monarchs and their private chambers, I could easily imagine the Portuguese royal family celebrating Christmas in the Great Hall with the biggest tree money could buy and the most elaborate baubles imported from Bohemia. On cold winter nights, German composers and writers would entertain them. The king was of German origin, which explained many of the Germanic influences on some of the buildings. The best French chefs would travel across Europe to cook for the European elite in the royal summer house.

Ferdinand's grandson, Carlos I, continued to reside in what was supposed to be a holiday home on the palace grounds. He surrounded himself and his wife, Amélie of Orléans, with the finest art of the era. But whilst admiring his extensive collection, I also felt a tinge of sadness for the doomed ruler. Carlos was soon to be assassinated together with one of his sons. His wife would become known as the last Queen of Portugal. It was from Sintra that she left Portugal as the 1910 revolution disposed of the royal family and everything it entailed.

Even though I felt somewhat sentimental about the old regime, I also knew that such lush and opulent riches as one can find at Pena Palace could only be brought into existence off the back of the suffering of others. While the kings enjoyed the company of Strauss and drank Glühwein by coal furnaces, millions of poor people struggled to make ends meet, many starving or living hand-to-mouth. That said, it felt nice to airbrush out the harsh realities of the past and spend a day surrounded by world-class art and architecture, to stroll the gardens, wandering from an enchanted grotto to a folly, envisaging a different life for oneself. But as the cold December afternoon darkened, it was time to return to the real world. Unlike Ferdinand II, we had no magic wand or copious amounts of gold to fund our final house renovations. We had but some meagre savings that we planned to use to finally make our own living quarters liveable and presentable.

SIXTEEN
WE NEVER LEARN

'We need to get a quote from a plumber and an electrician,' were my famous last words in December as I looked over the spreadsheet on my laptop.

After returning from Lisbon, we spent the first couple of weeks planning our remodelling project or, to be more specific, acting like adults and actually making a budget for our renovation. I was determined not to get caught up in the same financial fiasco we had when we renovated the guest apartments.

Since neither of us had a steady paycheck, it was paramount that we stuck to our very finite and limited budget. Consequently, compromises had to be made. This time around, instead of pulling prices of building materials and household goods out of thin air and using magical thinking to stretch our funds further, I used various online DIY shops as a guide to estimate the costs and then added them to my spreadsheet.

'I'd like a Chesterfield sofa,' I was still under the influence of our trip to Lisbon and full of posh aspirations.

Robert, too, liked the idea of 'classing up' our humble abode, but once we saw the price of said sofa online, we crossed it off the list.

'We can get a nice second-hand sofa,' Robert suggested.

'I don't think so,' I closed the subject. *Nice* and *second-hand* sounded like an oxymoron to me. Especially when applied to the item of furniture that one uses all the time. The idea of sitting on someone else's sweaty cushions with their biscuit crumbs and coins lost in the nooks and crannies of a tatty sofa was cringe-worthy.

'I'd rather sit on this old one forever.'

I gave the old chequered settee we had inherited with the house a loathsome look.

'I suppose you're here to stay with us for a little while longer,' I informed the hideous piece of furniture.

While many items on the list could remain in the house or be tossed out or purchased later, there was one fixture that we both agreed upon as being indispensable, namely, an underfloor heating system. Even though our living room contained a sizable fireplace, it did not provide uniform ambient heat across the whole area. Like most open-flame hearths, it tended to burn one side of your body while the other remained freezing cold. The whole area downstairs had many cold corners. As we were planning to knock down several non-structural walls downstairs to open up the space, we were confident that the lonely fireplace at the end of the room would not suffice.

'It means we'll have to pull up all of the floor,' Robert announced as we reviewed our plans.

I looked at the Mad Hatter's black-and-white chessboard-tiled floor at my feet. I was not going to miss it.

'Great!'

The next morning, we got to work. It was before Christmas, and the weather was quite miserable. Most days were unseasonably grey and rainy — the type of day the local expats would never photograph to share on their social media accounts. We removed all the furniture and household items from the ground floor, placed them on the patio, and covered them with a giant plastic tarpaulin. We moved the fridge, kitchen appliances, and food to one of the guest apartments, which we were going to use for cooking, eating, entertainment, and work during the renovation project. We would return to the main house at night and sleep in our own bedroom on the first floor. Our walk-in wardrobe prevented us from relocating completely to the guest rooms for the project's duration. I opened its sliding barn doors and looked at all the clothes and bits and pieces we had accumulated over the years and decided that moving the wardrobe's contents would require far too much effort than it was worth.

It is not that we are particularly stylish or elegant people who need various changes of clothing for different occasions. In fact, we both come across as a bit scruffy on any given day — a small hole or a stain on a piece of clothing has never been a deterrent to wearing it. We never iron our outfits and hardly ever keep them neatly folded. And even though our wardrobe seemed to be filled to the brim with untidy piles of garments stuffed on each shelf, I suspected I wore the same two pairs of pants and the same set of five T-shirts and two sweatshirts all the time. It was hard to justify the extensive collection of clothing we had acquired. But as we were about to embark on another nightmare renovation, there was no time to distract ourselves with Marie Kondo's life philosophy. To sort out our clutter, I would need to clone her a few times over and hire a whole team of Kondos full-time for a year. I looked at my hoarder's nest and slid the doors shut.

Once the downstairs area was ready for renovation, the whole house became a dusty building site again. The main task was to remove the old flooring to make space for the pipes for the new underfloor heating system. While Robert was busy with an electric jackhammer, he also removed the old plaster cladding from the interior walls to reveal the original stone from which the cottage was built. It took us a couple of weeks to finish this stage. While Robert chiselled away layer after layer, I loaded wheelbarrows full of rubble and dumped them behind the crinkle crankle wall. Once the work was done, we were going to cover the debris with topsoil and plant some lavender bushes.

I find it very difficult to become enthused by physical labour, and combined with freezing cold temperatures outside and a constant drizzle, we worked at a snail's pace. We obviously needed help, but our old Spanish builder, Dani, was busy with his olives and would not be free until the end of April. And I didn't want to risk hiring anyone else to help us. However, we already had bookings for April, so everything had to be done before spring. We were on our own. Whatever Dani and his helper would have done in a day took us three.

Since we were both more accustomed to sitting on our butts, staring at laptop screens, and occasionally falling down the rabbit hole of something we'd read online or becoming indignant about a social media post, the hard labour quickly got to us. I started to look for shortcuts.

'Maybe we don't need to remove the whole floor,' I suggested, wiping the sweat from my brow with my grimy beanie.

I leaned against one of the remaining walls to catch my breath before wheeling out another load of rubble. We'd been working like donkeys and only removed the floor and the wall cladding from the adjacent downstairs bedrooms. In our defence, the floor in those bedrooms had been ten centimetres, or four inches, *above* the rest of the downstairs floor, and we had to excavate quite deep down to make a level space for the insulation, the water pipes, the layer of cement, and new tiles. We had also removed all the non-load-bearing walls downstairs.

'What do you mean?' Robert was cleaning his protective eyeglasses of dust. His faithful jackhammer rested in the corner by the pile of plaster and cement rubble.

'Why don't we put the heating pipes over the old tiles,' I gestured at the remainder of the downstairs area, the chessboard living room and the library, which was still tiled.

I could see Robert was warming up to the idea, but there were a few problems.

'It won't work. We need space for the pipes, the top layer of cement, and new tiles. We won't be able to open any doors if we just build on top of the old tiles.'

It was a valid point. Raising the floor in the new living room, kitchen, and library by ten centimetres would mean we could not open the main door to the upstairs staircase. But I would not be dissuaded from finding a way to reduce the amount of hard labour I had been condemned to perform.

'If we continue digging the floor out, it will take us another month,' I explained my plan. 'But if we just remove the old tiles and then cut the door off at the bottom so that it clears the raised floor, we'll be done in the next few days.'

I emphasised the word *just*, which gave Robert something to chew over as I confidently put my beanie back on and rolled out another load of rubble.

'I think it's a good idea,' I heard him say as I re-entered our living room with the empty wheelbarrow.

We worked on it for another half hour. Still, since I had just saved us a couple more weeks of backbreaking labour with my clever suggestion, we decided to light the fire in the guest apartment, open a bottle of red, and research the siren call of our planned heating system. As always, we sought wisdom and advice from our best friends, some random guys on YouTube.

'Look, we can save a lot of money if we do it ourselves,' I heard Robert say.

I stepped away from the frying pan to watch the instructional YouTube video on his laptop.

'You simply set up a bunch of black irrigation pipes, connect them to a manifold and then pour cement over it.'

'How are we going to heat the water in the pipes?'

We knew we could not install an electric heating system because our mains electricity supply was weak and unreliable.

'We can connect the pipes to a water boiler at the back of the fireplace, and Bob's your uncle. We only need some black pipe, a manifold, and cement.'

It all seemed very straightforward, even to me, who usually frowns and looks confused when confronted with any plumbing project.

A little too simple, I mused as I tossed some fried onions, but I did not want to curb Robert's enthusiasm. At least, not immediately. As soon as I added some mushrooms to the pasta sauce and put it to simmer, I had a few minutes to question his cowboy idea.

'It sounds very cheap,' I stated the fact. 'Why do they charge forty euros a square metre in Leroy?'

In our search for the elusive underfloor heating system, we had already spotted a kit in one of Europe's most prominent DIY hypermarkets, Leroy Merlin, which had recently opened in Granada. There, we were quoted four thousand euros for our project, which excluded the labour and the cost of a specialised fireplace. Based on his extensive YouTube research, Robert's cost estimate was less than half that.

'They just want to make money,' was Robert's explanation. He blamed the price on corporate greed.

But I wasn't convinced.

'I think we should run this idea past Fran,' I proposed as I drained some pasta.

Fran was the plumber who helped me sort out our pool the previous spring. I felt he would know about various heating systems, and I was quite right.

The next day, we were standing outside his shop in the industrial area, staring at a cross-section of an underfloor heating kit displayed in the shop's window. I had to call a number on a small sign on the shop's door, informing us that he had left the shop to attend to an emergency and that potential customers should call him. True to his word, he was with us in twenty minutes. During that time, we had calculated that the price of his kit was more or less the same as what we were quoted in Leroy. This made me more suspicious of the YouTube hacks that Robert had endorsed the previous night.

'First, explain the YouTube idea to him and see what he says. Then we can compare the price with his kit. If it's the same price as Leroy, we'll go with Fran,' we agreed on this strategy before Fran arrived. 'At least he is local and can come over and fix the system if there're any problems.'

There was no doubt that employing a local business would always be better for us than some anonymous corporation that would be impossible to contact once the heating system was in place. By now, I'd had Fran's number in my WhatsApp for many months, and whenever I had any pool-related problem, I would send him a photo of the fault and a question. He always responded to my queries in a matter of minutes.

Once we were seated in his office at the back of the shop, Robert outlined the idea we saw on YouTube and asked if he could quote us for the parts involved in such a system. As Robert drew an elementary outline of the system we planned to install, I saw the horror in the plumber's eyes. But he was very polite and patiently listened to what, in hindsight, must have sounded like a most preposterous concept. I can only compare it to a couple of people off the street explaining to a surgeon how they were planning to amputate a leg with a handsaw and some leather straps.

Shocked by our ignorance, Fran took the piece of paper and pencil, flipped it over, and started to draw something resembling a Victorian steam engine with valves and gauges, safety valves for when the water was too hot, and various thermostats and regulators.

'If the water in the pipes is over 50°C, it can break the pipes, and you will have to remove the whole floor and do it again,' he enlightened us as we listened in dread. 'Also, you need safety systems; otherwise, the whole thing may explode under pressure.'

It dawned on me that we were devising some kind of Victorian steam bomb. We didn't need to discuss anything further. We looked at each other, thankful that we had managed to avert a total disaster and hired Fran on the spot. We did ask him to send us a quote so we could budget it into the project, but there was no doubt that we would not get involved in installing the pipes.

We left the plumber's shop and ticked it off our to-do list. I looked at the next item on our agenda.

'We should pop into the metal fabrication workshop and ask for a price of a supporting beam,' I reminded Robert.

In our quest for an open-plan living room, we had torn down all but one wall on the ground floor of our stone cottage. While the other walls were non-load-bearing, judging by their thinness, the one wall in the middle of the space was much thicker and appeared to hold part of the structure together. A few days earlier, Robert paused his demolition work to ask my opinion about whether or not the thick wall in the middle of the house was load-bearing. Since I had no clue, we went online to do further research. There was a consensus among the YouTube construction experts that if we were to remove a load-bearing wall, our dwelling might cave in and collapse on itself like a house of cards. The idea gave me many sleepless nights and made us both question the initial design of the ground floor. We had asked various builders, Spanish and English, but none wanted to commit either way.

'If you remove a little bit of the wall by the ceiling, you'll see if there's a ceiling beam at the top,' our old builder, Dani, advised via WhatsApp. 'If there's a beam, you can take down the wall.'

'You should put a supporting beam in place first and then remove the wall,' Ángel, the owner of the brickyard in Montefrio, advised us when we stopped by his shop to collect some sand and cement.

Whether there already was a supporting beam holding the house together or not, putting an additional beam in place before we knocked down the wall sounded like a reasonable precaution. Since the structural integrity of the edifice and our livelihood were at stake, we decided to err on the side of caution and added a steel beam to our shopping list.

The steelworker whose workshop we visited after Fran's was of the opinion that a steel beam was essential to our progress and proceeded to sell us the biggest and the heaviest that he had in stock. Since it was four metres, or over thirteen feet, long, it would not fit in the back of the car, so we had to go back with the trailer to bring it back home.

As soon as I saw the beast, I felt ominous about transporting it. On paper, a four-metre beam seemed manageable, but in real life, it transpired that it was tough to move around; it weighed three hundred kilograms or six hundred and sixty pounds. There was no way in the world we could lift it off the ground if it fell off the trailer. The owner of the steel workshop used a small crane to position it in the trailer we had parked right outside his business. There was a lot of shouting back and forth to rearrange the beam inside the trailer. As it was leaning against the trailer's back wall, we noticed considerable strain on the trailer's hook and the vehicle. It was almost lifting the car's back wheels off the ground.

Since the journey home was on curvy and narrow mountain roads, I wasn't convinced it was the safest way to travel. We worried that the weight of the beam would eventually flip the trailer and the horrendous, unmovable obstacle would land in the middle of the Alcalá-Montefrio road, causing mayhem. That little stunt would become legendary in the area.

Whom would we call to help remove the beam from the road if it fell off the trailer? I wondered as I rehearsed all the possible scenarios in my head.

'We need to change its position,' Robert announced. He must have gone over the same catastrophic possibilities in his head.

We spent another twenty minutes instructing the crane operator how to place the beam at the back of the trailer. We made a multitude of fine adjustments to find a sweet spot for the behemoth and then tied it down with some rope. I wasn't sure that we would not cause chaos on the road, but it was time for us to go. The trip home was one of the most nerve-racking we'd ever had. While Robert drove steadily up and down the hills, I faced the car's back window, watching the giant beam like a hawk. Should it shift its position in the trailer, we'd have to stop the vehicle.

We arrived home with no mishaps. Once parked on our driveway, we both breathed a sigh of relief. Whatever might happen next, at least we were not going to cause a major traffic incident. It took us another half an hour to figure out how to remove the beam from the back of the trailer. We needed to empty the trailer to transport the rubble from our floor excavations. Since we were generating a seemingly endless amount of broken bricks, rocks, and chunks of plaster and had already filled the space behind the crinkle crankle wall in a matter of days, our neighbour kindly suggested that we use our rubble to fill in a vast washed-out ditch on his land.

With some rudimentary understanding of physics and leverage, we managed to get the beam off the trailer. As it landed on the ground, it occurred to me that it was far too heavy for the two of us to install just below the ceiling. We'd need a team of strongmen to hold the thing up in the air and place it into the two holes that Robert had prepared. Discouraged and quite disheartened, we let the beam rest on the grass for a few days.

'I'll ask Tish's friend, Mike, to come and help us,' I announced one morning. 'He's done many renovations in this area and has a construction company.'

We did need professional help with the construction, and the English builders were the only ones available on short notice during the olive picking season. An added advantage of getting Mike on board was that he was also a licenced electrician, so I hoped to kill two birds with one stone.

'Ok,' Robert was getting as tired of our struggles as I was. 'Let's see what he says.'

SEVENTEEN
LAUREL AND HARDY GET TO WORK

'Y'ou'll never get this thing off the ground,' were Mike's first words as he exited his Berlingo.

He was pointing at the ginormous beam on the ground.

'Are you planning to build a block of flats?' he joked.

'You could build a five-storey parking lot on this beam,' he kept the quips coming even though we were not laughing.

I took an immediate dislike to Mike but, against my better instincts, decided to endure his inane remarks if we could finish our project before April. Mike and his assistant arrived one afternoon to assess the work and to give us a quote. While Mike was of a Rubenesque stature and complexion, his sidekick, Steve, was rather gaunt and grey. They both chain-smoked and gabbed incessantly with each other and anyone else unfortunate enough to be in earshot. A good half hour went by, during which they discussed the weather, Spanish meal times, cars that they owned now and in the past, their motorbikes, the Spanish way of parking, and 'the Spanish' in general, including a long tirade from Mike on how lazy and shoddy Spanish builders were before I managed to direct them into the house and was allowed to explain the job at hand.

While a lot of heavy lifting had already been done by Robert, it was just the first step of the renovation project. Now that we had a blank canvas, we had to put insulation on the exposed ground, lay the new floors over the heating pipes, make channels for new electric cables, switches and lights, set up a plumbing system for a kitchen sink that had now been moved, then replaster the walls and ceilings, and retile the floor. We also needed to decide if we should tear the middle wall down and, if we were to tear it down, how we might use the steel beam we had purchased.

As I explained to Mike the various switches and plugs I wanted to install in the new living room and kitchen, it struck me as strange that he wasn't writing anything down. He wasn't even sketching where I wanted the lights and plugs, which implied that I would repeat my instructions many times in the future.

'How will he send us an estimate if he doesn't know how many plugs he needs to order or how much cable to buy?' I asked Robert later that day.

'I don't know.'

Even though Robert and I were sceptical of Mike's ability to memorise everything, the contractor did not doubt his abilities. A few days after his visit, he sent me an estimate without details or a breakdown of the costs. It was just a number on a rather empty piece of paper. The price was clearly pulled from thin air.

Why, oh why, did I convince Robert to give this cowboy a chance to work on our house? I'd need a PhD in advanced psychology to answer this question. All the facts were staring me right in the face. He was unlikeable, rude, obnoxious, and couldn't even provide a simple estimate.

'You're lucky he doesn't have to do any roof work,' my friend Keith commented when I presented him with my plan of hiring Mike and Co. 'He'd never be able to get up there.' Keith unkindly, although accurately, was referring to Mike's portly physique.

We were told that Keith and Delia had had their own house renovation project assessed by Mike three years earlier but decided not to hire him as most of their work required repairs on the roof, and Mike himself might have created more damage up there than he might have managed to fix.

I decided to take the moral high ground and not judge a book by its cover. I even felt a little smug thinking that I was better than Keith and Delia by giving the man a second chance and overlooking his apparent misgivings. I was also quite sure that Steve did most of the hard labour, and even though he was as thin as a rake, he did appear strong and willing to work.

The day after I informed Mike that he could start as soon as he was available, I received Fran's quote. It could not have been more different from Mike's 'quote'. It included two pages of very detailed drawings and a page with a table where every spare part, pipe, valve and screw was accounted for and added to the total. The universe was sending me a message not to employ Mike, but I refused to listen for some reason.

'Let's try Mike and Steve,' I had to convince Robert, who was very leery about the duo.

I suppose one reason I had my hopes pinned on Mike was that there was no language barrier. By now, I could speak pre-intermediate Spanish, but the nuances of electrical and plumbing vocabulary escaped me. I wanted to find someone nearby who could come to our house and do minor repairs whenever an electrical appliance gave in, there was a leak or a pipe burst. Since Mike lived not far from us, I contemplated the idea that he might be our go-to person in case of a domestic emergency. While Fran had been exceptionally helpful with our swimming pool issues, his shop was a thirty-five-minute drive from our house, and his WhatsApp messages weren't always clear to me.

Like many native Spanish speakers, Fran habitually shortened whole words to one or two letters. The same way many people who communicate in English write *TY* instead of 'thank you' or *BTW* instead of 'by the way'. Consequently, if he was in a hurry fixing someone's water heater or a leaking toilet, he would pepper his text messages with *pq*, *xfa*, and *q* and many more random collections of consonants, which made no sense to me and only confused the old Dr Google Translate. With time, I deduced that *pq* or *pk* means *porque*, which means *why* or *because,* depending on the context. *Xfa* is short for *porfa,* which, in itself, is short for *por favor,* which means *please.* The letter *q*, as I found out over the years, is a bit of a wild card and can stand in for any word that starts with *q*, but most often, it stands in for *qué?* with its various meanings and usages. Once I got the basics of text messaging in Spanish, I could decipher that *eske* meant *es qué,* or *it's that.*

In addition to these common abbreviations, Fran also used his own idiosyncratic shorthand. Once, it took me a good half an hour to figure out his answer to one of my questions: *voy palla.*

I'm going to palla? Where the heck is 'palla'? I scratched my head, looking at the translator and then back to the message on the phone. I only put two and two together when he arrived at the house to fix the pool pump and figured that he had meant *voy por alli,* or *I'm coming there.* With time, I figured out that the best way to decode these enigmatic dispatches was to read them out loud and assume that the speaker had a habit of giving up on the last syllable of each word, something that most speakers of the *Andaluz* dialect do as a matter of course.

But while communication with Fran was a linguistic challenge, trying to get through to Mike turned out to be virtually impossible. As he and Steve set themselves to work on a cold and drizzly winter morning, I watched them like a hawk. While they retrieved their tools and other bits and pieces from their small van, I wanted to review the jobs they were expected to do to ensure we were on the same page. It soon became apparent that the obstinate man, who refused to write anything down, had missed several details related to the work I wanted him to do and had misunderstood others.

'I'm quite sure you didn't mention this,' he blamed me for the gaps in his knowledge.

How can you be so sure if you didn't write it down, I wanted to ask, but he had already walked away.

It just so happened that a little earlier the same morning, Fran had arrived with his assistant, Bruno, to set up the pipes for the underfloor heating system. As soon as I explained to them where the fireplace with the hot water would be and where we would keep all the necessary equipment and the controls, they rapidly commenced with the work. It was a pleasure to watch. Things inside the house were moving fast, and I did not need to linger to ensure everything was done right. Outside the house, a different series of events was unfolding.

That morning, Mike and Steve were to set up drainage pipes for the new kitchen area. Robert had already dug out a channel for the PVC pipes all the way from the middle of the ground floor to the main exit pipe at the side of the house. While Fran and Bruno moved like highly motivated worker ants determined to build a whole colony in a day, Mike and Steve's operation resembled a Laurel and Hardy performance. And it might even have been quite entertaining to watch were we not paying good money for the sorry spectacle. There was a lot of huffing and puffing, scratching, gasping, cursing, and smoking. Plumbing connections of various shapes and sizes were scattered all around, and tools were strewn across the ground and blamed for their unwillingness to cooperate.

Because I was brought up in Poland in the eighties when state-employed plumbers and electricians had a famously bad reputation for shoddy workmanship, I had learnt from the adults around me that if you wanted something done correctly, you had to watch a tradesman's every step. Since I had already witnessed Fran's work on many occasions, I focused my energy on the newcomers. I noticed an hour had passed, and nothing of consequence had been achieved. They'd reached some kind of a hiatus in the job. When I inquired, it turned out that there was a small bump in the middle of the channel that Robert had made for the exit pipe. Steve repeatedly placed the PVC pipe on top of the bump, where it would seesaw up and down.

'We could cut the pipe here and connect it on the hump,' I overheard him suggest to Mike, who was lighting another Marlboro cigarette.

'Yeah, let's do that,' the boss agreed.

I looked at the channel and their little obstacle with disbelief. I turned my back and marched off to Robert to inform him of what was happening and to tell him to tell the men to remove the small bump before they laid the pipe. By now, I had found Mike's demeanour gallingly unpleasant and didn't want to confront him. But, Robert had not warmed to Mike and Co. either and was unwilling to talk to them.

'They're *your* builders,' I was informed. 'You better talk to them because I might shout at them.'

I did not want to make a scene, so I marched back. By now, I knew the whole hypothetical arrangement with Mike and Steve as my new go-to handymen would never materialise. It was now a matter of damage control.

As a teacher, I am used to lacing negative feedback with a big helping of something positive. And so, before I pointed out that what they were planning to do was totally wrong, I stood for a few minutes and thought of something positive.

'That's a good quality PVC pipe.'

That remark compelled Mike to lecture me on the inferiority of Spanish PVC pipes compared to English pipes. I wasn't really listening as I was bracing myself for the critique I was about to deliver.

'You need to remove that small bump in the channel,' I finally blurted out. 'You can't put the pipe over this bump.'

It was never going to be an agreeable exchange: a Polish woman telling a British plumber in his late fifties how to do his job. I could see the sparks in his eyes as he controlled his anger. He had enough sense not to take it out on me but started to boss skinny Steve around instead, who was now in a slightly hyperactive panic mode and was running up and down, figuring out how he might resolve the offending bump in the channel. Out of nowhere, they came up with a jackhammer and levelled the channel for the pipe in a matter of minutes. I could hear a lot of muttering and cursing in the distance but decided to ignore it. The two must have reached a consensus that I was their sworn enemy.

As I stood under the patio to protect myself from the drizzle, I had to admit that the atmosphere on my construction site was not great. Robert had disappeared inside and was distracting Fran and Bruno with his Spanish jokes while they were trying to concentrate on setting up a complex network of looping pipes that, once covered with cement, would be impossible to change. Outside, my disgruntled English workers were plotting a coup and acting like forced labour. Tired of being the project manager for the morning, I went inside the guest apartment to warm up and make myself a cup of tea. A few minutes later, there was a knock on the door. Mike and Steve were done for the day. It was only noon. Because Fran and Bruno had occupied the whole living room and kitchen as they installed the underfloor heating pipes, the English duo could not think of anything else they could do on-site until we covered the floors in concrete.

I didn't argue with them. I ensured they packed all their tools up, as I had already decided I would not be employing them again. That evening, I sent Mike a message regretfully firing him and his assistant. I didn't tell him the truth about why I could no longer work with him. I said something about our budget and that we could not afford his expertise. I knew he didn't buy my explanation because a couple of days later, his wife contacted me to ask if he had offended me or Robert in any way.

He's just really direct and honest, and it sometimes rubs people up the wrong way. She wrote and attached a ridiculously large bill for the quarter-day's shoddy work that her husband had done for us.

I almost fell off my chair when I saw what he was charging us. I could have had two Spanish builders work for three full days for the same amount.

'At least we cut our losses as soon as we saw that he was of no use,'

Robert wholeheartedly agreed with my decision not to engage Mike and Steve any further in our project.

In retrospect, we had had a narrow escape. Yes, we overpaid for dodgy work that had to be fixed by Fran the next day, but we avoided a potentially massive bill from Mike and Steve and having to redo all the electrical wiring and connections. In the years to come, we met several families in the area who had fallen prey to Mike's 'construction business' and had lost thousands of euros of their hard-earned money. Some even sued him but never saw a penny in compensation.

That December was the last time I spoke to Mike. Three years later, he passed away suddenly. He left one morning for a job in a town an hour's drive from his village — his reputation was evidently radioactive by then, and he had to cast his net far and wide to find his hapless customers. He had felt pain in his chest at lunchtime and died in the emergency room just a few minutes after his arrival at the hospital. I often wondered what an appropriate epitaph would be for a man like him. What was his life's project?

EIGHTEEN
NEW BEGINNINGS

Once we had let Mike and Steve go, we were on our own again. We set up the cement mixer by the patio and spent each day mixing cement and laying a new floor over the heating pipes. Since it had rained heavily that December, a cement truck would not have been able to get up our driveway. It was too slippery from the mud. So, we had to mix several cement trucks' worth of the mixture ourselves. Every few days, Robert would bring a trailer full of sand and more cement bags. Once we had positioned the trailer by the cement mixer, I'd stand on top of the sand pile with a shovel and cast generous helpings of sand into the mixer below while Robert added cement and water.

By now, we'd mixed cement so many times we could quickly tell if it was the right consistency. It was a very different operation compared to two years earlier when we stood by the mixer with written instructions and fussed over the concoction like a dessert chef making sure the cake mix was perfect. With experience came some modicum of confidence. We were now like those great Italian *nonnas* who could cook traditional dishes without consulting a recipe. I quite enjoyed mixing the cement. It was productive, albeit slow work, but it was better than demolishing walls and clearing out the rubble.

'What about the electric cables?' I put my shovel into the mound of sand and asked while the cement churned.

'Why can't Fran do the electrics downstairs?'

'He's not an electrician,' I didn't understand Robert's idea.

'Yes, he is. It says so on the side of his van.'

'Really?' I couldn't recall seeing anything written on the side of Fran's van but decided to double-check.

Later that day, in a series of WhatsApp messages, some more intelligible than others, we established that Fran was, in fact, a plumber *and* an electrician. I really can't explain what fog had come over my mind that I never realised he could work in both areas. Perhaps in my naivety, I assumed that a tradesman was either one or the other. The new information was a godsend. Fran agreed to do all the electrics downstairs at a fraction of the cost of what 'Mingy Mike' had quoted us. Robert had devised this somewhat rude nickname for him after we'd paid his extortionate bill for half a day's work.

We had spent that Christmas living in the guest apartment. Because we were also working on paying writing projects and renovating the downstairs in our free time, the pace of our work was sluggish. We had finally convinced ourselves that the wall in the middle of the living room was not load-bearing and so slowly but surely tore it down too. It was the first week of January 2018 when I received an email from a woman called Belén. At first, I had no clue who she might be, but from her message, I figured out that she was the language school owner who had needed a teacher the previous October. She said she still had my CV and desperately needed a teacher as her previous teacher had been awarded a government post in another city.

My first impression of Belén was that she was not particularly well-organized. It was already the first week of January, the day before Epiphany, and the school term was to start in five days.

Why didn't she contact me earlier? I wondered.

I was even more puzzled when she asked if I could stop by the school the same afternoon for a job interview. I was in the kitchen making chocolate mousses and preparing a variety of tapas for a little party I had planned for the next day. Were I in my mid-twenties, I would have dropped everything and run off for the job interview. But as I was a veteran teacher and a somewhat blasé one at that, I was not going to spoil my entertainment plans for an opportunity of getting a job.

'It will set a bad example,' I told Robert as I typed my response. 'If I run to her now. She will expect me to do the same in the future. She can wait until Saturday.'

I told her about my situation and a few minutes later received Belén's answer. She'd see me at her school in Alcalá la Real on Saturday morning. The next day, we enjoyed a spectacular January afternoon with some friends. The skies were clear and deep blue in colour. The sun was bright, so we sat outside, drank copious amounts of cava, and enjoyed a potluck Epiphany lunch. I'd asked our friends to bring any leftovers from Christmas, so the table was full of English, Dutch, and Belgian holiday specialities.

Sarah had brought some homemade mince pies and cider. Liv and Julian fried a fresh batch of Dutch waffles sprinkled with edible New Year decorations, and Stefan and Emma shared a box of Belgian chocolates from Antwerp. We also had a variety of European finger food snacks. Keith, who was not a keen cook and had just spent another Christmas alone, contributed some festive beverages. His wife, Delia, was away in the UK. She preferred to spend her winters there, where she basked in the comfort of the central heating in her daughter's apartment. While Robert barbecued some meat to go with the *patatas bravas*, I showed our friends around so they could assess our progress on our latest building project.

While for regular people, the topic of DIY projects and house renovations might be mind-numbingly boring, for many expats who have followed a similar path to ours, it was a never-ending source of diversion. I outlined our construction ideas as we walked around the new cement floor. Everyone provided little updates about their own ongoing projects.

Liv and Julian were working on renovating their 16th-century hacienda, which they hoped to transform into guest accommodations. Stefan and Emma's guest house had been finished for years, but they continued to make improvements. Keith had his share of DIY adventures and regaled us about the revolving door of Workaways who'd come for short periods to do home repairs on his property. Céline and Leon owned a very narrow townhouse that had been extended into a cave; they were constantly figuring out how to fit themselves and two huge *galgos*, Spanish greyhounds, inside the tiny space their house provided them with.

As we sat down to eat, the atmosphere was lively. Everyone was chatting across the table. We laughed at each other's DIY misadventures, including our acquisition of a monstrously heavy steel beam still lying useless by the fence. I hoped the grass would grow around it in spring to hide its hideous presence. We hadn't seen each other throughout the fall, and it was nice to have a house full of people once again. It was almost twelve months ago when, a few days after Epiphany, I was left alone in the house to fend for myself with no car and few acquaintances. I looked around at the faces that were now becoming part of my life. They weren't strangers anymore. I had made two resolutions the year before to transport myself around without having to ask for favours and make new friends. I put a mental tick on both goals and took a long sip of cava as I admired my work.

As the cool of the afternoon set in, we moved to the guest apartment, where we lit the fire and drank traditional Christmas liqueurs accompanied by a variety of local goat and sheep cheeses. It was a jolly event, and I made a mental note to make it an annual one. 2018 was starting well. We still had money in the bank and several ongoing translation and writing projects to support ourselves through the winter. We were building new friendships and looking for ways to settle in this new place we loved so much. And while I kept my promise to host an Epiphany potluck party every year, I only had two more opportunities.

Epiphany Day in 2020 would be the last one we would spend in the company of our new friends. The ties of friendship we all tried to establish over the following two years would be shattered by the pandemic. We would all experience the lockdowns on our own, alone at home. One may ask whether it was worth devoting so much time and energy to nourishing a spirit of camaraderie that turned out to be so lacklustre and ephemeral. Of course, it was.

In the same way, it's worth cultivating beautiful flowers in the summer, even though we know they will die in the cold of the winter. They may not be alive when the inevitable frost comes, but their memory keeps your heart warm at night and gives you hope for the following summer. But the sadness of withered friendships was yet to come since, in January 2018, we were just starting to get to know each other.

'I'd like to invite everyone to the local fiesta in Frailes,' Céline announced as the party was winding down. 'It's in April, but it's so popular that I need to buy tickets for us soon.'

We all agreed to reunite in Frailes, all but Keith, who said he had to check the schedule of the UK rugby matches that particular weekend. He was strange that way. He always seemed to enjoy himself at social gatherings and chatted away with everyone, but his first response was always a resounding 'no' whenever he initially received an invitation. There was always an irrelevant errand to attend, a cricket or rugby match to watch on TV, or some other inconvenience he had to clear first. It made him appear quite ungrateful for the invitations extended to him. I hope that when I am seventy years of age, I might accept any invitation to mingle with people with a bit more grace and decorum.

Because of the glorious weather we had enjoyed on Epiphany Day, I did not expect to be stuck in a blizzard when I ventured out for my job interview a few days later. I was leaving the school after the interview when I received a text message from Robert asking me if it was snowing in Alcalá. I was still in the town at the time, on a small hill with views of the Moorish fort stretching before me. There was no snow anywhere to be seen. I texted him back and told him not to worry.

It's all clear here. I'll be home in 30 mins.

My interview was short and sweet. Belén was desperate to find a new teacher to start on Monday when the students returned from their Christmas break. It was the start of the second trimester. She wanted me to confirm that I could teach on Monday while we chatted in the office, but I needed a few hours to review the numbers and logistics. The job would entail me having to go into town four times a week. I wanted to check if my fuel costs would be more expensive than what I was to earn. The salary was the regular hourly fee received by English teachers in the area. It was nothing to brag about, but it would give us some financial backup, especially through the winter months when we had very few guests.

I sat down in the car, opened the calculator app on my phone and did the maths. As I suspected, I would not make a fortune, but we wouldn't have to worry about money. In my first forty years on this planet, I realised that few things in life are as stressful as not having any money in the bank. The feeling of financial dread can be overwhelming, and the anxiety stays with you every hour of the day.

At night you lie awake, reviewing your accounts, hoping there is a forgotten sum of money somewhere waiting to be found. Unpaid bills haunt your dreams one after the other, and you shuffle them around in order of importance. We should pay for the electricity first because the internet company is slow, they won't notice a missing payment for a few days. Then we can take another loan on the credit card, and hopefully, by the end of next month, we will get some more money coming in. As soon as any money comes in, it gets swallowed by unpaid debts, and you're back at square one again.

As children, we are told that money does not bring happiness. This may or may not be true. I have never been in a position to verify this. But I can attest that having just enough money to get by gives you peace of mind and the freedom to take on other projects. And so, even though I was going to be paid a little more than a local cleaner, the steady paycheck would bring some long-sought-after stability. I thought back to the times when we had no money, and I decided that once I got home, I'd text Belén and tell her to count me in.

I was still going over the pros and cons of my new prospects when it occurred to me that what started as a light rain had rapidly turned into a heavy snowfall. Soon, the windscreen wipers could not get the snow off fast enough. I slowed down and didn't think I was in trouble until I reached the first hill outside town.

Suddenly the car lost power. I pushed on the accelerator, but the vehicle refused to go forward. It moved a millimetre at a time, shuddering and jerking. It was very unnerving. I had no control over the vehicle.

To make matters worse, despite the snail's pace that I was moving at, the rear of the car started to swerve left and right. That's when I got very scared. It was time to call it a day. As soon as I saw a small parking bay on the side of the road, I parked there. I put on the hazard lights and called Robert.

It felt like ages had passed before he arrived in the four-by-four. I had a lot to worry about while I waited. I saw other drivers skidding past and almost falling off the roadside. Some were able to continue driving despite the foot-deep snow; others, like myself, parked on the side of the road and waited. On noticing a woman in distress, some drivers stopped and came over to check on me. One man tried to help by spraying some magic concoction from a spray can onto my front and rear wheels. They told me my car was a rear-wheel drive, so it struggled in the snow. I tried to drive it with the magic spray on the wheels, but the vehicle veered uncontrollably sideways, and after moving a mere ten metres, I felt even more panicked. I didn't want to get stuck in the middle of the main road and get hit by another out-of-control car coming the other way down the hill. Very, very slowly, I reversed back to where I had been parked a few minutes earlier.

Now I was really apprehensive. The blizzard was just getting started. Soon, visibility had been reduced to just a few metres. I switched off the engine because I didn't want to run out of fuel. I left the hazard lights on and hoped for the best. In a matter of seconds, the windscreen was covered in snow. I was getting entombed. Very carefully, I got out of the car and cleaned the screen with my hands. For whatever it was worth, I didn't feel comfortable sitting in a rapidly darkening ice coffin. I remembered that by law, we were obliged to carry high-visibility jackets for when we stopped on the side of the road. I put one on and waited. Another half an hour had passed when I saw our white four-by-four approaching over the hill. I hooted the car horn to attract Robert's attention. There was no way to tell one parked car from another at this point since they were all covered by two feet of fresh snow.

Robert spotted me and parked the Nissan Patrol on a side road about 50 metres from where I was stranded. I told him of the events of the last hour and the problems I had had controlling the car. I also informed him that a snowplough had just driven past on the other side of the road, and I hoped it would soon come back on our side. He didn't seem interested in this girly solution of just waiting for the municipal services to clear the road. Perhaps there is something about how mothers brought up their boys in the past that made them believe they were nothing short of Superman. Robert ignored my comments about the car being impossible to drive and sat in the driver's seat.

'We'll take this car home first, and when it stops snowing, we'll come back for the Patrol,' was his plan.

In all fairness, he did manage to drive up the hill a good 20 metres longer than I had managed before the car started to behave like a child throwing a tantrum. I could see the horror in Robert's eyes as the car began to twist and veer on the road. The roads hereabout only have two lanes and are not designed for driver error. If you drive off the road, there's usually a very long drop before you will come to a stop under an olive tree at the bottom. He managed to get the car to the side road where he had parked the Patrol.

We sat in the car for twenty minutes, wondering what to do and watching a few daredevils take their lives into their own hands as they negotiated the snow-decked hill. Fortunately, a snowplough came past, travelling in the direction of our house.

'Let's follow the snowplough in the Nissan, and then we'll collect this car when the road is properly cleared.'

It was as good a plan as we could make. Several other drivers seemed to have had the same idea since a small convoy had formed behind the snowplough. We locked my car and jumped into the Nissan. Half an hour later, we arrived home. I could not believe the landscape. The trees were covered in a thick, heavy layer of pristine snow. The green olive hills I had left in the morning were gone and transformed into a Snow Queen's paradise.

Bobby was provided with perfect camouflage for the first time as he romped around curiously in our field. Only his brown head was sticking out above the blanket of snow. It was the heaviest snowfall I had ever seen in Andalusia. The branches of many olive trees actually broke under the weight of the snow, and the icy conditions caused several serious accidents on the Granada-Cordoba highway. People were trapped on the side of the highway for many hours. Reading this news by my cosy fireplace, I considered myself very lucky.

'But how are you going to get to work?' Robert asked after I announced my decision to take on the teaching job.

It was an excellent question, which I didn't have an answer to. When I got home, I told Belén I would teach at her school. But I also checked the forecast for the next ten days, and there was more snow to come! Not having a clear idea of how to go about something had never before stopped me from doing it.

'I don't know,' I said as I looked at the winter landscape through the window. 'I'll worry about it on Monday afternoon.'

NINETEEN
LITTLE JESÚS

F ew jobs are as rewarding as being a kindergarten or primary school teacher. Imagine a job where your clients run to you with a smile and give you a warm embrace each time they see you. Working with children has always been a highlight of my teaching career, and I have often complained about the little respect primary school teachers get from other teachers and parents. If you want fame or glory, this work is not for you. You work with children because a hug, a drawing, or a card is enough recognition for your work. You work with children because watching them grow and develop is the most pleasurable experience. They are also the least fussy of learners — they don't complain when they don't understand something, trust your judgement, and are willing to go on any educational adventure with you. Plus, they are goofy and funny and, most of the time, a pleasure to be around.

With that being said, when I entered my first class at the language school in Alcalá, it had been twelve years since I had last talked to a group of primary school students. I was rusty and apprehensive about how the children might respond to me. I had to dig deep into my memories of teaching kindergarten in Al Ain in 2005, my first foray into working with kids.

We had been in the Emirates for just three weeks when a Canadian neighbour in our compound told me that a private primary school where she worked as a librarian desperately needed kindergarten teachers. I called the principal and was asked to stop by the same evening for an interview. I had master's degrees in English Literature and Art History but no real teaching qualifications. However, I also had zero teaching experience with children.

Until then, I had only taught sullen teenage goths in a depressing Swedish town in the middle of a pine forest. The town boasted a car factory, where most of my students' parents worked and where most of my pupils would end up working. To say that their prospects in life were gloomy and depressing would have been an overly optimistic assessment of the situation. The bleak milieu was not helped by the interminably long, dark winters during which the snow would be up to your hips on the side of the road.

I still remember the cold, dark mornings of my first teaching gig when I had to push my way through chain-smoking hordes of teenagers to enter the school building. The 'kids' would give everyone who tried to enter the premises a dirty look, send each other some secret eye signal, and then giggle inanely behind your back. I soon found out that most of the school's teachers used the back entrance to avoid having to walk past the snarky crowd of thugs that would gather at the front of the school. That first experience did not inspire me to become a teacher; quite the opposite.

In hindsight, I have no idea why the school principal in Al Ain let me teach the four- and five-year-olds. He must have been in a very tight corner.

'As long as you're from Europe and speak only English to the kids, the parents are happy,' a Finnish teacher at the school explained.

It was a private school following an American curriculum. The parents were Arab expats from Palestine, Syria, Jordan, Egypt, Iraq, and many other places in North Africa and the Middle East. The parents were mostly overachievers, including doctors, bankers, and managers of international companies. They came from challenging socio-economic circumstances and expected their progeny to supersede them in their life ambitions. As such, they naturally had very high expectations of the school and its teachers. To say that during my first week of teaching their children, I did not meet these expectations would have been an enormous understatement. My first venture into primary education was a total disaster. The kids ran amok around me. At the end of each day, the books, toys, pencils, and crayons were all over the classroom floor, and my mind was in a similar state of disarray.

I don't recall any teaching taking place. It was only thanks to my assistant, a kind and patient Libyan lady, Salma, that the children didn't poke holes in each other's eyes or go home with soiled pants. Seeing that I was clueless and had no idea when the children were crying to go to the toilet or dying of thirst, she taught me a few essential words in Arabic, including *hammam*, which means 'toilet' and *ma*, which means 'water'. She also trained me to use the Arabic kindergarten teacher's keyword, *halas!* which freely translates to *stop it now*, *that's it*, or *that's enough*. This delightful word has a multitude of uses depending on the context and your tone.

Why I wasn't fired from this position after the first week of mayhem was a mystery to me and still is. But the rumours that I had no idea of what to do with the kids must have reached the principal's office because in the second week, the smartly dressed Egyptian vice-principal, Ms Kamal, stopped by my classroom to tell me that the cleaning staff had complained about the state of the room at the end of each day. I was indignant.

Why don't you try to spend a morning with these monsters, and then I'll come by and assess the room's tidiness? I wanted to say.

But since I was only twenty-seven and had limited options in life, I decided to give teaching a go. I begrudgingly listened to her suggestions.

'Why don't we combine some of your lessons with Ms Shaza?' she continued. 'Just this month so that you can find your way.'

While I didn't like admitting defeat, I was also aware of my limitations. Ms Shaza was an Arabic teacher. Every day, the children would spend two hours with me, as I pretended to teach them English, and two hours with her, who actually taught them all the things that small children should know, like the letters of the alphabet, numbers, shapes, names of animals, and arts and crafts.

The first time we combined our classes, I could not believe my eyes. Even though she was in charge of double the number of students, all the wee rascals were sitting quietly on the mat, cross-legged, singing their hearts out, raising their baby arms to answer the questions about the alphabet and being positively adorable. I was now ready to learn how to be a teacher from this inspirational lady.

I observed Shaza every day and emulated her strategies. By the end of the first term, I had a group of perfectly behaved Muppet Babies who would stand in line when asked to, walk in an orderly fashion to the playground, and sit patiently with scissors in hand, waiting for my instructions during my arts and crafts lessons. Of course, my assistant, Salma, was invaluable in translating my instructions when needed and soothing the children in Arabic when they felt sad about something. I started my first year of teaching in the Emirates, not wanting to wake up the next day because of my fear of having to face eighteen miniature demons. But I ended the year by enrolling in a professional teaching course. It was the beginning of a career. As I had now decided to teach Spanish children, I hoped that the lessons from my past would still be relevant.

I was to teach various groups of learners from five years old to sixteen years old. The teens were not a problem for me — there is little difference between snooty teens whether they are from the Arabian desert, a Swedish pine forest, or the Andalusian olive groves. The other groups of ten- and eleven-year-olds were quite sweet and eager to learn. But one group of second graders gave me a whole new set of nightmares. In fact, one specific seven-year-old haunted me that winter and spring.

Little Jesús was ready to cause total destruction and bodily harm at any given time. He was unable to stay in the same place for longer than a nanosecond, and I doubt if I ever managed to sit him down for longer than a minute. As soon as I turned my back to check on the other children's work, he was already on the other side of the room chopping at a little girl's hair with a pair of blunt scissors or ripping pages out of another child's notebook. The only teaching that took place that term for that group was on the two days when Little Jesús was sick. As is a common feature of most young hooligans, Jesús had an immune system of steel and hardly ever fell ill.

I was at my wit's end with that seven-year-old. On a few occasions, I found myself chasing him around the classroom while other kids giggled in amusement. And on several others, I felt a strong urge to shake the living daylights out of the tiny brute, but I had enough sense and constraint not to act on that urge. It was time to ask Belén, the school's owner and manager, for advice.

As I recounted my trials and tribulations with this specific second-grader, I saw sadness and defeat in her eyes. The antics of the mischievous boy were not news to her. Why hadn't she warned me of his disruptive behaviour before I stepped foot in the class and made a complete fool of myself? I can only speculate that she had hoped that a new teacher would positively influence the teeny devil and make him change his ways. Well, in this case, I failed.

'Susana used to tell him to copy the songs from the Pupil's Book into his notebook,' Belén suggested. A tone of resignation was evident in her voice.

Susana was Jesús's previous teacher.

Since Belén was not forthcoming with any other ideas, like 'Let's kick Jesús out of the school!', I assumed that her obviously ineffectual solution was all she had in her repertoire as a teacher.

'We can't ask students to leave the school,' Belén read my mind. 'Other parents may protest. He's not a bad kid, but his parents are getting divorced, and no one ever says 'no' to him. His father only buys him things to compensate for the divorce.'

While I could sympathise with the child's stress, it fell on deaf ears.

I was a child of divorced parents, I thought to myself. *But I didn't bring a katana to my class and attempt to behead my classmates with it.* Needless to say, I had little patience for children acting out because they were going through tough times.

'I'll try to get him to copy the songs from the book,' I told Belén.

The next time I saw my minuscule nemesis, I set him up to copy verses from the book. Strangely, he seemed very happy to do that. I assumed Susana must have convinced him that copying things from a book was the right thing to do. I can't say it worked like a charm. But it usually did the trick for the first twenty minutes of the class, which gave me enough time to teach the other children some new vocabulary and practise our songs. As soon as we started our group games, Jesús would return to being his demon self.

I felt terrible having the child sit alone and mindlessly copy lines from his book like some unpaid medieval scribe. I could not imagine what educational purpose it had at all except to keep him quiet and in one place for a few minutes. But I had no better ideas to deal with Jesús's behaviour. He needed specialised help, and since I only saw him for two hours a week, I did not think I could provide such help. We were just a small language school in a small town. The school didn't have the scope or budget to help children with their psychological or emotional issues. Not having any other resources, I sought the help of *Supernanny*.

After his first experience of four minutes on the 'naughty chair', Jesús left his English lesson crying hysterically. Outside the school, he threw the biggest tantrum in front of his clueless dad, who was watching the spectacle from the driver's seat of his BMW, smoking a cigarette. His son threw the crayons out of his pencil case, bashed his school bag against the pavement, and swore that he would never step foot back in this school again. Belén called me outside to explain what had prompted this fervid drama.

'He was running and shouting around the class, and so he got to sit on the naughty chair for four minutes,' I looked at the frenzied boy lying now in tears on the pavement outside the school, making a religious martyr of himself.

'And *this* is not allowed at the school.' I handed his father a set of child-size nunchucks that Jesús would often bring from his karate classes to terrorise the other seven-year-olds in his English class.

I waited for an apology, but one was never going to be offered, so I returned to my classroom. What a lifetime in education did not prepare me for, a few evenings watching *Super Nanny* did the trick. I devised an arbitrary and somewhat random reward system to incentivise the children to behave well. Watching them work hard for the positive points I assigned for good behaviour, singing well, or colouring within the lines gave me a new understanding of the Foucauldian theory of power.

'I have no idea why they want these points,' I remarked to Robert one evening while relaxing with a glass of wine after work. 'But, by God, the kids will do anything for them. But what shall I say if some smart-ass kid asks me what these points are for?'

'Tell them that the student with the most points will get a gift at the end of the term.'

Thus, between the two of us, we had reinvented a primitive system of incentives through arbitrary rewards, and for fifty cents a class, for that was how much I was willing to spend in the Chinese shop on the rewards, I was able to bring peace and harmony to my lessons.

From then on, my other classes went smoothly. Once I got to know the children and the teenagers and familiarised myself with the syllabus, the work was easy enough. Considering I had been a teacher for almost fifteen years, it wasn't rocket science. I would spend my mornings mixing cement or plastering the walls in our new living room, then sit down for an hour and review the material I was to teach that day. I would then drive to Alcalá and work at the school until late evening. On many a cold and rainy day in February and March, I looked forward to the classroom's warmth. I now also had a genuine excuse for not spending the whole day on the building site that my house had become once more.

'I thought you wanted to start your own school,' my friend, Liv, commented once while we were having coffee in Montefrio.

'That's true, but I have no idea where to begin. I think I will stay at this school for a couple of years, observe Belén, and see how a private language school is managed. Then, maybe I will start a school here in Montefrio.'

That was the original plan, which was never realised.

While little Jesús used to test my professional pride and abilities to the extreme, there was another student in his class who would restore my faith in humanity and my vocation. Before each lesson, little Julia would walk in, look around the room, spot me, and beam with delight. She would then march across the room to give me the biggest hug ever. She did it for a couple of years until she became a tween. I did not know at the time that I would be blessed with the privilege of watching these children grow from Muppet Babies into young adults. Every September, they'd come back to the school taller and more confident in themselves. Over the years, I would get to know their families, their siblings and cousins and learn about their family lives.

Little did I know, but from my first day at the language school, I had begun to establish roots in the community. It was a new beginning.

TWENTY

A LO POBRE

T*he Dutch are such good hosts.* This pleasant thought struck me while I was gustily chowing down some blueberries and sipping cold champagne from a stylish flute. I was sitting comfortably on a modern swivelling bar stool in Céline's designer kitchen. Liv, Julian, Robert, and I had gathered at her townhouse in Frailes before the village fiesta. It was the first week of April, and unlike every other April I had experienced in Andalusia thus far, this one was freezing. We all arrived in our winter jackets, complete with woolly hats and gloves. I could see the abnormal weather putting a great strain on our hostess. Her townhouse was relatively narrow inside, and since we could not sit together outside in the garden or on the terrace because of the cold, we were slightly cramped in the confines of her living room. Still, what she lacked in space, she compensated with hospitality.

Stereotypically, a Dutch hostess not only aspires to provide the perfect luncheon or dinner for her friends but also usually succeeds at the task. I could tell from the carefully tailored selection of snacks that nothing on the table was there by chance. This was very different to the other nationalities that I have dined with in the past.

Poles, for example, like to serve their guests food that they never eat themselves.

'This is a traditional Polish dish,' a traveller from abroad will inevitably hear once invited to a Polish household for dinner. Proudly presented before the unsuspecting celebrant will be a bowl of sauerkraut boiled to death, adorned with prunes and chunky, fat-filled sausage, our pride and joy called *bigos*. Or, if the host is a real gourmand, a tower of *zimne nóżki*, 'cold feet jelly', made of pork trotters and knuckles, will be served. The trick to avoiding culinary disappointment when travelling in Poland is to never order a dish with the word *traditional* in its title. Most of these dishes take hours, if not days, to prepare and are only served once or twice a year — for a reason, I may add. Once the festivities are over, they tend to end up in the bin or the dog's bowl.

Poles are not alone in torturing friends from other countries with their culinary nostalgia. Many Brits often assume that whatever they serve to their guests enjoys international popularity and are indignantly surprised when their guests don't want to try mince pies or sausage rolls. They'll never forgive you if, during a Sunday roast, you remove a Yorkshire 'pudding' from your plate and set it aside, never intending to eat it. Adding pastry on top of a plate already plenteous with meat, vegetables, and gravy is a conundrum for most Europeans.

Even more inexplicable is the vacant indentation that occupies the middle of a Yorkshire pudding, something visitors to the Great Britannic islands assume was once filled with something edible. Perhaps the host had forgotten the filling of this nascent pie, or the intended stuffing was not up to scratch? And if your British host is genuinely patriotic, you will finish your meal with a dessert that will make any French food critic roll their eyes in horror — a trifle — a culinary experiment concocted by a team of disorganised six-year-olds who each was allowed to add a random ingredient to form a dish consisting of separate layers of soggy cake, jelly, custard, jam, cream, tinned fruit, and anything else found at the back of the kitchen cupboard, including flaked almonds or glacé cherries.

However misguided their culinary aspirations, the Poles and Brits often proudly adhere to their countries' traditions when hosting dinner parties. Americans, on the other hand, prefer a casual approach to dining. Whenever you are invited to an American meal, it feels as if you just popped in and surprised the whole family with your presence. Even if you arrive fashionably late, nothing is ever ready to be placed on the table, and it can take hours before the host offers you a glass of wine. In my experience, it seems as if the host was suddenly reminded that you were, in fact, invited to eat a meal together, and so within minutes of your arrival, you are assigned to be an assistant chef. Before you know it, you are busy chopping carrots and peppers while your partner is tasked to marinate some chicken wings in a shop-bought sauce. Even though Americans are more relaxed in their approach to dinner parties, they, too, resort to indulging in food nostalgia.

'This is American cheese,' a friend from Missouri once announced, full of national pride, when she saw me interrogating the glutinous, slightly luminescent substance that adorned a taco. 'I had to go to Dubai to get it in a special supermarket.'

I wished she hadn't bothered. The American cheese had the glossy consistency of a melted plastic Barbie doll and the same nutritional value, I presumed.

Considering my previous dinner party experiences, I was relieved to see that Céline had refrained from serving the gathered guests food infused with patriotic values and childhood recollections. Her selection of berries, nuts, and cheeses was devoid of any nationalistic pride. *Cava* flowed, and as soon as we exchanged the news of our ongoing renovations, Leon proceeded to give us a tour of his house. People often use the expression 'this place is a like a TARDIS' erroneously when describing a space just a little bit bigger than they expected. Céline and Leon's home was the first that I felt could be accurately described as a TARDIS. The reason was that more than half the house was inside a mountain.

The house's façade consisted of an entrance door and a small kitchen window to one side. Stepping inside, you found yourself immediately occupying a small, modern kitchen. Because of the limited space available, the kitchen housed several secret cupboards and drawers concealed behind plain marble surfaces. To the left, two steps up, we were in a miniature dining room that neither occupant of the house could use due to the limited ceiling height over the table. The purpose of the 'room' was unclear to me since most of Céline and Leon's family were Dutch and presumably were of the same, typically Dutch, statuesque height.

I had not seen a more impractical dining room set-up in my life, except for my neighbour Keith's dining room, where the distance between the back of the dining chairs and the wall was about ten centimetres, forcing one to sit upright with your belly pushed against the edge of the table. A dedicated dining room is a folly at best. When we misguidedly fit our modern, middle-class aspirations into an old-fashioned farmer's cottage, we can end up with Céline's dining room, which was perfect for a family of hobbits or Keith's cramped dining room, which would have been suitable for an annual meeting of the Slendermen Convention.

I could see that Céline's dining room was never used since it was filled with knick-knacks they had bought while exploring various expat flea markets that occupied the coast of southern Spain. The ornaments and other *objets d'art* were all potential craft projects for Céline.

'Look at these,' Céline picked up a pair of small oil paintings in ornate gilded frames.

They were small, intricately detailed portraits of a man and a woman. I liked them both.

'I'll use these frames for our photos.'

'You could paint over the gold with chalk blue or something else,' I suggested, as I am not a fan of gilded finishes.

I could see Céline did not agree with my shabby-chic upcycling idea and I knew she was not going to take any note of my advice. As I examined the aristocratic couple depicted wearing heavily embroidered velvet clothes, I wondered how many early Rembrandts, Vermeers, or Van Goghs had ended up as kindling in the past because the lady of the house preferred the fancy frame over the images painted on the canvas.

'Gold is nice too,' I tried to appease Céline's sense of household pride. 'It's very regal. Maybe you could just scratch some of it off at the corners.'

She was politely uninterested in my creative suggestion, so I changed the topic.

'And what's inside there?' I pointed towards a dark space behind the dining room.

'It's a bedroom.'

I walked over to a restricted opening in the wall, bowed down, and peeked inside.

'It's not our regular bedroom,' she clarified. 'It used to be a bedroom in the past. We only sleep in there when it's very hot in the summer because it stays cool all year round.'

The space had the definite curved shape of a cave that had been scraped out manually with primitive tools. Despite being covered by a layer of plaster, the grooves made by crowbars and chisels were visible on the rounded ceiling and walls.

As I explored downstairs, it became apparent that, in the past, a Spanish family had used only this floor of the house. There was a big fireplace in the kitchen where they would cook, warming up the whole area. They'd eat in the minuscule dining room and then retire to the Lilliputian cave to sleep.

'The upstairs of the house was used to store grain and dry cured *jamón* and sausages,' Céline explained. 'But we've converted it into a bedroom and a walk-in closet.'

The house was one of several on a narrow village street not far from a large abandoned industrial estate that was in total disrepair. The front of the building resembled that of an English terraced house, ignoring the fact that it had been built into the side of a mountain. In the past, these houses were used as dwellings for landless day labourers, called *jornaleros.* For centuries, *jornaleros* were a common feature of rural Spain, especially in Andalusia, which boasted some of the grandest agrarian estates in the country. The plight of *jornaleros* has inspired many Spanish novels and paintings.

Working for a day's wage, they earned just enough to provide the most basic food for themselves and their families. On good days, when the sun shone, the ground was dry, and the olive season was in full swing, they'd work all day hitting the trees with long sticks, pulling nets full of olives from tree to tree, and carrying heavy baskets to a wagon so that the donkeys could take the harvest to the mill. Doing this backbreaking work, they'd make just enough to buy bread, a bag of beans or lentils, and rice to feed the family.

But it's not always sunny in Andalusia. Should there be a week or two of heavy rain, the work in the fields would come to a halt. Once their hungry children had finished the last ladle of the household's watery bean stew, the parents would need to borrow money to survive until the next day's job came along. And so, as soon as the sun was out and the landlord called for his workers again, they'd begin their heavy labour by working to pay off their debt. They were trapped in a vicious circle of debt, hunger, cold, and misery that was impossible for most *jornaleros* and their families to escape.

Nowadays, local landowners and farmers hire seasonal labourers from Morocco, Algeria, Senegal, Gambia, and North-West Africa to help with the olive harvest, asparagus cutting, and cherry picking. In winter and spring, the demand for day labourers is huge. But once the last cherry is picked from the trees at the end of May or early June, there is very little to do in the countryside. At least, there is not enough work for the many seasonal workers who live here from December to May. It must have been the same in centuries past. Those who were mobile and could travel — mostly single men — would move on to look for work in other parts of Spain. But those with small children at home or who had to look after sick or elderly family members were always on the brink of starvation.

If the spring was warm and wet, figs, grapes, and tomatoes would be available throughout the summer. But in the years of drought or when the crops were afflicted by disease, the pawnshops thrived.

Mothers with babies in their arms and little ones holding onto their aprons would stand in line to exchange the last of their meagre possessions for a day's supply of food. Nowadays, mothers are no longer forced to sit on the street begging for a loaf of bread, and fathers don't need to knock on the landlord's door asking for an opportunity to do a gruelling day's work for a few miserly pesetas. But the collective memory of those days remains alive in Andalusia. Many families who reside here are the descendants of *jornaleros,* and their grandparents still remember the time when food was scarce and the next paying job uncertain.

The hardships of the past are not only reflected in the architecture of Spanish village houses but also in Andalusian cuisine. Asked what food they associate with Spain, many outsiders will inevitably mention *paella* — a somewhat festive rice dish from the province of Valencia that includes many expensive ingredients, such as saffron. Those who have visited Spain may also mention the ubiquitous *croquetas* or *tortilla española,* the Spanish omelette. But ask any local man, woman, teenager, or child in the provinces of Granada, Jaén, or Cordoba about their favourite food, and you will hear the word *migas* repeated over and over.

When I first heard of this dish from my neighbour, Maria, she struggled to explain to me what it was, or rather, I struggled to make sense of the words she used. She repeated the Spanish words for 'bread' and 'fry', but they made no sense to me as a dish in itself.

'A French toast?' I tried to guess the dish, but she shook her head.

Seeing my confusion, she reached for her phone and translated 'migas', which came out as 'crumbs'.

Bread crumbs? I was even more puzzled but didn't say anything. *That can't be a dish.*

Mystified by the whole 'bread crumbs' story, I went home and researched *migas.* I discovered that it is a dish made of crumbled stale bread fried with garlic and other condiments that one might have at hand. In my time in Andalusia, I have often been served *migas* and can attest that it belongs to the category of nostalgic food. But I always ensure I taste it whenever it is offered and praise the chef. Notwithstanding this, I have the same enthusiasm for *migas* as I have for the British Yorkshire pudding, American cheese, or Polish *bigos*. It's a necessary evil of cultural exploration. *Migas* tastes exactly as its translation suggests, namely, 'bread crumbs'. If I could improve on the Google translation, I'd say 'fried stale bread crumbs'.

There are other Andalusian favourites that you may hear locals talk about with heartfelt sentimentality, but you will never see such dishes at an international cooking show or served at a beach restaurant on the coast. They are all one-pot wonders favoured by Andalusian housewives and country inns. *Puchero* is one of them. It's a chickpea casserole that grandmas and mums in various provinces of Spain garnish with their unique selection of meat, legumes, and vegetables. Numerous other stews and soups feature lentils or beans as the central ingredient. The objective of these dishes is clear: feed as many mouths as you can for as long as you can with cheap, nutritious, heart-warming food.

If there is a theme to Andalusian cuisine, it's *waste not, want not*. An Andalusian classic made famous beyond the borders of Spain by the writer Chris Stewart is *patatas a lo pobre*. This dish advertises 'poverty' and 'desperation' in its very name. Bones and offal are typical flavour enhancers in most such Andalusian dishes. Kidneys, brains, and hearts are sold in local supermarkets next to more modern cuts, such as chicken breasts and pork fillets. *A lo pobre*, or 'poor man's', is a description that could be easily attached to Andalusian gastronomy.

With this in mind, I was ready for the culinary explorations at the Frailes' fiesta. Once we finished the *cava*, we got our umbrellas and went into the drizzle to join the annual village celebrations at the bottom of the hill. Because of the unusually cold April that we were experiencing, the Town Hall had set up a huge tent to protect everyone from the freezing temperatures and the intermittent rain.

We were waiting patiently in a queue outside the tent with our tickets in hand when I saw Leon getting itchy feet. He was watching the crowd like a hawk and must have spotted several other men like himself looking for the best tables inside the tent. While we all stood patiently, waiting for the gate to open, joking with each other and making passive-aggressive remarks about how we would storm the tent, someone pushed into the queue from behind. Leon could not take it anymore.

'I'll see you inside,' he said.

He threw away the cigarillo he had been puffing on tensely for the past ten minutes, flattened his perfectly trimmed moustache, and dove into the crowd with a determination that I had only seen before in my grandmother and her friends, who used their seniority and matronly bulk to piously shove their fellow Christians out of the way in order to secure the front pews before Easter mass. Leon had assured us we would get the best seats in the house. While I myself was not a fan of shoving and jostling for position in a crowd, I appreciated having someone in my company who didn't mind doing so.

It took us another fifteen minutes or more before we reached the entrance to the eating area and handed in our tickets. Inside the tent, we were presented with fifty or more long tables covered with white paper tablecloths and set with plates and bottles of wine. Next to each plate, there was a humongous piece of bread. In most cultures, it would have been a meal on its own. But wolfing down massive amounts of bread throughout your meal is mandatory in Andalusia. For this reason, every guest was assigned their own sizeable baguette.

I soon spotted Leon, who had singlehandedly 'reserved' six adjacent chairs by putting various items of his clothing on them. I looked around and was grateful for his sacrifice. The only tables that were still unoccupied were right by the music stand, next to a set of giant speakers, or outside the tent, behind the stage, next to the public toilets. If we had followed the polite queueing etiquette, we would have spent the afternoon either shouting at each other across the table like maniacs because of the music volume or watching an endless stream of people going in and out of the loos. We all thanked Leon profusely as we settled down at our well-located table.

Unaccustomed to Andalusian traditions, an outsider might have been tempted to open the bottle of wine presented to the table and pour everyone a glass. But the custom at such parties is to savour the view of the bottle of wine and begin the festivities with a small beer. As soon as we were seated, we were served a round of cold beers and a selection of cold meats prepared by local butchers. These included very rustic-looking cuts of white sausage and *morcilla*, Andalusian blood sausage. We polished these off with bread dipped in copious amounts of olive oil. The degustation of sausages and beer had given the waiters time to seat everyone and serve tapas. An hour into the party, I noted that all the tables were occupied, even the ones out in the rain and *en route* to the *pissoirs*.

As is common with people who have managed to avoid calamity by pure chance, we made several conceited comments about the poor saps seated behind the stage, wiping the gentle raindrops off their plates. Soon, we were served a hearty bean stew with chunks of pork, and the bottles of wine that had thus far been left untouched on the tables were ceremoniously opened. It was a great afternoon. We shared food and drink, but more importantly, new experiences. We were bonding with each other and making new friendships. The conversation flowed while we joked about the freezing temperatures, our Siberian attire, and never-ending DIY projects.

'With all this rain, we won't need to buy water this summer,' Robert announced cockily. 'Our tank is full.'

'It's been raining almost non-stop since February, hasn't it?' Julian stated the fact.

'Yes, and we've been collecting the rainwater from the roof into the tank.'

Robert and I were so pleased that our scheme had worked and looked forward to the summer when we wouldn't have to worry about the house's water supply. Little did we know that, while we were busy exploring Andalusian culinary traditions, a disaster was brewing back home.

TWENTY-ONE
THE WATER BREAKS

We arrived home from the fiesta in Frailes late in the evening, so I only noticed a stream flowing by the side of the house the following morning. I was on my way to the guest apartment to make myself a cup of coffee when my path was cut short by a small river running down the patio. As Julian observed the night before, it had been raining almost non-stop that winter. I thought the hills behind the house were so saturated that they were starting to flood and seep down the valley, but I was wrong. As I looked around the corner of the house, the source of this impromptu deluge was apparent. Our steel water tank, the pride and joy of our household, which was supposed to save us from another drought, had detached itself from its concrete foundation, and the eighty thousand litres of precious liquid that we had managed to collect over the winter were now cascading down the hill and onto the guest patio.

I like to keep a positive outlook on life and always try to search for solutions when faced with a calamity. But in that instant, even I knew we could do nothing but watch the water drain away. The deluge from the giant container was unstoppable. There was no patch or tape we could apply that would have been able to withstand the pressure. It would have been like trying to seal a slashed artery with a Band-Aid. I crossed the little river, entered the guest living room, sat on the sofa, and stared out the window. At that moment, I felt like I might never be able to get up again. It was so disheartening to lose all that essential resource. I shed tears of frustration.

We had worked every morning in the cold, mixing cement and plastering walls, living surrounded by dust and dirt, and then working long hours every afternoon at the language school — it was all too much. The one thing that had given me hope for the future had just broken down catastrophically. I was working myself into hysterics and adding up my miseries, one upon the other, fuelling the tears streaming down my face.

It was my second mental breakdown in this 'dream house'. The first one had occurred four years earlier, a month or so into our house renovations. Back then, we were living in a building site with no roof and thus were regularly flooded by the torrential rains of that winter and spring. The water flowing down the walls frequently shorted out our electric cables and left us in complete darkness. Since I already felt sorry for myself, all our past misfortunes in the house came back to me in a rush of calamity and cataclysm. But I didn't have time to continue my pitiful sobbing as I heard Robert enter the guest apartment. I wiped my face dry with my tatty work gloves.

'Have you seen what's happened?' he asked me innocently. But his observation only infuriated me.

'Have I seen what's happened?' I mocked rhetorically. 'What am I? Blind? I hate this house!' I was now shouting and peppering my words with F-bombs. 'I can't do it anymore! It's one step forward and ten steps back!'

I was angry at the house, the forces of nature, my life, everything. I was on a rampage and must have gone through a whole page of synonyms for 'faeces' before I sat down again. Now that I had run out of expletives, I decided never to speak to Robert again and committed myself to an ungodly sulk. I blamed everyone else for my hard luck.

'The concrete seal at the bottom of the tank wasn't strong enough. It should have been much thicker,' Robert explained and blamed the builder who had advised him on the thickness of the cement that held the tank in place. Now that we had identified the culprit of this disaster and cursed him, his mother, and many generations of his offspring to come, I wanted to know how we could fix the tank. But at that moment, any remedy was beyond my imagination.

'Where will we get another five thousand euros to build a new tank?' I asked.

'We don't need to build a new one,' this time, Robert was the optimist in the relationship. 'We just need a new foundation to seal the bottom of the tank properly.'

'How will you lift a four-metre-tall tank above the ground?' I struggled to understand his plan.

'No, we won't lift it. We'll get inside the tank, smash the old concrete inside and all around it, and then pour new foundations inside and outside.'

'How much will this cost?'

'A few hundred or so. The labour and the cement trucks.'

While I wasn't over the moon about wasting more money on the tank, Robert's cost estimation was much better than what I had sorrowfully anticipated.

'But first, the water has to drain out completely.'

It broke my heart to watch all that liquid drain away. I'd spent the previous two years struggling to supply the house and guests with running water and could not bear to look at it going to waste, flooding the patio and then running out onto the field. Several days later the little river behind the house ceased to flow. In the meantime, our old builder Dani stopped by one day to assess the damage and to see whether Robert's plan to fix the tank was viable.

He must have noticed that I was still upset about the damage because he reassured me profusely that he and Robert could repair it in two days. But the job would have to wait until May when he would be done with his olives.

'We can use the well until the tank is working again,' Robert reminded me that our well, which we hadn't used for two years because of the drought, was full again.

There was no more time that April to feel sorry for myself. May is usually one of the busiest months for tourism in Andalusia. The first guests of the season were coming on the 1st of May, and before that, we had to vacate their apartment. To do so, we had to finish our living room and kitchen and prepare the rest of the house for guests. As always, when faced with an inevitable deadline, I made a list of things to do and put it on the fridge in the guest kitchen. There were dozens of small and big jobs on the list, but the main one was 'build a kitchen.'

The original plan was to buy a kitchen, but since then, our costs had doubled, and we had to prioritise what needed to be done that spring and what could wait until the indefinite future when we'd have saved up some money again. The heating and the floor tiles were essential. The kitchen and the sofas could be purchased in the future.

'We can build a kitchen,' I informed Robert while reviewing my December spreadsheet.

The 'we' in the sentence was the exclusive 'we'; it excluded *me* and was used in my statement as a form of spousal encouragement. I had no idea how to build a proper kitchen. I wouldn't know where to start. But I knew how to draw one, so after a few days of walking around the empty room with the tape measure and pencil, I presented Robert with my drawings.

'What am I supposed to do with this?' he asked me as he looked at the notebook with my design.

'Build a kitchen.'

'From this?' he pointed at my artistic endeavours. 'There are no measurements here and no details. How am I supposed to know how much wood to buy?'

I had to admit that my design was sketchy at best. It resembled one of those futuristic drawings made by an avant-garde *haute couture* designer: a few fluctuating lines were drawn freehand, a zigzag shaded with a thumb, and *voila!* It was an illustration that conveyed feelings and the vibe I wanted for the kitchen, but it had no specific instructions on how one might go about constructing it. The only measurements I had included were the length of the walls, which was only tangentially helpful to my aspiring carpenter/husband.

'I need something like this,' Robert showed me a professional cupboard design plan from a carpentry website, awash with exact joinery dimensions.

All I saw were hundreds of meticulous measurements.

'It's too detailed,' I announced.

When *I* make things, I prefer to use the method that I developed as a child. Back then, I would spend hours sewing clothes for my Barbie dolls. I must have been ten or eleven when I received the best gift of my childhood — a tiny sewing machine that was made in Germany and worked just like a real machine, minus the possibility of piercing an inquisitive child's finger with a super-sharp needle. Since I didn't have any actual designs for my dolls' clothes, I used to draw creative inspiration from the women's magazines that my mother had lying around the house. I would lay the doll flat on a piece of fabric and draw the shape of the dress, skirt or shirt around her, a seamstress's silhouette. I would cut out the approximate shape and duplicate it onto another piece of fabric. All I had to do was sew the two pieces together.

As anyone who has ever taken up a needle and thread can predict, my first attempts at miniature *poupée-couture* were a fiasco. I had failed to account for the fact that dolls were three-dimensional entities and had some girth to them, however skinny my Barbies seemed. I was always keen to learn from my mistakes. In my second *collection de mode*, I cut out two pieces of fabric in one go and added an extra centimetre to the design. This way, my Barbies could fit easily into their new, albeit not very well-fitting, clothes, all of which had a distinct 1990s hip-hop feel, well ahead of its time in post-communist Poland.

Thirty years later, I was none-the-wiser about practical design and applied the same principles to my new kitchen. I grabbed the notebook with my sketches from Robert and wandered over to the corner of the room that was to become the kitchen. I lifted my design to my eye level, closed one eye for good measure, and proceeded to demonstrate how accurate and easily implementable my design plan was.

'Here's a cupboard, then space for a fitted fridge, next a cutting surface, and, as you move to the left, a space for a cooker. You see,' I beckoned him over. 'It's perfect.'

Even though Robert was deeply dissatisfied with my vague blueprints, there was nothing else we could do about our need for a kitchen. So, he spent some time writing down additional measurements, calculating how much wood he had to buy and of what lengths and sizes. The following morning, we hitched the trailer to the car, and with a scrap of paper containing his calculations resting on the dashboard, we drove to the sawmill outside Priego de Córdoba. It was a family business that stretched over a vast property and consisted of several warehouses, workshops, offices, an intricately designed wooden pavilion, and a huge house where the owners resided. Both Robert and I had always been in awe of this small but significant business.

Their primary business concern was the construction of pallets from pine wood. If you live in Andalusia and have ever had anything delivered on a pallet, the chances are that it came from this specific sawmill. Truckloads of pallets could be seen leaving the property at regular intervals every day. How they came up with the business idea was a mystery to me. Still, I admired the determination of a family who, surrounded by olive farms, decided to clear some of their land of olive trees and turn it into a profitable sawmill. It was the type of thinking that renders one either a successful entrepreneur or a lunatic. I was sure there were times in their family history when the founder of the sawmill doubted their decision.

The area around Priego is not abundant in wood, besides olive wood, of course. The few scrawny holly oaks, or *encina*, indigenous to the area are protected by strict laws prohibiting one from felling them. If you plan to cut down a tree that is ten years or older or of a specific diameter, you need special permission before you do so. You face a fine of thousands of euros if caught red-handed cutting down a protected species.

Any pine trees, or *pinos*, that you might spot in some people's gardens have a purely decorative purpose. Since these trees are so rare in this dry climate, they appear somewhat exotic to the locals. Poplar trees, or *alamo*, grow happily in our area and are often planted in parks and by city roadsides to shade the walkways. But there aren't nearly enough of them around to start a pallet-building empire. The scarcity of local wood suitable for running a lumber yard made me think that the young man who started the business in the 1960s had some moxie.

It was, in fact, the son of a local carpenter from Almedinilla who, in 1971, decided to focus his woodworking skills on making fruit boxes.

'So, you're going to make fruit boxes,' I imagined his father questioning his son's strange idea.

'Yes, just fruit boxes. I'm tired of fixing chairs and making tables.'

'I don't understand,' his father would say while planing down a tabletop. 'We have a good business. We're the only carpentry in the village. People come to us all the way from Bracana and La Rabita to make new furniture and fix their old pieces.'

'Yes, Dad. But once we fix their chairs and tables, they never come back. If I make fruit boxes, all the farmers and cooperatives will buy them. Then, they send the fruit in boxes to shops in Madrid, and I have to make more fruit boxes. They'll always need more boxes.'

'But Pablo, I have been working so hard to teach you how to work with wood. It doesn't take a genius to make a fruit box.'

'Exactly! I can train some people to do it and make hundreds or thousands of boxes every day.'

'Out of what wood?'

'Pine.'

'You're *loco,* son,' his dad would dismiss the idea. Quite rightly, as there might be enough pine trees in the area to make a few hundred fruit boxes, but definitely not enough to start a whole enterprise.

'I can buy pine wood from Germany,' the son would insist.

The young Pablo must have convinced his dad because fifty years later, the business was thriving and selling not only pallets but also wooden garden furniture, home décor items, gazebos, and garden sheds all over Spain and Portugal, all made out of German pine but manufactured by a team of twenty Spaniards in the countryside outside Priego. The spirit of adding value to a basic raw material was palpable in the compound. Both Robert and I enjoyed visiting this lumber yard to admire the various products they had on display and to watch this tight-knit family at work. It was always a pleasure to see.

Once Robert had paid for the lumber in the office, a young man, the son of the business founder, jumped into a buggy, and we followed him to collect the planks for the kitchen. Since it was starting to rain, he showed us which pile was ours and left us to load the wood onto the trailer. We must have loaded half of the wood from the stack onto the trailer when a thought occurred to me that it was an awful lot of lumber for just one kitchen.

'Are you sure it's all *our* wood?' I hesitated.

'Yes, he said so.'

'But it's quite a lot.'

'I made exact measurements according to your design,' Robert said indignantly. He would not admit to making a mistake in his calculations, even though some doubts must have crept in.

It's enough wood to build a small kitchen and Noah's Ark afterwards, I thought to myself. But since I was cold and wet, I kept these unkind observations to myself and continued to help load the wood. We were running out of time that April, and there was no time for bickering.

TWENTY-TWO
ARCTIC MAY

A French family with two young children was due at our place in two weeks, but we were still living in their accommodation and unable to relocate back to our house. To make matters more stressful, the May holidays that year coincided with some other French national holidays, and it appeared that all of France had decided to come to Southern Spain to enjoy a few weeks in the sun.

Soon after Dominique and her boys were to stay with us, we expected the arrival of more French families until the end of May. We had no option but to make haste with our projects. While Robert worked every day building a new kitchen from scratch, I spent my mornings cleaning grout from the floors and painting so we could move back into our part of the house. I had to squeeze in as much work as possible before lunch because, in the afternoons, I would drive to the language school in Alcalá to teach. While our preparations to receive Dominique and her family were in full swing, one thing bothered me about their stay.

I could remember quite distinctly a conversation I had with her in January. She called me in person to ask if they could use the swimming pool in May.

'I've just made a booking for two weeks in your *gîte*,' I heard a pleasant woman with a strong French accent over the phone.

'It's Dominique, right?' I had seen the booking appear on my phone a few minutes earlier.

'Yes, that's me. I wanted to ask if we can use the pool during our stay. The children are excited about it.'

'Yes, of course.' I assured her with the same confidence as if she had asked me if they would be allowed to drink coffee in the morning. 'The pool is always open on the 1st of May.'

My last words to her now reverberated through my mind each time I went outside wearing a winter jacket. I felt terrible for having promised something totally out of my control. It was just a week before their arrival. Unless Moses himself came back to Earth and decided that the eleventh plague was boiling water across the planet, there was no way my arctic-temperature swimming pool would be in a condition acceptable to humans. I was bracing myself for a wave of complaints. But it was too late to cancel their stay. And while I was hoping for a miraculous change in the weather, my to-do list magnetically attached to the fridge was getting longer every day.

Under normal circumstances, the turnover of rooms between guests is not extremely time-consuming. But on this occasion, I did not consider the fact that we had been living in the guest accommodation for several months, and the cleaning required to make the apartment ready for the guests entailed more than mere dusting and vacuuming. It's hard to explain what it is about us humans, but it seems that once we settle down in a place, the grime we naturally produce spreads in an almost uncontrollable fashion.

We moved our possessions out of the guest accommodation the day before Dominique's family's arrival.

'That's enough time to prep the apartment,' I told Robert.

But little did I know. Once our belongings were out of the way, I started scrubbing, dusting, polishing, and vacuuming with a vengeance. But the more I cleaned, the more dirt I uncovered.

How come I didn't see all this before? I thought to myself as I stared at the small patch of black mould that had formed at the top of the ceiling above the staircase. Right next to it, a family of spiders was jauntily hanging off a wooden beam and admiring their aerial empire. It looked as if they were living the good life up there, judging by the size and complexity of their web.

Once I had vacuumed the spiderwebs, cleaned the mould, and begun to paint the wall with a fresh coat of white paint, I noticed a multitude of small marks and stains of various provenance: handprints, a spot of ketchup, pointillist insect poo, forensically-intriguing scratch marks, water stains, and many more minor defects.

Have I been blind all this time? I quizzed myself as I spent a few unhappy hours painting.

The more I scrutinised the apartment, the more faults I discovered. Each time I looked at my watch, hours seemed to have whizzed past. Since it was evident I wouldn't finish the job in time, I called in Robert, who was putting together our kitchen, to help me with the guest lodgings. All hands on deck were required if we were to welcome our first guests of the season in style.

It was three o'clock on the day of their arrival when I finally finished mopping the floors and closed the door to the guest apartment. The place was ready just in time. We were lucky that their flight to Sevilla had been delayed and that they had to wait an hour before collecting their rental car. This gave us time to jazz up the outside area with some bouquets of fresh camomile and clean the leaves and sand that had accumulated over the winter from the bottom of the pool. Even though the water was glacial, we set up the pool furniture as if it were the middle of summer since we wished to make a good first impression.

I was wondering whether to put out the cushions and mattresses on the sun loungers when the decision was made for me. I heard a clap of thunder, and in a matter of minutes, we were engulfed by a torrential storm. That's when Dominique messaged me:

We're 10 mins from the house. See you soon.

I looked at the smiley emoji that punctuated the text.
She won't be so happy when she gets here, I thought to myself.
The frustration was overwhelming, and if the guests were not just about to arrive, I would have thrown in the towel. But since calling it quits and lying down for a few hours to calm my nerves wasn't an option, I collected two umbrellas from the mudroom and stood under the patio, ready to hand them over to my guests as they exited their car. Disheartened, I cursed under my breath until I saw a small rental car appear on the driveway. I put on my big hostess smile and rehearsed my hospitality welcome lines. The wind had picked up by now, and the torrent was almost horizontal.
At least they won't be asking about the pool.
They parked the car but remained inside for a few minutes before they summoned the courage to venture out into the pouring rain.
Welcome to Mordor! I wanted to say as they scrambled out of the car, but I bit my tongue.
They were positively shell-shocked. Instead of the clear blue skies and glorious Spanish sunshine, they had imagined before their trip, they were welcomed by a mini apocalypse. Dark clouds hung low over the olive hills, and a dangerously strong wind was turning the umbrellas inside out. I led the way to their apartment as we fought against the elements like intrepid polar explorers. A huge puddle had formed on the guest patio, which meant we all had to skip over it to get to their front door. As I opened the door, I realised the torrential rain had managed to seep under the door, pushed there by the pounding wind. The floor in the living room was wet, and there was a steady drip from the ceiling above the staircase. The wind-driven rain must have gone under the roof tiles. I apologised profusely and reassured them that this was not the usual status quo. Basil Fawlty would have been proud of my performance.

Unless the whole building decided to cave in and collapse on top of our heads, I could not imagine making a worse first impression. As I marched to my headquarters to get a mop and a towel to deal with the water on the floor, I noticed that the pool was now covered in a thick layer of leaves that had been blown from the surrounding trees. It looked like we had abandoned it all winter and hadn't bothered to clean it for the past six months.

Thank you, I gave the pool a sarcastic nod and decided to deal with it when it stopped raining.

When I returned to their apartment to mop and dry the floors, I expected the family to tell me they were leaving. But they seemed to be making themselves at home. The fire was roaring, and the place looked cosy despite the small leak above the staircase. Instead of asking me for a refund and a recommendation for another guest house, Dominique asked me whether I could serve them breakfast the next day. It was Sunday, and all the shops in the area were closed, which meant they arrived with no groceries.

'We're going to go out to eat in Montefrio tonight,' she explained. 'But it would be nice to have breakfast here before we go to the shops tomorrow.'

Even though I didn't serve breakfast to our guests anymore, I felt I could not refuse their request. The next day, Robert and I got up early to assemble parts of our kitchen so that I could prepare their breakfast. The problem was that while he was helping out in getting the apartment ready for the guests, Robert had not been able to finish constructing our new kitchen. Before I could prepare the breakfast, we had to mount the new countertop and fix the sink into a hole that Robert had cut out in the countertop the day before. The cupboards had no doors, and all the food preparation was done on the dining room table because the untreated countertop needed to be varnished before we could use it. To say that the kitchen was improvised would have been generous. However, it did have running water, a stove and a fridge, so I got on with the programme. I just hoped that poor Dominique wouldn't catch a glimpse of this madness if she were to pass by outside, so I closed the shutters of the kitchen window.

I consulted the contents of my fridge and shelves hoping for gastronomic inspiration. Had I known that I was going to make breakfast for the guests, I'd have been prepared. But as it was, I had to improvise with the limited ingredients that we had in the fridge. I decided to focus on the presentation and distract my guests from the measly scraps of cheese and boiled eggs I had on offer. There was no fresh fruit in the house, which bothered me until I remembered I had a generous supply of a strawberry concoction I had made earlier that month.

I'm not a horticulturist, so I can't explain why, but somehow the cold and wet spring that we were experiencing had resulted in an abundance of strawberries in Andalusia. They were being sold for one euro per kilogram in the shops, which was a once-in-a-lifetime bargain. Each time I went to the supermarket, I'd come home with several kilograms of strawberries. I couldn't stop myself. But even I, an aficionado of all berries, wild or cultivated, could not consume the quantity of strawberries I felt compelled to purchase, so inevitably, I made jam from them. Or, to be more specific, I intended to make jam.

It soon became apparent that my casual approach to making jam and marmalade was not working on these strawberries. My usual method, which anyone who can differentiate between a jam and marmalade will find simplistic at best, was to take any fruit that was plentiful on our land, like figs or quince, cut it up, add some sugar, cinnamon, vanilla, lemon, and boil the mixture until it was of the right consistency. Then, I'd put it in clean jars and call it a day. But the strawberries I had bought refused to fall in with this procedure. The boiling mixture I had on the stove would not thicken. No matter how much sugar and lemon I added or how long I boiled them, the strawberry concoction just would not jellify. I was loath to throw the strawberry *ragout* away because it tasted delicious, so I called it 'strawberry sauce' and poured it into glass jars with the idea that their teleological function would become apparent one day.

Scratching my head about how to add a little panache to my beige breakfast spread, I remembered my stock of strawberry sauce. I assembled four table glasses and layered them with Greek yoghurt and my strawberry mixture. I congratulated myself on the visual effect. The strawberry sauce was a deep red and looked very enticing. It was the focus of the breakfast and distracted the guest from the rest of the meagre offerings. My years of dedication to *MasterChef* had finally paid off. As I brought the tray to the guests' apartment, the strawberry sauce instantly mesmerised the children. I needn't have bothered with anything else. With the guests' mood and the weather clearing up, I could begin to relax.

'So, I don't think we'll be able to use the pool?' Dominique addressed the elephant in the room while buttering a piece of baguette.

'I don't think so. I'm so sorry,' I went on to explain how it was an exceptionally cold spring. 'You're welcome to use the sun loungers and relax in the pool area.'

She executed an exquisitely French eye-roll, which, I admit, was not particularly pleasant to be the target of. I apologised for the umpteenth time and left them to eat their breakfast and make plans for the day.

At least they're staying. I thought to myself as I returned to clean up my makeshift kitchen.

When I arrived home from school late that evening, I was surprised to hear children laughing by the pool. Even though it had stopped raining, it was still chilly outside. I approached our patio and saw Dominique and her husband drinking beer with Robert. Bobby was on his best behaviour under the table, hoping for a serendipitous piece of cheese to fall his way. In the pool, the two young French boys were chasing wooden sailing boats from one end of the pool to the other.

'Robert made these wooden boats with Raphaël and Mathéo this afternoon. They are so excited. They have never been in a carpentry workshop or made anything with wood. It's unbelievable!' the boys' mum informed me.

I could understand now why everyone was so relaxed. Few things will make a parent as happy as when someone else looks after their children for free for a couple of hours. I got myself a small beer and joined my contented guests, who bombarded us with questions about the house and life in Andalusia. The new holiday season was officially open.

TWENTY-THREE
QUICK-CHANGE

While April was a difficult and stressful month with impending deadlines and me juggling teaching and house renovations, the month of May became unbearable. We were still setting up the new kitchen and finishing the refurbishment of our living room. With a steady stream of holiday guests to look after, school to go to in the afternoons, and our regular freelance writing and editing jobs, there weren't enough hours in the day or days in the week. To make matters worse, a few months earlier, I had agreed to travel to Saudi Arabia to give a series of guest lectures at several female-only universities in Riyadh.

'Why don't you cancel it?' Robert suggested.

'I can make more money in a week in Saudi than in a month teaching at the school.'

It was difficult to overlook the financial benefits that a working trip to Saudi would bring, especially considering the financial burden all our house renovations had put us under. But while holding workshops and talks at these universities was not an issue, securing a travel visa to Saudi Arabia was, to put it mildly, mission impossible. For this reason, I didn't get my hopes up about going. I had run the gauntlet of obtaining a Saudi visa the previous year. And even though I had a professional team of author-promotion experts to support me by completing the necessary paperwork and making phone calls, my visa did not materialise on time, and I did not go on the trip. The memory of receiving a series of updates on my phone about the status of my flight and its departure while I was home sorting out a pile of firewood was still vivid in my mind. If Spanish red tape is hell on earth, then all I can say is that the Saudi bureaucracy has learned from it and taken it to another level.

'I don't think my visa will be ready on time,' I admitted to Robert.

It was Tuesday morning, and I was supposed to fly on Saturday. My passport was still with a fixer in London, and we were running out of time for the courier service to bring it back to Spain.

'What happened the last time?' Robert could not remember exactly at which point of the visa application process the publishing company's intricately laid plans fell apart.

The trials and tribulations of getting a Saudi visa were so complicated and confusing that describing them would make a great bonus chapter of *Finnegan's Wake*. So, I'll spare everyone the mental torture of doing so.

'The invitation letter from the Ministry of Foreign Affairs listed me as an Assistant Professor, but the letter to the Saudi Embassy in London said that I was a Lecturer. So, they couldn't complete the application in time,' I cut the very long story short.

One of the main issues with obtaining the permit to enter the magical kingdom was that all the paperwork had to be submitted in Arabic. Still, no one on the author promotion team at the publishing house in the UK could read Arabic. Hence, most visa applications contained minor discrepancies that were lost in translation. Unfortunately, whoever processed the final paperwork at the Saudi embassy was a stickler for details who possessed a great talent for spotting minute errors in the visa application paperwork. Whoever this jobsworth was, they did a great job in undermining the Saudi economy that was not related to oil exports. They must have relished in the pleasure they enjoyed by destroying people's business trips and important meetings.

When I woke up on Wednesday morning, I was still unaware that frantic emails had been exchanged between the conference organisers in Saudi, the author team in the UK, and my visa fixers in Madrid and London for the past few hours. As I discovered, the letter of invitation from the Saudi Ministry of Foreign Affairs, a key document in addition to the letter addressed directly to His Highness the Ambassador, had me listed as 'male'. Since Friday was not a working day in the Kingdom, we had two days to fix this confusion regarding my gender.

Preparing for a 'no-show' on my part, the university in Riyadh had found a Scottish lecturer who could be flown in from Dubai as a proxy to read my slides in case I or any of the other European speakers didn't show up. Morag, the Scottish substitute, had written to me to ask for the slides and a walk-through of my presentation so she would be ready if needed. It was not the first time she had had to present other people's work in Saudi because of a failed visa application.

The days before my uncertain departure were extremely stressful. There was a constant barrage of emails from all the parties involved in organising the lecture tour; *ad hoc* solutions and contingency plans had to be put in place. In the meantime, I had to entertain my guests, teach, finalise my talks, and brief Robert on how to turn over the apartments during my absence.

Finally, on Thursday evening, I received a phone call from Cambridge that my passport with the visa inside it had been dispatched from London and would arrive in Madrid at the publisher's office on Saturday morning. So, instead of flying from Malaga to France and then to Riyadh as originally planned, I had to ask Robert to drive me to Madrid city centre, a quick four-hour drive one way, to collect my travel documents and then to Madrid airport to catch a flight to Dubai. I would spend a couple of hours at Dubai International Airport before a very short flight to the capital of Saudi Arabia.

To say that the day of my departure was a super stressful morning would be an understatement. It was only when the wheels of the plane retracted that I could breathe a sigh of relief. I could not believe that *I was actually on my way*. I took out my laptop and decided to finish my presentations.

People's opinions on working in public spaces are often divided, with some finding it impossible to focus on their work while others chat around them. I belong to the group who do their best work in transit, on a plane, train, or at a busy airport.

My attitude to working in public spaces might result from the fact that access to the internet in public places used to be limited, and thus prevented one from procrastinating and distracting oneself with pointless internet searches. Another reason might be that, as a teenager, I had a forty-five-minute commute to school on the bus every morning. Since my house was at the start of the bus route, I was always guaranteed the same quiet seat by the window. As soon as I got on the bus, I'd do all my homework and study for the exams. I have carried this work habit into adulthood because the noisier the place and the more commotion around me, the faster I get to work.

At home, in the solitude of our quiet library, I often find it impossible to get any work done. Under such conditions, issues that have been on the back burner for weeks suddenly need my immediate attention.

What does J Lo's 'jungle dress' look like? I'd start to wonder for no other reason than someone had casually referenced it in a conversation several weeks ago.

Did Ally McBeal have a baby? Was it hers? I'd question an off-hand remark made by a podcaster.

Is garlic really good for you, or is it a myth? My thoughts wandered to the particularly spicy curry I had eaten the night before.

I needed answers to all these imponderables immediately. Each of these lines of inquiry would lead me down a bottomless rabbit hole.

What happened to Calista Flockhart? I'd start falling down the hole. *Who knew Versace was a woman?* I'd stare amazed at a photo. *But have any real scientific trials on garlic been conducted?* I'd dive deeper and deeper into the unknown. After an hour or so of this mindless research, I'd realise it was time to stretch my legs and go for a little walk outside. I'd find myself in the garden and decide it was time to do some impromptu weeding. Once I was done dead-heading the geraniums, I'd notice a decorative tile that I had purchased months earlier which needed to be hung on the wall today, immediately, right now!

It's time for lunch, I'd announce to no one in particular after an hour of pottering around.

After lunch, it was time for a nap and then the dogs would demand to go for a walk. By the time I was back at my desk, it would be late afternoon, and I'd have lost my train of thought. If killing time was an Olympic sport, I'd have several gold medals.

For these reasons, sitting on a plane, literally tied to a chair, and not having access to the internet always proved to be a very fruitful time for me. After a couple of hours of focused work, I added the final touches to my workshop materials and mentally rehearsed my talks. I was quite pleased with myself and asked for a glass of Chardonnay. While I searched the in-flight entertainment menu for new films, the attendant brought my drink, and the crew began the meal service.

I do love being on a plane, I thought to myself and surreptitiously raised my glass to my fellow passengers.

I felt like a dowager from one of those Agatha Christie novels where people dress up for dinner and are served five-course meals. I loved everything about my little meal: the tray, the tiny containers, and the cutlery in a bespoke paper wrapper. Everything on the tray was so neatly arranged and perfectly sized. It was a real work of art. Consuming my meal entailed a choreographed dance; every movement had to be planned in advance. If I took the lid off the rice dish, where could I put it since I wanted to eat the rice with the chicken, which was in another minuscule dish with a lid? I took my time arranging and rearranging the lids, the salt and pepper sachets, the cutlery, and the glass of wine on my miniature table. Once everything was how I wanted it, I turned on my TV show and enjoyed my meal.

Where else can you put on headphones and enjoy your favourite programme while others run around serving you food and drink? You can't do that in a restaurant. When you go out to eat, you pay good money to talk to the *maître d'* and the waiters, and then you feel obliged to keep up a friendly conversation with your fellow guests. It's excruciating. It would be socially unacceptable to wear headphones and enjoy a show on your phone while people ran around serving your meal.

But on a plane, you are free of these social constraints. When your wine is finished, you politely gesticulate at the stewardess and point at the glass, not unlike a chimpanzee in a zoo demanding more bananas. When your beverage is brought to you, you have no social obligation to engage in vacuous chit-chat with the stylish lady who has served you. You are welcome, even encouraged, to ignore your fellow passengers and laugh or cry at your preferred televisual entertainment as you wish.

Suffice it to say, I had a perfect journey. The eight hours flew by. It was Sunday morning when I landed in Dubai and strolled around the airport in search of an abaya. I had an old one stashed in my carry-on luggage in case I couldn't buy one at the airport. I had bought my old one at Lulu Hypermarket many years earlier to wear for the National Day celebrations at the university I worked for. Since Western women who work in the Emirates are not forced to wear an abaya or cover their heads, the abaya I owned was more of a prop. Anyone who had spent any time in the Gulf could see that it was a cheap ten-dollar outfit, something a maid or a cleaner might quickly throw on to carry the rubbish out to the municipal bins. If I were to appear in this tatty robe at a prestigious university, I would make a poor impression.

Back at home, I am not particularly concerned with my attire and often refer to myself as 'Miss Lidl' since I buy much of my clothing from the middle aisle at the German supermarket giant. But in the Middle East, I felt obliged to make an effort. After all, I was representing a global textbook publisher and hoped to continue working for them.

I'm sending the author team this bill, the feminist in me decided as I browsed the over-priced black garments at the airport souvenir shop.

I felt despondent at having to spend the little money I had on me on an abaya. The prices were more than I would typically spend on my whole summer collection from Lidl. I felt it was a bit unjust for the female staff members to be forced to purchase outfits that we would never wear again. I chose two abayas; both had beautifully embroidered sleeves and matching headscarves. Then, after watching a few tutorials on YouTube on how to tie an appropriately modest headscarf, I proceeded to the airport bathroom to transform myself into a sheikh's Western wife.

I still had time to kill before my flight, but I wanted to get comfortable wearing the headscarf and the abaya. The last time I wore one at my university in Abu Dhabi, I tripped over the long cloak and almost fell down the stairs. While an abaya is typically quite loose, it's not designed for fast walking, running, or negotiating escalators. Another thing I didn't want to happen in Saudi was for my headscarf to slip off my head while I was on the street or in a conference room full of Arab men.

I looked unrecognisable in the bathroom mirror. I glanced at the Arab girls standing at the marble bathroom sinks, fixing their headscarves and applying lipstick. I was a stranger in this world, an impersonator. I felt like an undercover spy. I gave a suitably inane pout for the mirror, checked my headscarf, and exited the bathroom. I expected someone to call out in shock at my transformation. But no one cared. I joined the black wave of abayas marching down the airport walkway and disappeared into the crowd.

After all the effort I had made in disguising myself, I was somewhat surprised when I reached my departure gate to see that most women there were not wearing an abaya. I checked the screen for the flight details. It indicated that Riyadh was our destination. Unless the Saudi religious police had been disbanded in the last ten hours since I left Andalusia, I was perplexed why so many women at the gate were not covered up. I had been explicitly advised by the team in the UK to wear an abaya before I boarded the flight. Not wanting to become a self-appointed *Mutaween*, or religious police, by questioning the women at the gate as to why they had failed to cover their hair or wear an abaya, I kept my mouth shut. I also knew from my time in the Middle East that there was one set of rules for the locals and another one for Westerners. Since I was the only foreign woman on the flight with no male companion, I remained silent and took out my Kindle.

The flight was a disaster. There was no wine served or TV series to watch. I spent the forty minutes talking to another EFL teacher from Jordan who was returning to Saudi after a short holiday break. She taught in a desert town which was a seven-hour drive from Riyadh. I wanted to be kind and sociable, but she put me off when, ten minutes into our chat, she asked me whether I had any children. When I said no, she fell silent for a few minutes as if she did not know how to continue with our conversation. According to her social contract, women were expected to while away the flight by talking about their offspring and showing each other photos of their babies and hubbies.

'Why don't you have children?' She came back, breaking *my* social contract.

It's not your business, I thought, but we had just taken off, and so the awkward silence following my retort would have been agonising.

'Because I don't want to have children.' I must have said something very confusing to her because she remained speechless for a while.

'It's not necessary to have children to be happy,' I felt sorry for being a little mean and decided to hold out an olive branch.

'Is there a problem with your husband?' I heard in response.

I wasn't shocked by her directness. In fact, I was expecting this question. It wasn't the first time I had had this conversation. I had worked with Jordanian, Palestinian, and Syrian women before. While I was being respectful of her 'choices', she was not going to let the topic go. She wanted me on 'Team Baby'. I took out my headphones, connected them to my phone, and decided to hold my tongue for the rest of the flight.

Twenty minutes before we were to land, I noticed a sharp increase in bathroom traffic. Just before the seatbelt light was illuminated, indicating we were about to land, I removed my headphones and looked around at my fellow passengers. They had all transformed themselves from wearing skinny jeans and tight T-shirts into uniform rows of black shadows. The once vibrant and cheerful congregation of females had metamorphosed into fully-covered, law-abiding Saudi citizens. The mood in the aircraft cabin became sombre as the plane initiated its descent. I mentally braced myself for the new world order I was about to be cast into.

To say that the week that followed was informed by a riotous exercise in conspicuous consumption would be an understatement. If Marie Antoinette rose from her grave and went on a royal visit, she would simper in mock despair: 'Guys, it's too much!' As an unaccompanied woman, I had no choice regarding what I did with my 'free' time between the workshops and the talks. One evening, I visited the hotel's rooftop pool, expecting a relaxing swim while admiring the sunset. The pool staff almost fell off their chairs when I exited the lift. It was explained to me in a polite but firm tone that I could come back between two and five in the afternoon.

'But that's when most people are at work,' I pointed out quizzically.

'I know,' a Filipino man blithely responded as if I failed to understand this clever idea of opening the pool to female guests only during the hours when one might expect them to be at work.

Suitably chastised, I scooted back to my hotel prison cell with my tail between my legs, threw my abaya onto an armchair, laid myself out on the bed, and stared at the ceiling in sullen contemplation.

Fortunately, I didn't have a lot of time to myself. As a guest of the university, all of my lunches and dinners were arranged for me according to a pre-planned schedule. Each day, I ate my meals with a different group of people, always in the company of a chaperone. While Riyadh's cultural scene was rather dead, to say the least, its restaurants were styled after a live version of *MasterChef*. During my stay, I tasted food I had only seen or heard of on TV. Making plans, my hosts were posed with a dilemma. Should we go to a Japanese, French, Korean, or German restaurant today? Every breakfast, lunch, and dinner provided to me was a veritable feast. I thought I had eaten my fill of international experimental cuisine when a Japanese chef presented an array of French *amuse-bouches* by lifting a smoke-covered cloche. This was just the start of the gastronomic experience he was to provide us with. He then proceeded to serve a soup in a bowl made of bread, savoury *mille fois*, followed by a collection of chicken popsicles. When he asked if I wanted to taste his deep-fried ice cream, I drew the line.

'Deep fried ice cream?' I repeated with astonishment.

'Yes, it's delicious,' said Fatima, a Saudi university dean who was ordering food for the table. She was a petite woman with very short dark hair.

I liked her a lot, even though I never understood why she had returned to this women's penitentiary after being awarded her doctorate in Michigan. But then, here, in the middle of the Empty Quarter, she was someone of some importance. In the States, she would have just been yet another immigrant, a 'nobody' in many people's eyes.

And while fried ice cream might lie somewhere at the pinnacle of culinary technique, at least for me, I wondered whether such a dish is necessary. Ten thousand years ago, we were foraging the forests in search of berries and rabbits to survive. Now, we were freezing perfectly good food to then deep fry it.

'When I tell my students about fried ice cream, they'll never believe me,' I told Fatima.

She clearly did not understand what I was talking about. She would have been even more confused if she had seen the menus in most restaurants in rural Andalusia. Humble meat and potato dishes constitute the staple fare. Your typical Andalusian would not dream of hiding a plume of smoke under a cloche, impaling chicken balls on a skewer, or serving soup in an edible receptacle.

'Did you enjoy your stay?' she asked me on my last day.

'Yes, the teachers were great. I even met one of my old colleagues at the workshop yesterday,' I told her. 'Martina, we used to work together in Abu Dhabi.'

I didn't tell Fatima how sorry I felt for Martina when I met her. While a teaching gig in Saudi Arabia might have been appealing to a young teacher who was desperate to get some overseas teaching experience, for someone who had been teaching for almost thirty years, had written language textbooks and run academic departments, like Martina had in the past, working in Saudi Arabia was purgatory, a state of limbo filled with the dead souls of teachers' past. I wasn't being smug in my disparagement of life in Saudi Arabia. In many respects, the teachers working there enjoyed much more comfortable lifestyles than I did. They all had air-conditioned apartments and money to spend on fried ice cream.

But I couldn't help feeling like a day visitor at a high-security prison. As I walked the university corridors dutifully protected by my prison guards, aka my 'chaperones', I sensed the inmates' emaciated arms sticking out from behind mental bars, their hands trying to touch my shoulders as if freedom were contagious.

'I was so excited to hear you're coming to give a talk,' a Pakistani teacher approached me after one of the sessions. I felt a sudden bolt of pride in my work, even though I suspected she was exaggerating.

'So, can you tell me...' I braced myself for a question about writing textbooks. '...how do I get a visa to Spain? How did you do it?'

'I live there,' I was taken aback by her naïve enquiry.

'Yes, exactly. How? I want to move to Spain.'

'It's part of the European Union,' I started to explain the practicalities of being a resident in the EU.

'So, can I apply? Can you help me?'

Apply for what? I wanted to ask, but her desperation was unmistakable, and I didn't want to crush her dreams.

I had no clue about the paperwork involved in getting a Pakistani national to Spain. All I could offer was some generic advice and wish her well.

As I boarded my flight to Dubai and then Paris, I could not help but feel a great sense of relief flood over me. I found my week in Saudi to be particularly emotionally draining. When I wasn't being closely chaperoned from the university campus to an up-scale restaurant by the conference organisers, I was left alone, trapped in my hotel room with nothing to do. Walking alone on the city's streets would be uncomfortable as everyone would stare at me. Even inside the hotel grounds, I was constantly fixing my head scarf and worrying that an inopportune gust of wind might reveal that I was wearing jeans. No sports or leisure facilities were available to female guests, and the TV in my room was permanently tuned to Egyptian soap operas.

As I stepped out into the transfer terminal at Charles de Gaulle Airport and merged with the crowds of passengers hurrying to catch their connecting flights, I felt joyously exhilarated to be back in the free world, where no one cared a damn what I was wearing or doing. The sense of liberty was palpable. Gone were the shiny marbled floors of the Arabian airports, their red carpets, gaudily gilded bannisters, and sparkling chandeliers.

Here, in the heart of a dark and grey commuter hub in Europe, there was no glitz and glamour. I spotted chewing gum on the cement floors. A scruffy poodle had been released from its flight crate and was doing its business in a corner, paper coffee cups and sandwich wrappers were left nonchalantly abandoned on stiff plastic seats, and empty water bottles were scattered along the walkways inside the airport. Another essential Middle-Eastern element was mercifully missing from this landscape of emancipation. There were no slaves, or 'overseas labourers' as they are called in the Gulf, obediently cleaning, polishing, and sweeping for sixteen hours a day at a wage that could not be called 'minimum' by even the most thoughtless of us.

I arrived home late in the afternoon on the 15th of May. Even though I felt drained and thoroughly fatigued after three flights and a two-hour drive from the airport, I decided to attend the San Isidro fiesta held that night in my neighbour's barn down the road. San Isidro is a holiday celebrated in rural communities throughout Andalusia and many other parts of Spain, including Madrid, where San Isidro Labrador, or 'Isidore the Farmer', was born. It is said that the saint spent his holy life ploughing fields and doing miracles, such as softening hard rocky ground with his feet so that a well could be easily dug.

Over four hundred miracles are attributed to this extraordinarily industrious *jornalero*, some completed with the help of his wife. According to Christian mythos, Isidro felt sorry for his fellow day labourers and would often instruct his wife to keep a pot of bean stew simmering on the stove throughout the day in case he came back home from the fields with a group of hungry men. His hagiographer describes that on one occasion, Isidro came home with a larger crowd of starving peasants than usual, and soon his wife Maria ran out of stew.

'The pot is empty', she discreetly informed her pious husband, who was busy regaling the men with a story of how God had sent some angels down to Earth to plough his fields when he was so busy praying that he had forgotten about his work.

'But some of them have not eaten,' Isidro whispered back.

I imagine that being poor *jornaleros,* he and his wife had only one room which was used as a dining room, kitchen, and bedroom. The situation was now quite embarrassing as his hungry guests sat at the table waiting for the promised meal while the hosts scrambled to find something to eat.

'Can't you make some more?' the clueless husband asked.

Sure, I'm going to whip a stew out of my... his wife had a variety of witty responses available, but she chose not to share them in front of their oblivious guests.

'Let's see,' Isidro pulled on his wife's arm and directed her towards the wood stove where the empty pot was resting.

See what? Maria thought to herself, and some unkind suggestions crept into her mind, but being a good medieval wife, she kept them to herself. Or so we are told by the considerate hagiographer. There is a reason why poor Maria de la Cabeza, as she became known, was never canonised. Perhaps the scribe added a footnote in his account of this miracle only for the Pope's eyes.

'Look! The pot is full!' Isidro clasped his hand in wonderment and began to serve a delicious stew from the miraculously refilled pot.

I'd pay a lot of money to travel back in time and see Maria's face as she saw this miracle unravel. She'd spent years, day after day, making stews for the hungry vagabonds that her husband kept bringing in. She must have been livid when she saw the pot full of food. She had hundreds of other jobs to do, including protecting her scrawny chickens from foxes, overseeing the birthing of calves, chopping wood, cleaning the chimney, fixing the leaking roof, baking bread, and making preserves for the winter. I imagine the list of chores of a medieval farmer's wife was endless. Most wives would make a pot of stew every few days as it was economical and time-efficient. They'd prepare a whole pot and be released from slaving over the stove for a few days. This poor woman had spent years cooking for a small army of hungry men, a battalion, day in and day out, only to discover that her devoted husband could refill an empty pot just by using his magical powers.

'Why didn't you tell me you can miraculously refill the stew pot!?' I could hear her raised voice late that night once the guests had left their cottage. 'I've spent years making stews out of a pitiful handful of beans and rice that we have saved for our family, and now I find out you can make food by dint of sheer willpower! This is outrageous!'

I imagined her throwing down her tea towel and going to bed very, very angry.

Legend also informs us that Isidro and Maria took vows of abstinence and moved to separate houses after their son was saved from drowning in a well. I suspect that the miracle of the self-replenishing stew pot was the straw that broke the camel's back. It was bad enough for Isidro to use angels to do his field work while he sat in the chapel all day, but to keep his magic powers secret from his wife and make her cook for no reason would sorely test any obedient wife's patience. The resentment that ungrateful women show to their godly, male companions may be why her husband was canonised four centuries later while his wife, Maria, was only 'blessed' and bestowed with the strange nickname of *de la cabeza*, which translates as 'Maria of the Head'.

The San Isidro party in Pedro's barn was a simple affair. We stood outside the building for a couple of hours chatting to our neighbours, drinking beers from small bottles and being served a selection of cold meat on paper plates. Inside, some elderly couples were dancing to live flamenco music, and men were playing cards. Shells of roasted sunflower seeds, a favourite accompaniment to Andalusian drinking, smoking, and playing cards, were liberally scattered all over the barn floor. The music was too loud for me. I would not have been able to talk to anyone above the noise, so we remained outside and watched the sunset over the olive hills. We left around 10 pm, just as more people started to arrive. I explained to my neighbours that I was very tired after my travels, but they didn't seem to understand where Saudi Arabia might be and what kind of place it was. They had even less idea of why I would travel there in the first place. I didn't feel like it was necessary to dwell on my trip.

As we left, I was happy to be back in a place where men and women drink, eat, dance, sing, chat, and have fun together. It was a different world. In hindsight, we should have stayed longer at the fiesta. It was the last San Isidro that we would enjoy for many years to come. A year later, one of our neighbours was found dead in his car near the river. He had suffered a heart attack while working on his land and must have made it back to his car to rest. He was found late at night by his sons, who had gone out looking for him. That year, the festivities were cancelled out of respect for his grieving family. And in the years to follow, a pandemic swept the country, which meant that all public gatherings were banned. Several years would pass before we could meet again to dance, drink, and enjoy a life of freedom.

TWENTY-FOUR
GOLDEN YEARS

H ave you ever stabbed someone with a knife?' the Romanian woman incongruously asked me while I passed her the sugar.

We were sitting on the patio, drinking coffee, gossiping, and discussing what plants were resistant to drought when Ioana posed this question. Vince and Ioana were house-sitting at Keith's house. They lived in Rotterdam, but Ioana was originally from Romania, which she liked to remind us of in every conversation we had with her. Being in her early sixties, she revelled in stories of the communist hardship her parents had endured. She herself had escaped the regime in her early twenties. As a student, she went to the Netherlands on a scholarship and never returned home.

How Robert met the couple was never explained to me. But this momentous event had taken place while I was in Saudi, and, on my return home, they became a constant feature in my life. They were like an annoying aunt and uncle who lived next door and constantly popped in because they felt bored. Ioana and Vincent had little understanding of the fact that we had work to do and used to check in on us almost daily. The majority of their impromptu visits were justified by an endless series of mundane queries that could have quickly been resolved with a WhatsApp or a short text message.

'We were wondering if you peel the bark off the grape vines in the spring?' was the compelling reason for one of their visits.

'I'm not sure what …' I responded as they exited their car.

By the time I had a chance to compute the reason behind this latest spontaneous intrusion, Ioana had marched over to my grape vines to explain what she had meant.

'In Romania, my family had a beautiful vineyard.' This was another prominent theme in her stories, namely, everything in 1970s Romania was the best and the most amazing. 'The grape vines were really thick and lush in the summer. I think it's because they used to peel the bark in the spring.'

It takes an Eastern European woman to be able to read between the lines of what another is implying.

I know my grape vines have old, dry bark hanging off them. Thank you for pointing it out, my eyes exclaimed, but social etiquette dictated what actual words I would use.

'Would you like a cup of tea or coffee?' I said instead.

Ioana always wanted a cup of coffee, some biscuits, and then another cup. Oblivious to the fact that Robert and I had writing work to do in the mornings and that I had to be at the school until late in the evening, Ioana and Vince would sit by our patio for hours, accepting fresh pots of coffee and retelling us their life stories.

I realised that I must have spent too much time with Brits in the past because there was a definite cultural distinction to be made with respect to how Vince and Ioana accepted my hospitality. When I offer a cup of tea or coffee to a British friend, I am consistently confronted with instant rejection.

'I don't want to be a bother,' Keith would say.

'It's not a bother at all,' I'd reassure him.

'Only if you have a kettle on already.'

'It's no hassle, don't worry.'

We'd go back and forth like this a few times, and only after I had sworn on my grandma's grave that I was just about to make a cup of tea for myself would he accept a cup of said beverage. It was always a lie on my part. I was never about to make a cup of tea in the middle of the day — I'm not as madly in love with hot beverages as the English are. A cold beer or a glass of wine, yes, I'm usually about to have one, or at least wish I could have one. But I'm also a polite hostess, so I always lie to my English friends and pretend that the kettle is always about to be switched on.

But Ioana and Vince did not follow this ritual. They always instantly accepted my offer of hospitality and then overstayed by accepting more refills. They must have been on their fourth cup when Ioana inexplicably asked Robert if he had ever stabbed someone with a knife. I wasn't really listening. I was getting somewhat frustrated because we had planned to visit the plant nursery outside Alcalá together, but instead, we sat with these uninvited guests for two hours, drinking coffee and reviewing random traumatic experiences from our past lives.

Ioana's stories reminded me of some of the stories my Romanian physiotherapist had told me years earlier in Al Ain. Marisa was an outstanding therapist, and her massages would make my back pain melt away. But instead of gentle spa muzak in the background, her massages were accompanied by the whiny, complaining voice of a middle-aged Eastern European woman re-living Ceausescu's catastrophic reign. Her stories included arbitrary strangers in times and places that were both simultaneously distant and too familiar to me.

Distant in that I was only a child when the Iron Curtain fell. The world of apparatchiks, brown suits, vodka-drinking, and chain-smoking adults wasn't really my world. But it was also very familiar in that, as a child, I had heard of men and women being imprisoned for hiding US dollars from the authorities. Possession of any foreign currency was illegal in communist countries. I knew of people in my neighbourhood so deprived of any hope for freedom or joy in life that they drank themselves to death or found other means to commit suicide. These were familiar tales of the effects of communism on people's everyday lives. My own grandfather was sent to a communist prison in the late 1950s for stealing a bucket of coal to heat the house where his family was freezing to death in the cold Polish winter. Coal was considered government property, and stealing it from his place of work made him an enemy of the state. I knew others, uncles, brothers, and fathers who had served time in jail for misdemeanours or for spreading Western propaganda by listening to The Beatles or wearing jeans — such violations of your basic rights were part and parcel of growing up in a communist country.

It must have been the reason why, even though Ioana had an arresting hook for a conversation: *Have you ever stabbed someone with a knife?* Her question failed to arouse my interest. I only heard some scraps of a story about someone in her Romanian village who killed someone else over a bag of potatoes or something like that... I couldn't retell her fascinating story because I was herding them back to their car so I could prepare myself for work later that afternoon.

'Will you come over for lunch next Saturday?' Ioana inquired once I had managed to get her inside their vehicle.

'Yes, we will. It's perfect because we have two families from Baena coming for Saturday night, so we might want to make ourselves scarce and give them all the privacy they need,' were my prophetic last words.

We had started our third summer season as hoteliers and hosts of a rural guest house, and I had developed an ability to predict which guests were being dishonest with me. After the fiasco of the first summer when we had to kick a family from Sevilla out who kept on multiplying in numbers from one day to another, I had developed a sixth sense for picking out troublemakers who would inevitably leave a negative review of our little establishment.

A man from Madrid once made a booking for him and his wife. Two hours later, he asked me if his seventeen-year-old daughter could join their party. Five hours later, he sent me another message asking if the daughter's friend could accompany them. When I said I'd have to charge the daughter and the friend for the extra beds, he changed his mind about bringing them. The next day, he asked me where he could collect the key to the property.

'Don't worry,' I replied in Spanish. 'We live here. We'll be here when you arrive.'

That same afternoon, I received a phone call from the online booking company. A formal complaint had been made about us for misleading potential guests. According to the agent, the guest had not realised that the pool would be shared with other guests. We were given a firm warning with a wink since the booking agent understood what had happened after I explained to her that they wanted to bring an unspecified number of friends to our rural retreat.

Afraid that we would suffer a repeat scenario where a guest booked as a party of two but many more individuals would arrive at our property, I had developed a habit of sending a welcome message to the person who had made the booking which specified the number of people who were included in the booking. Several times in the past, I had received impolite messages from guests who were planning to arrive as a large, unannounced group and were disappointed that their cunning plan of turning someone's home into 'party central' had not come off.

'I'm sorry for the inconvenience. You're welcome to cancel,' I'd answer politely.

'It's not for you to decide whether I stay at your house or not!' one angry woman wrote back to me when I caught her in a web of lies about the number of people she intended to include in her party. I showed the exchange of messages to Robert.

'What is she thinking?' I was really amused by her lack of knowledge about the world of small business. 'Does she really think that she can come here to my house after sending all these rude messages?'

Robert, unfortunately, hardly ever saw the humour in our customers being rude. He became very indignant and made an action plan in the event that she and her friends were to show up.

'Look! She's already cancelled,' I heard a ping on my phone and showed him a message on my booking app. He calmed down.

But despite all my efforts to distinguish between honest guests and cheats, nothing had prepared me for the disaster that was about to unravel before me.

'How many people are coming?' Robert asked me the night before the impending debacle.

'There are two couples, and one couple is bringing a child,' I passed on my interpretation of the booking.

Both couples had booked separately but informed me that they were one party of five. I sent them welcome messages specifying the number of people in each booking and assumed that they'd have the decency to correct me if they were planning to bring more guests.

The next morning, a good two hours before the normal check-in time, two cars appeared on my driveway. As soon as they had parked, numerous children of different ages started to spill out of the vans. I tried to count them off as I greeted the adult guests, but between the raucous riot rapidly developing on my driveway and deciding what I should do with all these people, I was at a loss for what to say to them.

'How many children are here?' I asked one of the adults while a fourteen-year-old boy rudely pushed me out of the way with his inflatable shark and went straight for the pool. Several smaller children followed him. None of the youngsters bothered to say 'hello' or introduce themselves. I felt like a lowly footman at Downton Abbey.

Shall I unpack your luggage for you too? I wanted to ask the young masters but decided to focus my energy on the people who were paying for this extravaganza.

'So, how many children are here?' I cut short their warm greetings.

A short, dark-haired man, who looked like an accountant or another type of office worker due to his clean-shaven face, smooth hands, and lack of muscle, was jovially explaining to me whose child was whose and which one was whose cousin. He kindly informed me that there was 'no problem'. 'They can all sleep together,' he told me once he had concluded his very confusing genealogy.

I peered over the hedge and saw at least four children in the pool already and a couple more still getting their pool toys out of the boot of one of the cars.

'They can't all sleep together,' I informed him. 'I've only prepared one single bed.'

'No problem. Isn't there a sofa bed in one of the apartments?'

'Yes, there is.'

'And Sara can sleep with us. It's a king-size bed. I read on the internet,' a chubby woman with burgundy-coloured hair chipped in while blowing cigarette smoke over everyone. Her female friend seemed unaware of how their 'check-in' was proceeding and remained focused on unloading a multitude of beach bags and coolers full of food and beverages from their car.

The four adults offered up several congenial solutions to their accommodation arrangements, but in a tone that suggested that it was my problem to house them and their extended family and friends. It was time to get real.

'Look! Your booking is for four adults and one child. But there are at least four additional children here,' I was still unsure precisely how many extra children there were because they were scattered all over the property and constantly running up and down, chasing each other for no apparent reason but with great hilarity. It was impossible to get an exact head count under the circumstances.

'But they can all sleep together. No problem,' another mum tried to convince me as if these overly energetic children could be squashed into any old space for the night.

'I'm very sorry, but you'll have to pay extra for each child.'

'OK,' the accountant kept a firm expression, but I could see his weekend getaway was turning into ashes in his mouth. 'How much?'

'Thirty euros per child.'

They retreated to the cars to discuss this development and agree on my terms in private.

While they were in conference, I noted that a small football team was splashing all the water out of the pool.

Should I have asked for more? I regretted selling myself so cheap.

'OK,' the burgundy hair came back to me with their decision. 'It's not a problem. We'll stay.'

'You can pay now with cash or card.'

Once I had received the money, I spent another hour preparing extra beds for the little army of young firecrackers. As I walked back and forth from the storage room where we kept all the guest sheets and towels for the apartments, I noticed that while the husbands busied themselves with the barbecue, the two women had started to set up a party area on my patio table right outside the main door to our section of the house. This was a very peculiar development. Both apartments had their own outdoor dining spaces, but it dawned on me that these areas were set for couples or families of four. The large table on my private patio could easily seat ten people and was fully shaded. It was perfect for their intended purpose, but it would have made the next twenty-four hours of my life a living hell.

I could see that they were planning to spend the afternoon barbecuing pork chops, drinking *Alhambra* beers, and rowdily swimming together. They'd probably go for a nap at 5 pm to resume at around 8 pm. I was quite certain that they'd be barbecuing more pork chops around 10 pm and sit and drink shots right outside my front door until the early hours of the morning. It would have driven Bobby nuts. I was sure that there was a limit to how much smell of grilled meat a Bodeguero could take. It would have taken a highly trained circus dog not to bang on the door and try to scratch his way out all night, knowing that the people on the other side were eating cheese and serving meat. This setup was not going to work.

While Red Hair was assertively shouting instructions to the children in the pool, I approached the quieter of the two women. She was arranging paper plates and serviettes on my patio table. 'I'm sorry. But this area is private. It's not for guests.' I tried to be as diplomatic as one can be in a foreign language.

The meek woman called over her burgundy friend, and they started to shout at each other in indignation. It's not easy to understand another language when people get angry and yell at each other. Apparently, now that they had paid for the extra guests, they felt like they owned the whole house.

'But where are we supposed to eat together? The table on the terrace is too small!' the pushy one was working herself up.

'Why don't we move this big patio table over there,' I pointed to a shaded spot on the walkway ten metres away from my front door. 'There's a lot of shade under the bay leaf tree.' *And I won't have to listen to your conversation all night.*

Begrudgingly, they called their husbands over and moved the table and the chairs. I was confident that this minor inconvenience would be reflected in their review of their stay. I went inside and vented my frustration to Robert.

'Of course, they can't sit right outside our door all night,' he agreed.

'Why didn't they rent an isolated Spanish *cortijo*?' I was angry.

I was referring to numerous *casas rurales* in the area, which are usually owned by Spanish families who rent their summer houses to tourists in the weeks that they don't use them. These properties are usually quite basic but charming old cottages, often inherited by a group of siblings when the family's patriarch passes away. The owners of such houses don't live on-site since they prefer the comfort and amenities of town life. Because the accommodation they provide is so simple and rustic, the owners don't mind how many people arrive and what they get up to while on the property. The obvious downside of this type of establishment is that they are very uninspiring. They are furnished in the cheapest way possible, often with hand-me-down sofas, cheap second-hand tables, and a random selection of chairs, plates, and hideous curtains. If you are lucky, you are provided with wine glasses and plates. A swimming pool is optional and, if present, often consists of a tiny, above-ground pool or an irrigation deposit that might accommodate just a couple of people at a time.

Suppose your endeavours in the hospitality business are informed by the principle that people go on holiday to experience something that they don't have at home. In that case, this type of basic *cortijo* fits the bill. Staying in such accommodation is like travelling back in time to your late grandma's house in the 1980s. Even the most experienced hotel inspector would find many of these properties challenging to advertise successfully. Alex Polizzi would have had a field day in any one of them.

'Darling! Darling!' she'd have gasped in horror. 'What's all this tat on the shelves?' she'd point to a dusty collection of ceramic figurines portraying busty milkmaids and feral geese in various farmyard poses.

'I'm not trying to be rude, darling, but honestly...' she'd roll her eyes, break the fourth wall, and continue with her inspection.

'Oh, God! This sofa looks like it washed up on the beach ten years ago. The attention to detail here is obviously lacking.' She'd pick up some tatty, stained, and mismatched armchair cushions and rearrange them as if that would solve the hotel's low occupancy rate.

'The tiled floor is gorgeous, but the furniture is awful,' the camera would zoom in on an overbearing set of fake mahogany grandma's cabinets and the red checked upholstery of the dining table chairs.

'I mean, I've never seen an uglier bed in my whole life,' she'd open the door to the master bedroom and showcase a dusty four-poster bed with head- and footboards sculpted in subtly erotic mythical motifs. 'I can't stand the bed, the nightstands, and these hideous lights. And what's with the swan towels? Why does every failing hotel put swan towels on the bed?'

She'd grab the offending avian towel sculpture and fold it neatly back into a square, as a towel should be. As a big fan of Alex Polizzi, I know that swan towels drive her insane. She'd already be fuming when she inspected the *en-suite* bathroom.

'I don't know what it is,' the camera would do a tracking shot of the avocado green bathroom fixtures. 'Whether it's the geometrical pattern on the tiles, the pink shower curtain, or the lonely, abandoned pubic hair on the washbasin, I find this place pretty depressing.'

'You don't know that the other *casas rurales* are like that,' Robert challenged my narrowly opinionated view of our competition.

'Yes, I do,' I've been checking the photos they have posted on the booking sites. *And imagining myself to be an Andalusian version of the Hotel Inspector*, I might have added smugly, but I wanted to spare myself some dignity.

Spying on my competition wasn't something that I did on a daily basis. But, being naturally very nosy, I wanted to know what other B&Bs and guest houses looked like inside and to get an impression of what people said about them. I felt that I had a pretty good idea of which places were much nicer than ours and which were not. The difference in style and attention to detail was usually reflected in the rates that were being asked for by the property owners. However, this wasn't always the case.

I could see why my current guests had preferred to stay at my house over some of the cottages in the area that would have made Polizzi scream in horror. But I was disappointed when I realised that these guests had tried to trick me into securing a lower price for their accommodation. I was also disappointed in myself for not immediately turning them away when they arrived *en masse*. I could see their negative reviews being written before my very eyes. From the moment I requested payment for the extra guests to my setting a limit on their use of my private patio, things would only get worse once they sat down together and had a chance to exchange notes concerning their discontent.

'Let's take Bobby with us; otherwise, he will bark at the door all afternoon as they walk back and forth,' Robert suggested, and we went off to have lunch with Ioana and Vince in Keith's house as per their previous invitation.

'I'm sorry to tell you, but Ioana is feeling terrible today. Her arrhythmia has been bothering her, and she's had to take her medication which makes her sleep,' Vince informed us as we sat down on his veranda. Bobby had run off with Keith's dog to play in the garden. On any other day, I would have suggested that we return home, but I could not face my guests again and needed a safe place to while away the late afternoon.

'I hope she feels better soon,' I commiserated.

'She needs surgery, so we may have to return to the Netherlands for that before we commit to buying a house.'

Like many semi-retired digital nomads, Vince and Ioana were on a constant lookout for suitable properties wherever they went. They had viewed several properties in our area while house-sitting for Keith, but nothing was ever quite to their taste. Their house search made a good, neutral topic of conversation for us, and it definitely kept them busy.

'Keith and Delia are buying a house in the Midlands,' Vince announced as he poured us some wine.

This was news to us.

'But they have a house here?' I was slow on the uptake.

'As I understood, they were visiting a friend in the village where Keith grew up and saw a *For Sale* sign in a new development. They liked the house, especially the central heating and modern kitchen. I think they've put a deposit down.'

We knew Delia had recently inherited her late mother's estate, but I assumed she'd use the money to finish her yoga retreat here in Spain and finally give up on travelling between the UK and Spain. They'd spent the last three years preparing to open a vegan yoga retreat. For most of that time, Keith was alone in the cottage while his wife made some money in the UK. With the help of an endless stream of Workaway volunteers, they had renovated their cottage to accommodate groups of yoga practitioners. There were four twin rooms, each with *ensuite* bathrooms, a communal kitchen and dining area, a yoga studio in place of the old attic, and a brand-new swimming pool. Constructing all these facilities had taken a lot of work and money. It was difficult for me to understand why they'd abandon their project without finishing it.

'I think Delia wants to be close to her granddaughters,' Vince explained.

We spent the afternoon in the shade of the patio, gossiping about the owners of the house in which we were sitting and outlining alternative plans for their lives as if someone had asked us to. Giving unsolicited life advice is my area of expertise, and it appeared that both Robert and Vince had their own ideas, too, regarding what Delia and Keith should and should not have done with their life in Spain.

One of the reasons I wanted to return to Europe from the Middle East and grow roots here was to avoid the revolving door of expat friendships. I was saddened to hear we would lose two good friends and neighbours. I also felt a little angry that Delia and Keith hadn't tried a bit harder to make Andalusia their permanent home. But then they weren't the first, nor the last expats to come here with high hopes, do a little bit of renovation, throw a lot of money into a building, and fly back home with an unsellable cottage in the middle of nowhere and an empty bank account.

I couldn't blame Delia for giving up. Running a bed and breakfast or even a guest house once you have retired can be exhausting. Keith was already in his seventies, and Delia had just turned sixty. Why would they want to spend their golden years scrubbing toilets, ironing sheets, washing an endless supply of dishes, sweeping leaves around the house, and have complete strangers write a critique of them and their lifestyle after each stay?

It was late at night when we arrived home. Our guests' party was still in full swing. They'd just set up the BBQ for a second round of pork chops. I could see bags of rubbish, paper plates, and beer tins scattered everywhere across the patio and in my flowerbeds.

'Hola!' One of the men shouted jovially as he saw us approach the house, 'Why don't you join us?'

We declined in unison. I didn't particularly like these people; we didn't belong in their party. I was also too tired to spend another hour speaking Spanish. They all looked like they were having a good time, so I hoped that, against all odds, they might write a positive review of their stay or not write anything at all. My hope was misguided, of course.

'I wouldn't want to do this when I'm in my sixties,' I told Robert as we entered our house and locked the door behind us.

TWENTY-FIVE
THE HOUND OF BERRUGUILLA

'I think we need to get some Workaways to do some maintenance work,' I informed Robert as I sat at the dining table in the kitchen, working on a draft of a coursebook.

That spring, we were seriously overwhelmed by work. Because we had spent the winter renovating our kitchen and living room, some areas around the house and guest apartments had been neglected. And now, with guests coming and going, teaching at the language school, Robert translating a book, and me working on a new coursebook, there were not enough hours in the day to attend to the garden and do house maintenance.

'What maintenance work?' as usual, Robert was mournfully surprised that there was work to be done. 'What do you want them to do?'

'Let's make a list.'

I took out a notebook, and we went around the house and garden and compiled an impressively long list of jobs that a couple of Workaways could do. At the top of the list were: weeding, trimming the jasmine hedges, cleaning up the fallen leaves, painting the main gate, revarnishing the wooden window frames, moving the firewood that had been delivered in early April and left on the driveway, removing a small pile of rubble leftover from the winter renovations, and plastering some walls in the utility room. Other minor repairs could be postponed until we had more time.

'I can't see how they can do all this?' Robert was sceptical.

'I don't expect them to do *all* these jobs, but they can do some.'

The first couple of volunteer workers who stayed with us were Romanians, Georgeta and 'Eddy', a nickname he bestowed upon himself presumably because his real name was too confusing for foreigners to pronounce. They reported that they had just escaped from working for a crazy lady in Marbella. According to their tales of woe and suffering, their host had made them scrub clean an empty swimming pool with toxic acid but hadn't provided them with gloves or eye protection. Even though Georgeta's high-pitched, whiney voice annoyed Robert, good work was achieved daily and with a positive attitude. I didn't need to supervise anyone, and the couple provided us with humorous entertainment as they recounted their Workaway misadventures. An added bonus was that whenever Ioana appeared for one of her pop-in visits, she had a new captive audience to share her stories with.

'Maybe I was wrong about the Workaway system,' I told Robert as we waved Georgeta and her boyfriend goodbye after their week's stay.

I went to the kitchen and crossed a few items off the to-do list posted on the fridge.

'They were very good at gardening,' Robert agreed.

'The next ones are coming in the first week of July. They're a pair of architecture and engineering students from Paris.'

'How are they going to get here?'

'Raoul, the boy, is going to borrow his brother's car, and they'll drive here.'

I was still drinking my morning coffee one morning in early July when I received a text message from Chantal, the female counterpart of the new Workaway couple.

Is it OK if we come tonight? Our air conditioning in the car has broken down, and it's too hot.

I was expecting them the following day, but I didn't mind if they came a day earlier. It was almost 40 degrees Celsius, or 104 Fahrenheit, in Spain that week, and so I imagined them slowly roasting inside a beat-up Citroën all the way from the Arc de Triomphe, past the Sagrada Familia in Barcelona and then along the humid Mediterranean coast. To combine work and pleasure, the couple had chosen the scenic route to our house instead of the more direct one from the north via the Basque Country and Madrid.

We were sitting inside the cottage watching TV very late in the evening when I received a text message from Raoul.

We're here, it read.

I couldn't understand. *Where are they? Under the sofa?*

Where are you? I wrote back, convinced the couple were lost and at another cottage.

Outside the casa, I read the reply.

I was puzzled as to why they'd sent a text message from immediately outside the house instead of knocking on the door, calling out, or hooting the horn. But then, I have observed that extreme reliance on their mobile phone has rendered many young people quite handicapped when it comes to simple social interactions.

Young Raoul made a lasting first impression on both Robert and I. As is typical of the youth today, they suffered from an inability to stand up straight, so they were both lazily leaning on the side of their car, staring intently at their phones. As we approached them, Raoul spotted us and decided that this was an opportune moment to lift his T-shirt up to his neck and begin scratching his exposed belly. To add a further *panache* to his performance, he yawned maniacally a few times and stretched his arms into the air, gesticulating like someone suffering from St. Vitus' dance. His whole performance took place before we had the opportunity to say hello or shake hands. It was evident that Chantal was the brains of this operation. She immediately put away her phone when she saw us exit the house, stood up straight, and put a friendly smile on her charming face. In the meantime, Raoul continued with his impromptu convulsive yoga regime and twisted his arms behind him as if he wished to be rid of the offending appendages.

Once we had shown them to their apartment, we decided to reunite early in the morning, when it was still cool outside, to brief them on the jobs that needed to be done. Back in our living room, Robert fumed about the young man's lack of good manners and inability to 'act normal', but I decided to take the high ground and give him the benefit of the doubt.

'I think he was nervous and tired,' I assured my tense spouse.

The following morning, I was sitting on the patio enjoying the fresh morning air and listening to the birds when Chantal appeared. She was right on time and explained that Raoul needed a few more minutes to prepare for the day's work.

'That's OK,' I assured her. However, I also didn't want them to waste the cool of the morning. I explained to her that if they started early in the day, they could finish their work by noon when it started to get unpleasantly hot. As per the agreement, volunteer Workaways were supposed to work five hours a day, five days a week, in exchange for food, accommodation, and pleasant social interactions.

While I was explaining to Chantal how to organise her days to avoid working in the heat and blazing sun, I expected to see Raoul show up, but he was nowhere to be seen. I could see Chantal was getting uncomfortable while we waited for her boyfriend.

'Why don't I start work?' she offered. 'I'm sure Raoul will be here any minute, and I can tell him what to do.'

'OK,' I agreed, as the clock was ticking.

I showed her my list of jobs, and we agreed on which ones they could do.

'Today, please prepare the other guest apartment because we have a family with a baby arriving tomorrow. I'll show you where the cleaning products are and what to do.'

As I left Chantal cleaning the windows of the guest apartment, her young man was still conspicuously absent.

Has he gone AWOL? I wondered.

I decided to check and knock on his apartment door to see if he was there. I turned the corner and saw him sitting on the stoop of the guest accommodation tying his shoelaces in slow motion. A comatose sloth would have had a greater sense of urgency than Raoul. I was watching the *Matrix's* 'bullet-time' in real life — each movement of the shoelace was time-sliced and held suspended in time and space.

Once he saw me, he called out a friendly 'hello', but his mouth remained a full second behind the sound. I stood by his side for a few minutes, updating him on what Chantal and I had discussed. As we chatted, I became concerned about whether he would ever stand up and get to work or if he wished to imitate Rodin's famous statue by becoming a live version of it.

In the days to come, Raoul would provide Robert and me with plenty to vent about, especially concerning Gen Z and the future of our planet. I was particularly taken aback seeing the young Zoomer pose as if he were re-enacting a series of scenes from famous paintings. Sitting on a stone by the potato patch, he posed for Dürer's *Melencolia*. Another day, instead of trimming the hedges, he assumed the position depicted in Van Gogh's *At Eternity's Gate*. Cézanne's *Sorrow* seemed to be based on our Raoul as he cleaned the gate, and David's painting of *The Death of Marat* perfectly captured the state of young Raoul's soul whenever work had to be done.

Reclining was his definite area of expertise. While the European masterpieces of doom and gloom seemed to reflect Raoul's outlook on manual labour, he really should have sought a job at the Louvre School of Art as a model for recumbent figures. It did not matter if he had been tasked with varnishing a window frame or blowing the leaves off the patio with the electric leaf blower; he always managed to squeeze in a quick lesson in the noble art of reclining. With practised ease, he'd find a convenient tree trunk or a large rock to lean against, his arms splayed across the ground motionless as if paralysed, and stare up at the sky hoping for heavenly intervention from St. Joseph, the patron saint of workers.

I worried that the young man was suffering from the effects of anaemia or some immune system disorder that made him excessively tired each time he was tasked to do a job. He spent most mornings shadowing his industrious girlfriend while holding a rag in his hand, allowing him to pretend that he was doing something constructive should I see him by chance. Understand my surprise then, when later one afternoon, he asked me where he could go jogging.

'I try to run ten kilometres whenever possible,' he told me.

I showed him the path where he could run as far as his heart's content, and as soon as I finished my sentence, this modern-day Pheidippides had disappeared between the olive trees.

So, you can move quickly, I thought to myself. *You just choose not to.*

Raoul's only saving grace was his girlfriend, Chantal, who worked for the two of them and was always eager to learn new things. It was good to see that at least some work was being done around the house because, soon after their arrival, our usually sweet and relaxed Bodeguero, Bobby, decided to become a real menace to the peace and tranquillity surrounding Berruguilla. It all started with his annual visit to the vet.

'Why don't you take Bobby to the vet while I do the shopping,' I suggested one morning so that we could kill two birds with one stone and save ourselves driving to town and back twice.

Even though I had much more experience in dealing with vets and pets than my husband, I felt my time was better spent buying groceries for the week, as even at the age of fifty, Robert seemed to have a poor understanding of how to plan for the week's meals. In his mind, a trip to the supermarket was akin to visiting a novelty museum. Whilst I'd be busy packing into the shopping trolley the fruit and vegetables we customarily eat each week, he'd disappear for a quarter of an hour and return to the shopping cart with a box of sushi-flavoured popcorn or a packet of chicken livers. Sometimes both, implying that these constituted some kind of a meal.

'What am I supposed to do with this?' was my rhetorical comment to most of the novelty items he would sneak into the trolley behind my back.

Based on two decades of this shopping experience, I knew that if I left him alone with the shopping trolley, I'd end up with a set of mystery ingredients that even the best of contestants on *Chopped* would struggle to assemble into a meal.

With this in mind, we agreed that I would do the weekly grocery shopping while Robert and Bobby went to the vet to get Bobby his vaccinations. It took me about forty minutes to shop and pack the car, and while I stood alone by the car's boot, I wondered what was causing the delay.

Surely a simple vaccination should not take more than twenty minutes, I thought, but I couldn't see Bobby or Robert anywhere in the car park. I decided to walk over to the vet and check what the hold-up was.

Once I opened the vet's door, I was confronted by a scene of mayhem. In the centre of the waiting room was Robert holding Bobby in his arms. The vet's assistant was circling next to him, trying to stop Bobby from slipping out, while the vet followed everyone around in circles holding a loaded syringe in the air.

'Close the door!' All three shouted at me at once since Bobby had seized upon the moment of distraction, wriggled himself out of Robert's embrace, and was now on the floor running towards the main door. I closed it shut right in front of his little nose.

The humans in the room decided it was time for a little break from whatever they had been doing for the last half an hour or so. While Bobby hid in the corner behind a poster advertising dog toothbrushes and eyed everyone up and down suspiciously, I learned from Robert that our little protégé had escaped the muzzle the vet had placed on his head within ten seconds of it being put on and then proceeded to feverishly snap and growl at each appearance of the vaccination needle.

'Perhaps you should take him for a little walk in the park for half an hour to help him relax,' Beatriz, the vet, suggested. I was sure she needed a mental break, too, so we obliged and said we'd return in half an hour.

But walking on the lead on the city streets turned out to be more stressful for our *campo* dog than we had anticipated. Used to running free among the olive trees where the only scents he can smell are those of his arch-enemies, the multitude of wild rabbits that populate our area, the odiferous pavements of Alcalá soon became overwhelming for Bobby. First, he tried to hide inside a bush by the side of the pavement, and I had to drag him out of it. Next, he tried to wriggle his neck out of his collar in order to run for his life across the road. This was a perilous thing to attempt because the traffic in the town was unlikely to stop for him, and he would have been run over in seconds. So instead of taking a relaxing walk, we had to drag him back to the car with his back legs firmly planted on the ground and his head wriggling like a crazed Houdini as he tried to escape from his collar.

Some people who were walking by stopped and asked why we were being so cruel to this innocent little dog.

'He's afraid of the vet,' I had to explain to one curious grandma who enquired with some authority from behind her aluminium walker in the hope of saving the poor dog from his tormentors.

I felt terrible because it made Beatriz, whose clinic was just a few metres away, look like a monster, but there was no time to explain Bobby's fearful behaviour because I was getting very stressed and flustered. And the more stressed and flustered I became, the more frightened Bobby became. Miraculously, we managed to get him back to the car.

'We should take him for a run in the countryside,' Robert suggested.

We agreed that half an hour spent outside town might help Bobby recover his confidence, so we drove off and parked outside Alcalá in an olive grove. I put a lead on him so as not to lose him in the new environment, but I needn't have bothered. Bobby had turned into a rock and decided never to leave the safety of the car again. It was now sweltering outside and even more so inside the car. Everyone was exhausted and irritable, so we decided to call it quits. We returned to the vet to explain that we needed to postpone the injection.

'Can we make him sleep or tranquilise him?' I asked.

Beatriz raised her eyebrows and explained that the most effective sedative was in the form of an injection. Giving Bobby an injection to calm him down so we could give him his vaccine injection was a bit of a Catch-22.

'But there is a pill he can take,' she said. Give it to him tomorrow morning, and when he's sleepy, give him the injection.

'Me?'

'Yes, otherwise you'll have to pay for a new one,' she explained. 'I have activated the syringe. I've put it in a small cool box for you. You have forty-eight hours to use it.'

'But how?' Now I started to pant like Bobby anticipating the procedure.

'Like this,' she grabbed her assistant by the neck and pretended to pull some skin up. 'It's subcutaneous. It's very easy.'

I repeated what she had told me to make sure I understood her. I had never injected anyone or anything before and was starting to feel dizzy at the prospect. I returned to the car with my homework project in its little insulated box and a sleeping pill in my handbag. At home, I fortified myself with a glass of red and went straight to YouTube, where I watched numerous videos on vaccinating your dog. While I watched, I felt that administering an injection was a skill that one should practise hands-on instead of merely watching others do it. My confidence that I could inject Bobby fell to zero, so I went to Robert's workshop and told him to do it instead.

'OK,' was his answer.

'Don't you need to watch any videos?' I was puzzled by his nonchalant approach to what I had begun to perceive as a major medical procedure.

'The vet said it's subcutaneous, isn't it?' he checked.

'Yes,' I confirmed. The word *subcutaneous* was getting on my nerves by now. Until this point in my life, I had never heard it spoken aloud, or at least, I felt like I had never heard it before. Suddenly every other word was *subcutaneous* this and *subcutaneous* that.

'It's easy. You pull a little skin and inject it there. He has a fat neck. It will be fine,' Robert informed me and went back to turning an olive wood bowl on his lathe, a hobby he had taken up that summer.

At what moment everyone in the world had become an expert in subcutaneous injections was a mystery to me, but it was better him than me. I would not have had the nerve. All I had to do was make Bobby sleep so he would not bite either of us during the procedure.

The following morning, after a nice run together in the field, I put a little yellow pill in Bobby's wet food. Even though I pretended everything was business as usual, our dog must have sensed something was amiss. He ate all the wet food around the pill and left the lonely little dot at the bottom of his bowl. As soon as he was finished, he decided to squeeze himself into a corner of the sofa, shrewdly anticipating our next move.

'OK, this is how it's going to be,' I gave him a dirty look as I picked up his bowl to retrieve the pill.

I only had one pill, so I had to use it wisely. I decided to crush it into a powder so he could not pick it out from his food. But since he was aware that something suspicious was going on, I was certain he would not touch a second helping of his store-bought dog pâté. His second breakfast that morning had to be something irresistible. And so, with my morning coffee getting cold, I put on a small pot of pasta to lure my discerning dog. There aren't many things in life that Bobby loves more than pasta, except cheese, of course. I combined his two favourite foods and sprinkled the powdered sleeping pill on top with a dash of grated parmesan as an extra garnish.

The spiked, soporific pasta was gone in seconds. Now, all we had to do was wait. I called Robert so that he would be ready with the syringe. We positioned ourselves on the armchairs opposite the sofa and watched Bobby. This, of course, was a terrible idea since it made Bobby even more suspicious of our intentions. I could see his sleepy eyelids fall down and then suddenly rise again. After five minutes, he was resting his listless head on a cushion. But his ears were still pointing up in alert mode to let us know that he would be aware of any shenanigans on our part as he took a little nap. Ten minutes later, we were convinced that Bobby was fast asleep.

'Where's the syringe?' I asked Robert.

'In the fridge.'

'If you open the F-R-I-D-G-E, he will wake up immediately,' I whispered angrily. I didn't want to use the word *fridge* in case it was

248

one of the few words that Bobby understood, as it would definitely wake him up.

More heated whispers were exchanged about how to extract the syringe with the vaccine from the fridge without alerting the dog.

'I'll get it,' I decided. 'You're too clumsy.'

I used my best ninja impersonation and stealthily rose from the armchair and walked gingerly over to the fridge. I manipulated the rubber seal on the door to open it as quietly as possible. But it was no good. As soon as I opened the door, the bottles of sauces and condiments in the fridge door started to jingle against each other. I felt like a bomb disposal engineer who had just cut the wrong wires. I looked over my shoulder, but Bobby was still in a deep sleep. His sleeping pill appeared to be working.

That is until Robert came close to Bobby with the syringe. At the moment Robert was to insert it into his neck, Bobby jumped to his feet and turned into a medium-sized Hound of the Baskervilles, growling and snapping each time either of us tried to approach him. We spent the rest of the afternoon pretending to be busy doing other things but secretly watching to check whether Bobby had fallen asleep. He was evidently irresistibly tired and drowsy, but he refused to close his eyes for longer than a few seconds at a time. He was gallantly fighting the effects of the narcotic, trying to stay alert like Captain Willard on night watch in the Vietnamese jungle.

'I think he needs a bigger dose,' I deduced and sent Robert back to Beatriz to explain the events of the day. We still had twenty-four hours to administer the injection.

In the evening, Robert returned home with the pills.

'She was quite shocked that Bobby hadn't fallen asleep. She gave me a bigger dose but said it was enough for a Labrador, and we should not give Bobby any more than that.'

I could hear from Robert's account that our vet was uncertain about how we wished to proceed with the palaver of giving Bobby his injection. However, being a country vet, she was open to being flexible and letting the pet owner take on some responsibility. I had witnessed a farmer in her waiting room who described his dog's symptoms and demanded to get medicine for the dog without her actually examining the animal at the clinic. I felt thankful for her understanding.

The next day was Groundhog Day — Bobby went for a good run and then a 'special' breakfast of pasta with parmesan. I crushed *three* pills into his meal this time. The only difference in his behaviour that morning was that even though he seemed much sleepier than the previous day, he was also much meaner and more aggressive as he fought off the effects of the tranquiliser pills.

'He's an angry drunk,' Robert's observation was very accurate. Our Bobby lashed out blindly at everyone and everything in his exhausted rage.

I wanted to cry.

'How are we going to vaccinate this dog?' I gave up on being able to use the syringe, which would be viable for just a couple of hours longer.

'I don't know.'

TWENTY-SIX
FRANCE WINS THE WORLD CUP

F or the benefit of our mental health and Bobby's, we decided to postpone the injection until we had a better plan in place. I spent the next few days 'researching' various methods of vaccinating animals but was left none the wiser after my efforts.

'How do they vaccinate lions at the zoo?' I was sitting on the side of the driveway and expressing my frustration to Robert, who was busy painting the main gate with Raoul. To be precise, the young man was languidly holding the paint pot while Robert did the painting from atop a ladder. It was Chantal and Raoul's second week with us, and I had to admire the youngster's ingenuity in avoiding doing any physical work even while others around him were busy.

'Don't they use guns with syringes in them?'

My rhetorical question was lost on this youth, and Raoul proceeded to boysplain how zookeepers vaccinate lions. Since I had clearly run out of rational ideas myself, I decided to follow up on his idea and went online in search of a dart gun that would shoot a vaccine syringe into a living target. I found a selection of blowguns and darts, but judging from their size, they were for Texan longhorn cattle or South African rhinos. One of them would have easily pierced Bobby's skull completely if one were inclined to aim there. Also, I did not have the required canine vaccination to put inside the dart.

'Isn't there a vaccination in the form of a pill?' Robert asked as he came in to drink some water.

'Yes, there is, but it's not available for house pets,' I had been studying vaccination techniques for a couple of days and had become a bit of an expert. 'It's used for wild animals, but the dose is not accurate.'

As I explained this to Robert, a novel thought occurred to me.

'We should call the dog whisperer?' I informed Robert. 'I don't know why I didn't think of it before.'

'Who's the dog whisperer?'

'There's a guy on Facebook. He's called Trevor. I've seen him a few times advertising dog training. I think he lives near Alcalá.'

It took me some time to find the relevant post on the social media that I was referring to. Anyway, I found the whisperer's number and sent a WhatsApp message to him outlining our predicament.

What size dog is it? was his quick response.

It's a medium-sized dog, like a Jack Russell, but a little bigger. I sent a photo of Bobby next to Robert for comparison.

Bring him this afternoon, was Trevor's immediate reply. *I'll see what I can do.*

We found Trevor the Whisperer's house in a tiny village outside Alcalá la Real. On the way there, we stopped by the vet, and I asked her to prepare another syringe to take with us in a cool box. Bobby was sitting in the back of the car, sulking and refusing to interact with anyone. He must have felt cheated; instead of going for his usual afternoon run in the olive groves, he was returning to the vet's, or so he thought. Once we had parked outside the dog whisperer's house, he refused to leave the car. He sniffed the treats I offered in my hand with a look of betrayal and refused to touch them. And if he thought his luck had taken a turn for the worse, he was quite right.

A giant Belgian Shepherd appeared in the doorway of Trevor's house. Saskia would teach Bobby how to be a good dog by following her commanding example of excellent dog behaviour.

'Why don't you wait inside while we walk around the block a bit?' Trevor suggested after we convinced Bobby to get out of the car.

I didn't protest. It was still very hot outside that afternoon, so I was quite happy to sit in the cool living room with Trevor's wife while Robert walked Bobby. The house was relatively small, even by Spanish standards, but I had to admire how they converted what space they had into a canine spa and hotel. Unlike many expats who come to Spain and reinvent themselves as real-estate agents, builders, EFL teachers, or spiritual healers, Trevor had been a professional dog handler all his adult life and knew what he was doing. With his pension from the police force, he and his wife had left old Blighty behind and, with minimal investment, started a small business.

His wife, Marta, was in the middle of outlining how much better their life was here in Spain than in the UK — a topic that many local expats of all nationalities love to dwell upon, especially on sunny days — when the boys and the dogs returned from their walk. Bobby immediately jumped onto the sofa and hid behind me. I started to apologise and moved to chase the dog off the sofa, but the couple explained that the sofas were for the dogs who holidayed in the house when their owners went away. As Bobby settled down, Saskia lay at the foot of the piano and watched him attentively. She was a good teacher.

'The problem is Robert,' was Trevor's assessment. 'He flinches each time Bobby shows his teeth, and now the dog thinks he's the boss.'

I had to agree with this sage evaluation. I noticed that Robert's face changed each time he saw the syringe. Bobby must have also observed this and decided that since Robert was afraid of the needle, he should be too.

'He needs to relax a little before we give him the injection. Would you like a beer?'

I wasn't sure if he was talking about Bobby or Robert, but I accepted a cold beer. It took almost an hour before Bobby was finally vaccinated. In the meantime, the Brits in the room went over the usual topics of conversation that were on everyone's mind at that time: the imminent consequences of Brexit, the housing crisis in the UK, and immigration. Once they had run out of hot issues to address, they moved on to scoffing at their compatriots in Spain, namely the 'bargain-loving Brits in the sun', whom everyone loves to make fun of, even though we are THEM.

'OK, I'll give Bobby a nice bath now, and hopefully, he will relax,' Trevor announced.

I didn't question his idea, but I had doubts about how a warm-water ablution would tranquilise our dog, who hated getting washed. Ten minutes later, a damp and dour Bobby jumped onto the sofa.

'Here's a treat for him. It's dried liver,' Trevor passed me a piece of what looked like a desiccated brown stick.

'So do you think we'll be able to vaccinate him today?' I broached the subject of our visit.

'I've done it already while I was drying him off. He's good to go.'

I could not believe my ears. I was so happy I wanted to kiss everyone in the room.

'You truly are a dog whisperer,' I praised his ability to control unruly dogs.

'Not a problem. Instead of payment, you can make a small donation for the rescue dogs I help whenever I can.'

I put the equivalent of an hour's consultation in a jar marked with a dog rescue charity's logo. Afterwards, we arranged for Robert and Bobby to visit Trevor a few more times that summer to keep working on Bobby's (and Robert's) attitude so that we would not experience this problem in the future. On the way home, we stopped to buy some beers for the evening. The World Cup Final was that night, and France was playing Croatia. Our French Workaways had asked us if we could set up a big screen outside on the patio to watch it together.

'I'll make *gratin dauphinoise*,' was Chantal's tempting promise. 'I called my mum yesterday, and she gave me our family recipe.'

While I later rolled my eyes at the idea of having a family recipe for what I considered a simple potato dish, Robert was all ears. Like many an Englishman, potatoes form a constituent part of his diet. He refuses to consider it a proper meal if there are no potatoes for lunch or dinner. The idea of having one of his favourite potato dishes prepared by a bona fide Frenchwoman transported him to spud heaven. All the way home from Trevor's, my husband speculated on the secret ingredients Chantal's family recipe might include.

'I bet you they put thyme in it, or maybe marjoram or tarragon?' he listed off all the herbs that he could think of that sounded like something a French family might have in their garden.

As it transpired, Chantal had a secret recipe for making dauphinoise, and the secret was the central plot of the Stone Soup story. As she started her promised dish, all she needed from me were two Pyrex baking dishes, which was a reasonable request since the holiday apartment where she was staying was not equipped for baking. Raoul appeared in my doorway a few minutes later, asking if we had some potatoes. Apparently, they had forgotten to buy some.

'Only five or six,' he explained nonchalantly while scratching his belly under his T-shirt.

I went to the pantry and gave him eight potatoes for good measure since Chantal was preparing two dishes — one for us and one separate one for Raoul, as it was his favourite dish. He was about to leave when he remembered one more thing.

'And she's asked if you have some extra cream because we only bought one packet, and it's not enough for two dishes.'

I obliged as I realised that if I were not to provide the young couple with the ingredients for the meal that *they* had offered to bring to the football match, we would have nothing to complement the sausages that we were planning to barbecue.

'Don't you need some garlic?' I asked as Raoul was about to return to his girlfriend with his loot.

'I don't think so. The recipe does not require any garlic,' he informed me and went away.

Ten minutes later, Chantal appeared at my kitchen door.

'I've just spoken to my mum, and she told me there is garlic in

255

potatoes dauphinoise,' she informed me knowingly. 'I was also wondering if you have a tiny bit of nutmeg?'

Did you forget to buy that too? I would have said if I wanted to be facetious, but everyone was in a festive mood, so I bit my tongue and gave the young woman a jar of nutmeg.

She thanked me and returned to my kitchen half an hour later with two dishes ready to put in my oven to bake for an hour while we turned on the football. It wasn't the first time that summer that we had set up the big TV outside for a communal session of watching football, so by now, Robert was an expert at it. The TV was set up within minutes, and Robert and the kids were watching the game. As for me, I was not planning to get too involved in watching France versus Croatia. Up to that point in my life, I had watched two complete football matches and considered this experience enough to last me a lifetime. I could not imagine what might be different in each game.

Unless all the footballers involved decided to form a line and walk themselves off a cliff, I was not interested in applauding adult men while they ran after an inflated leather ball to score arbitrary points. But I also know that there are two things you can do to quickly antagonise many Europeans. The first is to show a dislike of their pooches, and the other is to trivialise the global significance of football. And so, I opened the window from my kitchen to the patio and pretended to watch the game while making a salad. And although I could not care less who was playing against whom and why, I did enjoy the spirit of community that afternoon, especially as the young French nationals were losing their minds as the game progressed. I wish I could give an exciting account of the match; it seemed thrilling from what I could apprise from the spectators' response. So it came to pass, as I was about to serve the 'stone soup' dauphinoise, France won the World Cup. *Hourra!*

Considering that Robert has as much interest in football as I do, I was impressed by how much fake enthusiasm he mustered for the game. We celebrated the French victory late into the night and watched the reports of Francophile celebrations in various European capitals on TV. A few days later, our French Workaways left to volunteer on a goat farm somewhere in the Alpujarra mountains. I wished them good luck as I knew they would need it with Raoul's work ethic and lack of common sense when it came to all matters agricultural.

'Could have been worse,' Robert assessed the young people's stay with us.

I had to agree. We did lose all our watermelon plants when Raoul decided that a set of identical plants growing in a line next to an irrigation pipe were most definitely a type of weed and pulled the juvenile plants and their roots out of the ground.

'He would have dug up all the baby potatoes if you hadn't stopped him,' Robert reminded me. 'I wonder how long he'll last on a real farm?'

It was another rhetorical question. I knew he wouldn't last long, but we did not keep in touch for long enough to find out what happened to them in the Alpujarras. But even though our Gen Zs had left us, they must have left the snowflake juju behind at Berruguilla because we were about to be inundated by a Millennial Wave.

TWENTY-SEVEN
THE MILLENNIAL HEATWAVE

In one of my more ditsy moments of the summer of 2018, I offered my guests yoga classes. I found the concept of providing a yoga retreat curiously compelling, and it sounded like something I might enjoy doing. In retrospect, I should have known better. I had been forewarned by my friend Claire, who, during our days in Abu Dhabi, used to spend one month each summer locked up in an ashram outside Delhi. While many aspirational yoginis might sign up for a stint in such a place for mental health reasons, she went there purely to lose weight.

'It was so easy,' she would tell me every September back at university, always five kilograms lighter. 'They locked me up in a room.

There was no fridge or access to a kitchen. Someone came in a few times a day to give me a massage or some other treatment. I did some group yoga every day and was supposed to meditate the rest of the time. I was given a small bowl of rice with steamed vegetables twice a day, so I had a lot of time to think about my life between the meals.'

I learned from Claire that on this journey of self-discovery, she was not allowed to bring anything to entertain herself, including books. To me, this sounded like a terrible way to while away your days, and I was certain that to Claire, who was used to being in five places at the same time and talking to several people all at once, it must have been mental torture.

'What did you do all day?' I asked in horror on hearing that books were not allowed.

'I watched some flies play on my window,' she told me in all seriousness.

'It sounds like a scam to pay thousands of dollars to be locked up in a depressing room, deprived of food and entertainment,' I was being honest with Claire.

'Definitely,' she admitted without hesitation. 'But how else am I supposed to lose weight? Caroline from HR pays a company to bring her powdered oatmeal and soup three times a day — that's a scam!'

I had to agree with Claire. The world of self-improvement, be it emotional or physical, is rife with swindlers. With Claire's ashram experience in mind, I determined that I would never organise a yoga retreat. Still, I was not dissuaded from partaking in a spot of impromptu yoga now and then. One July morning, while stretching by the pool and enjoying the cool morning breeze, I thought I could organise some yoga classes at my house. Finding a yoga instructor was not a problem. For some reason, Andalusia attracts a disproportionate number of 'spiritual healers' of all shapes and sizes: from the study and practice of yoga, through the magical effect of crystals and sound healing, to the art of Reiki and everything in between. Any gap in the marketplace where spiritual goods are traded is quickly occupied by entrepreneurs interested in all things psychic or metaphysical.

'It's not merely a massage; it's *therapy*,' Lucas's husband, Arie, corrected me once at a dinner party while I was innocently explaining to someone that he provided massages. He was pretty indignant about my mistake and decided to childishly sulk for the rest of the evening, scrolling through his Instagram feed.

'For someone so interested in mindfulness and spirituality, he spends an awful amount of time on his Facebook and Instagram feeds,' I told Robert on the way home. 'He's posted five times today about how much he loves the tranquillity of nature.'

'Really?' Robert, who didn't spend much time on social media, was surprised to hear this. 'He was just telling me how much he hates living in the sticks and how he missed the hustle and bustle of Rotterdam and its nightclubs.'

Armed only with a high-school certificate he obtained in his late twenties, Arie was lucky to have spent most of his adult life in Asia as a holiday representative for a Dutch package holiday company. It must have been during one of his stints in tropical Bali when he stumbled across the veritable gold mine called 'spiritual healing'.

It does not take a genius in economics to do the maths regarding how much money can be made on this snake oil business model. The investment in the enterprise is minimal — a second-hand massage table, a couple of clean towels, and a bag of cheap crystals. Arie grew a guru-like beard, developed the startling confidence of a diva, and had absolutely no qualms about taking money from vulnerable, recently divorced, or widowed women — for they constituted his primary target market. He called his shamanic massages 'therapy' and titled himself a 'therapist'. Should anyone mistakenly call him a 'masseur', they'd be his enemy forever.

But while Bali may have been teeming with lonely, middle-aged women eager to spend their deceased husband's life insurance money on finding the meaning of life, rural Andalusia was inhabited by down-to-earth farmers, skint Brits, and tight-fisted Dutchmen. None of them was interested in parting with their hard-earned dosh for something as ephemeral as what Arie was offering. For these reasons, Arie, who spent most of his time travelling from one European capital to the other on the prowl for new converts to his pathway to enlightenment, was hardly involved in house renovations or the B&B business back in Spain. In an attempt to keep his peripatetic husband at home for at least a couple of weeks at a time, Lucas suggested that they offer their establishment for yoga retreats. They converted every usable space in their cottage into bedrooms to accommodate their proposed yoga groups. The facilities were spartan, but I assumed that was aligned with the ashram experience one would pay good money for in India.

While Arie could have taught the yoga classes I wished to offer at my place — he was a healing maverick, and there was not a single branch of spirituality that he hadn't dabbled in — I did not think he needed any more fuel to boost his already overinflated ego. Instead, I found a middle-aged Essex woman from another village. Stella was a short brunette who used to work as a yoga instructor in the UK. She and her husband had recently moved to Andalusia, hoping to open her own yoga retreat among the olive groves. They purchased a dilapidated cottage on the outskirts of a small village and spent most of their days renovating it and making plans for their future business. Stella would advertise her yoga classes on local social media to make ends meet. Business must have been slow because she was more than happy to drive for fifty minutes to come to our small guest house to teach yoga and mindfulness once a week.

While my guests only occasionally felt like getting up at 9 am to do yoga, I had gathered enough participants from among my friends and neighbours to make the journey worth Stella's time. My friend Liv was a regular participant since the yoga sessions were a welcome break from renovating her guest house for the next season. Trish also came and brought with her a few other women from the nearby villages. And even Arie graced us with his presence on several occasions, which was a bit of a mystery to me because, from his own accounts, I assumed he had already reached the highest levels of nirvana and spiritual evolution. Yet here he was with his yoga mat stretched out between some middle-aged women, most of whom, like me, only did yoga occasionally and were far from fit or flexible. Or maybe he was feeling a little lonely, forsaken in the middle of nature, starved of the more sophisticated social gatherings he was accustomed to.

It's difficult to say because he did not seem to make any new friends in the area where he had bought his house. In fact, he appeared to be very successful at alienating whoever was stationed next to him during our mindfulness sessions. After the second session that he attended, I noticed that the ordinarily sociable and friendly women who were present discreetly moved their yoga mats away from Arie as soon as he positioned his next to theirs. *Maybe he has bad BO*, I thought to myself, but I couldn't detect any when I spoke to him after the class. The puzzle became apparent during the third session when the only place left in the shade for my yoga mat was between Arie and my friend Jessica.

Jessica was a young widow and was usually very outgoing and chatty. Since she spent a lot of her time alone in her cottage, it was very unlike her to keep her distance from people, especially if she had intentionally left home to meet new people.

Our classes took place in the shade of the bay leaf and nispero trees by the pool, facing the olive groves and a clear blue sky. We started the session with some deep breathing and Sun Salutations. The sun was lovely that morning. Stella was a great instructor and gave minimal but very clear instructions. I was enjoying myself until we came down to practice the Child's Pose, where you sit on your knees and stretch your arms out on the floor in front of you.

'Lengthen and widen the spine with each inhale. Sink deeper into the pose with each exhale,' I heard Stella's gentle voice over the chirping birds. 'Relax your shoulders downwards.'

I took a deep breath, and that's when I realised someone had relaxed their muscles a little too much. The miasma that emanated from Arie's mat would have been enough to make the most hardened sewer cleaner quit their job.

'Take five deep breaths,' Stella hummed her instructions in the background.

In the meantime, my eyes were popping out of their sockets as I tried my best not to breathe for the continuation of the pose. I snuggled my nose under my right armpit and hoped to fight off Arie's stench with my own BO, but it was a futile move. As we lifted our behinds to engage in the Downward Facing Dog position, I looked to my left at Jessica and Trish. Their knowing smirks indicated why they had moved away from Arie's mat at the start of the session. The rest of the session was pure torture for me. Arie unleashed a new silent killer with each pose intended to stretch or squeeze our long intestines. By the time we were in the Ragdoll position, I was a shadow of my former self and about to pass out from oxygen deprivation from holding my breath.

Fortunately, that was Arie's last yoga session with us. His presence had been humbly requested at a yoga retreat in the Alpujarra mountains for the rest of the summer, where he would provide his shamanic massages in a yurt. He told us about his upcoming adventure as we sat by the pool eating slices of cooling watermelon and relaxing after our exercises. Since Jessica and Liv were new to his shamanic scheme, he made a blatant sales pitch for his services. Listening to him, one might have wondered why modern medicine has not ceased to exist altogether since Arie claimed he could cure almost any disease with a simple regime of regular massages and a palmful of shiny crystals that get their energy from the rays of a full moon.

There is no doubt that Arie and his stories provided me and my girlfriends with hours of gossip and free entertainment for years to come. We were both fascinated and appalled by his evolution from a tour guide to a modern-day Rasputin and his sudden conversion from a happily-married gay man to a heterosexual husband. His future wife's wealth, which she had acquired from selling alternative medicines and holistic healing in Belgium, might have had something to do with his unexpected change in sexual orientation. To say that his life partner of twenty years, Lucas, was inconsolable and heartbroken would not give justice to the pain Arie had caused. But it's not unusual that those who profess to be deeply spiritual and mindful are capable of delivering such emotional blows against the most vulnerable.

Arie's antics were not our only source of entertainment. That August, we were inundated by Millennials, whose unifying feature was that they loved the *idea* of being in the middle of nowhere surrounded by nature but hated everything about the actual experience that was provided to them.

'There's no internet by the pool,' a skinny Dutch girl from Amsterdam informed me from her sun lounger.

I looked at her almost translucent white skin and the reddening freckles that peppered her nose.

You're going to get a heat stroke, I thought to myself.

It was over 40 degrees Celsius, or 104 Fahrenheit, and she'd been bathing in the full sun for several hours now. Considering that she weighed about forty kilograms, I was surprised that there was still any water left in her body.

'No, there isn't. You are too far from the Wi-Fi router,' I didn't know what else to tell her.

'Isn't there another connection?'

Where? In the oak tree? I wanted to ask.

'There is no mobile signal because of the mountain that lies between us and the village of Montefrio,' I pointed at the olive hill right in front of her.

She wasn't the first guest to ask me this question, and I was getting annoyed with this generation that thought Wi-Fi signals grew on trees. In the past, I'd heard professional educators sagely refer to Millennials as 'digital natives'. The concept revolved around the claim that, since they had grown up with digital technology, they were presumably naturally able to use any form without explicit instruction. The term was supposed to contrast them to my generation, who had sent their first email in their early twenties, or my mum's generation, who had learned how to use the computer by having her children shout at her and lose their temper while she tried to open a folder on the desktop with the same care and attention one would devote to launching a nuclear missile.

But while Boomers might occasionally struggle with modern technology, at least they have had to make an effort to use it. So-called 'digital natives', on the other hand, are the neglected children of technology. We all assume they have assimilated digital knowledge and use their smartphones intelligently. But this assumption has created a generation of digital naïfs who believe the apps on their phones can read their minds and solve any problem they may face. This may be true up until the very moment they lose their connection to the internet. That's when they transform from seemingly independent adults who can purchase flight tickets and schedule a journey from

Amsterdam to Andalusia to little helpless babies abandoned in the wild raised by a family of wolves.

I was getting old, and the social and conceptual gap between me and them was widening. The only positive aspect of hosting Millennials was that they avoided human contact at all costs. Thus, even though they might only be 20 metres away from me at the house, they usually sent me a WhatsApp message instead of asking me a question face-to-face. At least I didn't need to put my hospitality smile on when answering their queries.

Good Morning! I was wondering if you could tell me where we could find a boulangerie?

I woke up early one morning to see this message on my phone.

In Paris. I wanted to reply.

I thought of Montefrio's *panadería*. It would be a good lesson in life to be confronted by the bevvy of matrons who frequent the shop in the morning or be snubbed by the shop assistant when they inevitably ask for some delicacy that the Spanish baker had only seen on TV in a French travel or cooking show.

There's a great baker near the post office. I'll send you the location pin.

I never found out how their search for a *boulangerie* in Andalusia ended, for they didn't mention it to me, even via WhatsApp. I was certain that the local *panadería* did not meet their expectations of a perfect Parisian bakery replete with strawberry tartlets, colourful macarons, and freshly-baked *brioche*. I'm not saying that you can't find these in Andalusia. In fact, many Spaniards love a croissant for breakfast or a macaron for dessert, but such foreign pastries are usually sold in the big supermarket chains or in the more cosmopolitan bakeries of Madrid or Barcelona, where there is a demand for them.

'Why do you get so indignant about their requests?' Liv asked me.

'Because they don't live in the real world.'

The line between what's real and not real has long been blurred by the Instagram generation, who insist on continuously foisting their fantasies and aspirations on innocent bystanders.

'I can't eat figs,' another Millennial guest informed me. 'I'm vegan.'

Over the years of running a guest house, I have learned not to roll my eyes at guests, but this astounding piece of information tested my self-control. I looked at Liv, Julian, and the two other Dutch guests, Marike and Pieter, sitting at the same table for clarification.

'It's because wasps die while pollinating some fig species,' Pieter, a foodie, explained hesitantly.

'I'm very sorry,' I apologised for presenting a bowl of fresh figs under her nose. 'I don't think I have anything else.'

Pieter, who enjoyed cooking while on holiday, had made tiramisu for everybody, and so, with his permission, I invited Liv and Julian for some cake and cava. Since I didn't want to exclude my other guests, a young couple from Silesia, I invited them too. The problem was that Kasia was vegan, and the tiramisu wasn't. As I had learned, the figs weren't vegan either, so she was left to nibble on some nuts she had brought to the table. I hoped no miniature beasts were involved in the harvest of those pistachios.

'Where is Adam?' I inquired after her boyfriend, whom I had seen barbecuing in the blazing sun earlier that day, wearing nothing but overly tight Speedos and a Moroccan woollen headscarf wrapped securely around his sweaty forehead. It was an ensemble that stayed in the viewer's mind for years to come. I assumed that this fashionable ethnic-chic pool outfit was inspired by an Instagram influencer or some such. I didn't even ask why on earth he was wearing a woolly head covering in forty degrees heat.

'He's got food poisoning,' Kasia informed me. I was about to pour her some cava when she quickly placed her hand over the wine glass in horror.

'Oh, no! I can't drink this.'

'Wine is not vegan,' Pieter, who himself ate everything and seemed knowledgeable on the topic.

Is it because a fly might have fallen into the barrel and drowned? I wondered and made a mental note to refrain from offering her anything else to eat or drink in the future.

'You should try some of Sabina's zucchini bread,' Marike suggested.

The previous March, I bought a bag of zucchini, or courgette, seeds at a local nursery and, in my horticultural naivety, I planted the whole packet. I was now swamped with the fruit and constantly searched for ways to dispose of at least two to three zucchinis a day since I didn't want them to go to waste. It was an abundant harvest, and Robert and I struggled to consume the summer squash on our own. To slow down the plants' fruit production, I'd go out every morning and pick the open flowers before they developed into fruit. I'd fry the flowers in tempura at lunchtime and add them to a salad. That summer, we went through a whole zucchini-based diet. We had zucchini quiches, pancakes, and even zucchini 'spaghetti'. We sautéed, fried, boiled, stuffed, and baked the fruit until neither of us could bear to look at it any more. We liberally gifted bags of zucchini to neighbours, friends, and unsuspecting guests. Finally, I started baking zucchini bread which was quite nice as a novelty, but after a few loaves, it, too, became overwhelming. The good thing about the bread was that it was easy to freeze and serve in the distant future once our plants stopped producing the fruit. I also served it generously to guests, who loved it.

'Does it have eggs?' Kasia asked about my zucchini bread.

'Yes, it does,' I confirmed.

'So, you don't eat cake?' Liv, who spent most of her adult time in Zimbabwe and wasn't fussy about what she ate or drank, was now curious to find out.

'There are a lot of vegan desserts,' Kasia reassured the group of sceptics. 'When I feel like having something sweet, I make a delicious tomato cake.'

Her audience quickly turned their attention to the amaretto and coffee-soaked tiramisu Pieter had served.

'Oh! A tomato cake?' Liv was astonished on everybody's behalf. 'How do you make that?'

It's been my experience with vegans that you don't need to ask them twice to receive a long lecture on the wonderful techniques employed in preparing vegan dishes in an endless effort to make them resemble non-vegan cuisine. We learned from Kasia that she made her tomato cake from a can of tomato soup. I didn't take down detailed notes on the recipe since I prefer my cakes not to be canned soup-based. I never warmed to Kasia and Adam, who took turns getting heat stroke during their stay that summer, or 'food poisoning' as Kasia called it, since she adamantly refused to accept my advice that sitting in the full sun during the hottest times of the day caused vomiting and diarrhoea. As a result, neither of them saw much of Andalusia beyond their bathroom and the pharmacy in Montefrio. It was good to have Marike and Pieter as guests at the same time, as I would have thought that the world had turned upside-down and no one had sent me the memo.

Marike and Pieter were stereotypical Dutch in their physique and outlook on life — both were very tall and physically strong, gave straightforward opinions, and were pleasantly chatty. Within days of their arrival, we quickly became friends over their love of baking and Pieter's passion for carpentry. The camaraderie started with a slice of peach cobbler. By now, the fruit trees that we had planted during our first spring in Spain were bearing beautiful fruit. That August, our little orchard provided us with a bountiful supply of peaches and *paraguayo*, an exquisitely sweet, flat peach shaped like a small disk, and hence sometimes called a 'doughnut peach' in English. We were also the beneficiaries of copious amounts of figs, pears, and a variety of apples the size of golf balls.

Since we could not eat the peaches fast enough on our own, I made peach cobbler for the guests, which was a huge success. While many Americans might consider peach cobbler to be a classic, everyday dessert, I learned that it was a complete novelty for our Dutch, French, Spanish, and Polish guests. I myself had never tried it before and had only seen it briefly in an episode of *Criminal Minds* — where one of the detectives brings a delicious-looking cobbler all the way from New York to Quantico — so I did not have an exact idea of what it should look or taste like. Nevertheless, I assumed that a generous amount of cinnamon and vanilla never hurt any cake. While the word *cobbler* is self-explanatory to most English speakers and gave me a good indication of what the dessert should look like, it was extremely difficult to translate to non-native speakers, who seemed to be quite confused when I tried to do so.

'Is this a Spanish cake?' they'd ask me.

'No, it's an American cake. It's called "cobbler",' I could see the puzzlement on Marike's face.

'You know the main street in Montefrio,' I tried to relate the name to something tangible. 'It is built from stones like this.' I made a fist like a cobblestone.

My folk etymology was muddling at its best, so I abandoned my explanation.

'Can you make us another one?' Pieter asked. 'We loved it.'

They noted my bafflement.

'We'll pay you,' Marike explained.

'You want me to make a whole cake for you?'

It was a strange request, but they were both as tall as professional basketball league players, and I assumed they were up to the task of scoffing down a whole cake.

'Can you tell me when you make the cake so I can watch you and learn how to make it?' Pieter asked.

I wasn't prepared to be giving a masterclass in baking, mainly because I don't follow recipes to the letter and hardly ever use the exact same amount of ingredients, but of course, if this experience was going to ensure they had an unforgettable holiday, I was more than happy to oblige.

When selling a dream, it's essential that one focuses on the small details and lets the client's mind fill in the blanks with whatever fantasy they are trying to fulfil. Since I wasn't the typical 'farmer's wife' that they imagined me to be — I don't even own an apron or oven mitts — I had to improvise. In preparation for my cobbler masterclass, I searched the drawers for a wooden spoon and rustic-looking wooden bowl.

Anything that looked like it could have been used in the Middle Ages was put on display in the kitchen, including our pasta machine, which had been collecting dust after the novelty wore off, a meat mincer which was only ever used once twenty years earlier in Sweden to make moose sausages, and lots of rustic-looking bits and bobs which suggested to the observer that most of my days were spent processing meat, churning butter, and preserving food for the winter.

While my little baking workshop was a success, I discovered I had limited patience for teaching people how to cook. Even though Pieter was a keen student, watching him peel the peaches was tortuous, to say the least. It took most of my mental energy not to snatch the fruit from his clumsy fingers and do it myself in five minutes. Instead, we spent twenty minutes or so chatting while he struggled to grip the fruit in his now slimy fingers. Every other stage of the preparation process was equally frustrating for me to watch. There was a lot of indecision and second-guessing on his part, which I found exasperating. But we made it to the end in an amicable fashion, albeit the whole process took three times longer than if I had made the cake on my own.

'It's a nice bowl,' Pieter pointed to one of the olive wood bowls that Robert had turned that summer.

Once he was informed that Robert had a wood lathe in his garage and a mountain of scrap wood which he could practise wood turning on, Pieter spent most of his holiday in front of the machine, learning how to make small bowls and containers of various designs.

It was a good summer. The guests enjoyed the great Andalusian outdoors, swimming, barbecuing, and eating the fruit and vegetables from our land. The heavy rains in the winter and spring meant we had a bounty of potatoes, sweetcorn, and other vegetables we could share with others. While the guests relaxed by the pool, we explored several local *mesóns*, or rural inns, with our new circle of friends. It was just as I had imagined our new life in this beautiful part of the world might be.

TWENTY-EIGHT
OLIVE LEAF TEA

It was towards the end of August when I noticed an unusually large number of missed phone calls from a series of unknown numbers on my phone. Because our cottage has thick stone walls, getting a phone signal inside the house is impossible. As soon as I took Bobby for a walk and caught a signal on a hill, I would receive notifications that I had several missed calls. I was accustomed to seeing one or two missed phone calls, usually from telemarketers, but this time it was five or six calls a day.

'If they really need to get in touch, they'll find a way,' I waved them off.

I didn't have time to stand under the oak tree searching for a signal so that I could return strangers' missed calls. Between the guests, I was also preparing for my family's visit. We agreed that this year they'd land in Alicante, which was served by direct flights from Gdansk, my hometown. Having to collect them from the airport also gave us an excuse to visit Costa Blanca. Since it's a five-hour drive away, we booked an apartment by the sea to enjoy the beach together for a few days after they landed. We'd then all travel together in one car from Alicante to our house in Granada province. Bobby was going to spend the four days with Keith and Freddie, and the cats didn't care one way or the other if we were at home or not. As long as the tiny bathroom window was left open for them to go in and out of the house, and the feeder and water tank were filled to the brim, they could have stayed by themselves for a week until they'd noticed that their dutiful servants had gone on holiday.

It was the day before our trip to Alicante when I received a message from my boss.

Hi. Sorry to tell you, but I've decided to close the school. I passed my oposiciones in July and got a job three hours away from Alcalá. I won't be able to manage the school and drive to work every day.

There was a reason why Belén, a fluent user of English, did not translate the word *oposiciones*. It's a Spanish cultural quirk which does not translate easily into English. In summary, the Spanish *oposiciones* refer to a set of civil service exams. The court of Felipe II established the exam system over four hundred years ago to ensure that the uneducated masses had access to the best, most law-abiding, king-loving, and God-fearing teachers. It's a series of exams which take a great deal of time and money to prepare for, but once you pass the *oposiciones*, you are guaranteed a lifetime position working for the government. This guarantee discourages any kind of incentive or initiative from state employees, but it does allow civil servants to live their lives happily, albeit modestly, until the day they die.

My father doesn't think I'm a real teacher because I don't teach in a government school, she wrote explaining her decision. *Also, I need a good pension, and the government one is the best.*

When we bought our house in Spain during the financial crisis of 2012, I remembered reading about the Spanish civil service being a burden on the economy. Back then, I was unaware of the system of *oposiciones* and didn't know that civil servants included not only government workers such as town hall clerks, petty bureaucrats, and tax collectors but also policemen, doctors, nurses, teachers, and many other essential services. As I later discovered, over fifty percent of Spanish citizens worked for the government. I observed sadly how the *oposiciones* system discouraged private enterprise and promoted a life of quiet desperation in service to the state. Belén had run the language school successfully for three years, but she was already willing to throw in the towel in exchange for a steady salary and a guaranteed pension.

While I could see why she gave up the school, I myself would never have considered working in a government school again. My limited experience of teaching at school brought back a feeling of dread. I suffered a flashback of getting up when it was still dark to face a bunch of teenagers who didn't want to be there almost as much as I didn't want to teach them.

I'd rather clean toilets at Warsaw Central Station than teach in a government school again, I thought to myself.

I was annoyed that Belén had not informed me in June that there was a possibility I might not have a job to return to in October, for that's when the academic year started at most private language schools across Spain.

Good luck! I wrote back and finished the message with some good-luck emojis.

Would you like to take over the school? Another text message appeared on my phone a few minutes later. *I've told the parents I want to close the school, but they asked me if you and Marissa could continue. I gave them your number. If the landlady does not want to renew the lease, maybe you can rent an apartment in town and teach from there? You need to talk to her.*

I read this text a few times to ensure I got it right. This explained the mystery of the multitude of missed phone calls. I had considered opening my own language school before, but I planned to build up to it gradually. I didn't expect a ready-made school to fall from the sky and hit me like a ton of bricks. I put my phone down and took Bobby for a walk. I needed a few minutes to think it over. There were three weeks left before we were supposed to start teaching. Because I had only worked for Belén since January, I didn't have enough time to take notes on how one should place the children in their respective classes, prepare the schedules, decide what courses to offer, and order the books. I explained all this to Robert while I made myself a cup of coffee, still undecided about what to do.

'But the school already has students, and the parents know you, so it's a big advantage.'

'I know. Also, it's an established school. It's been in Alcalá for over thirty years, so I won't have to start from scratch.'

OK. I'll do it. I informed Belén that same morning via WhatsApp. *But I'm going to Alicante for a few days. I can meet you when I come back.*

Belén agreed to meet me at the school on my return to discuss the price of the school's assets, including the desks, chairs, projectors, and whiteboards. I was also going to meet the landlady, Puri, who was the founding mother of the school. Puri opened her French language school in the 1990s and ran it until her retirement a few years ago when she entrusted her life project to Belén.

Puri says her son-in-law has vouched for you, so she has agreed to lease the building to you. You can sign the lease next week, Belén wrote.

Who is her son-in-law? I was puzzled about who this mysterious advocate of mine could be.

Someone called Fran?

Great! He's my plumber. See you when I get back.

As I discovered later, Fran's character reference was crucial to my takeover of the school. Puri would not have signed a new lease with a stranger without it. Her husband was initially opposed to leasing the building since he had his eyes set on the ground floor commercial space and wanted to convert the classrooms into a spacious private garage and workshop where he could while away his retirement years. But I supposed he was unable to convince Puri to let her life project fade and wither since she wanted to see what else the school could offer to the inhabitants of Alcalá.

It wasn't the first time in my life that a total coincidence and a little bit of kindness had paid off in the long term. A decade earlier, I was offered the opportunity to write a series of textbooks for a top publisher simply by being friendly to their sales reps and editors who were researching ideas for a new textbook series. I was teaching at the university in Abu Dhabi when a sales rep asked me if I could organise a focus group for the editors who wanted to brainstorm some ideas with teachers in the Middle East. Only a handful of the faculty showed up. Some did not want to ruin their lunch break or preferred to stare at their computer screens while mindlessly munching on a sandwich instead of volunteering their professional feedback. Others were too busy on the prowl with their Tupperware container in hand, ready to gate-crash the other university departments' functions for free food.

I didn't dwell on what took place at the focus group meeting and thus didn't expect to hear back from the editors when I received an email two months later inviting me to write a sample for a new coursebook based on the research they had gathered during their visit to the UAE. I took on the task even though I didn't have a clue how to write a textbook. However, I was willing to learn and understood, at the time, that it was a chance of a lifetime. All I had to do was put my head down, work hard, and accept the feedback I received from more experienced people. Other EFL teachers have occasionally asked me how they might become textbook writers. I wish I could tell them there was a set of instructions to follow, a course they could take, or an office where they could apply. But there isn't. I tell them to be kind and outgoing, and hopefully, you'll get lucky.

I felt that, once again, fortune was smiling on me. Instead of having to start a school from nothing, I was handed one on a silver platter. It was a once-in-a-lifetime opportunity, and even though I faced a very rough and amateurish re-launch, I wanted to give it a go.

'What's this?' I heard Robert enquire as I was pondering my lucky stars.

'It's my tea.'

'Where did you get it from?' he did not seem impressed with the muddy concoction in my glass teapot.

'I made it myself.'

'From what?'

'From olive leaves. The Australians who were here last year told me that olive leaf tea is super healthy, and it's very easy to make too. I just dried some leaves in the oven and put them in a jar. I forgot I had it in the cupboard.'

'What does it taste like?'

'Horrible,' I had to admit that the brew had a hideous taste. 'But it's ok if you drink it with a lot of honey.' The bitter flavour was the main reason why I still had two full jars of dried olive leaves after a year in the cupboard.

It was clear that Robert did not understand why I would be drinking a hot infusion of dry olive leaves as he examined the soggy grey leaves at the bottom of the teapot in disbelief.

'It's supposed to be very good for you, even better than green tea,' I explained my madness and started to outline the health benefits of the potion, only to realise I was but one step away from putting oregano oil on a cut finger. Chila's wish to turn me into an Eastern European witch doctor was being realised.

Even though the tea tastes terrible and is somewhat bothersome to prepare, I perversely enjoy drinking it occasionally. I like that it is readily available all around my garden — all I have to do is go outside, collect some olive leaves, and dry them. While olive leaves are ubiquitous where we live, none of the shops hereabout sell olive-leaf tea. Above all, I enjoy that it is something that, with a little bit of effort and ingenuity, can be transformed into something beneficial.

The next morning, we set off early for Alicante. We drove past Granada and across the mountains towards Guadix, where we stopped for coffee and some sightseeing of the Roman ruins. Outside Guadix, we walked around Barrio de Cuevas, or the 'Suburb of Caves', to admire the famous cave houses, which once served as hideouts for the Moors, who had been persecuted by the invading Catholics over a thousand years earlier. Once the rulers of Granada, the Moors spent the last days of the Caliphate hiding in the mountains and caves that can be found across the province. The houses were still inhabited, so we couldn't look inside one. What we could admire were the long white chimneys that protruded from the side of the hills into which the cave houses were excavated. I felt at home in this new place as we continued our journey along the Mediterranean coast. The pink oleanders separating the carriageway, the snowy peaks of the Nevada mountains in the distance, the white fishing villages framed by ancient bougainvillaea and the modern cities with the Spanish supermarket chains and football stadiums we passed on our way to Alicante felt familiar to me. We weren't strangers here anymore.

Four years and a month ago, we moved to Andalusia to start a new life. We had left behind regular jobs and steady paychecks in search of something more meaningful; a life project and a sense of control over our own destiny. During that time, we had demolished parts of an old cottage and renovated it for holiday guests. We had got to know our Spanish neighbours and created a circle of friends. We had learned new trades and developed our social skills. We had practised a new language and successfully navigated a new culture. There were times when we were financially and emotionally broke, but we had never looked back or considered selling up and returning to our old lives. We had always looked ahead.

As we approached Alicante, I spotted a lone sailing boat on the horizon. I've always loved the sea, partly because of the great explorers who conquered it for us five hundred years ago. Sitting on the apartment terrace in Alicante that evening, I gazed at the sunset reflected by a tranquil sea and thought of the brave sailors who ventured into the unknown. Why had they done that? Why do some of us leap into the unknown, never to look back? I wasn't comparing myself to Columbus, of course. I was well aware that I would never be as brave or adventurous as he was, but I find inspiration in people who live their lives differently and won't settle for the same job for the rest of their lives merely to avoid the stress of modern-day life. I am in awe of people who travel beyond the horizon simply to see what lies in the unknown. Sometimes, they never return. Sometimes, they re-emerge scarred for life. But sometimes, intrepid explorers discover a new world, a new way of life, something different. I was willing to give it a chance.

My sister and her family were to land late that night, so we had a few more hours to kill before going to the airport to collect them. I poured myself a glass of chilled rosé and returned to the terrace to continue with my romantic contemplation of the maritime view. One would think that having agreed to start my own business, my very own school, I would have been feeling stressed or anxious. But surprisingly, I wasn't. The previous night, I had slept like a log and not once did I wake up to fret and worry over our future. I felt calm and confident as if this new life challenge was meant to be.

I can do it, I thought to myself. *What's the worst that could happen?*

A REQUEST

If you enjoyed *Olive Leaf Tea*, please don't forget to leave a review or share a photo of the book on your social media.

To receive updates about the next book in this series, read new chapters before they are published, and view additional artwork from the books, please subscribe to my website or follow me on social media:

http://www.sabinaostrowska.com
Facebook @sabinawriter
Instagram @sabina.author or @cortijoberruguilla

Under the Cherry Blossom: Things Fall Apart
(Book 4 to be released in 2024)

ABOUT THE AUTHOR

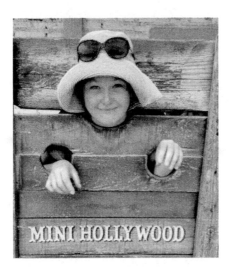

Sabina is a non-fiction writer. She has lived and taught English in Poland, Sweden, the Netherlands, the UAE, and Spain. Her memoir series depicts her and her husband's adventures of starting a new life in rural Andalusia.

She currently lives in the middle of olive groves outside the picturesque village of Montefrio and runs a language school in the town of Alcalá la Real.

For the occasional glimpse of Cortijo Berruguilla and the nature around Montefrio, follow her on Instagram @cortijo.berruguilla or Facebook @cortijoberruguilla

To get updates about new books, subscribe to her website or social media:
www.sabinaostrowska.com

Chat with Sabina and other memoir authors
and readers in the Facebook group,
WE LOVE MEMOIRS:
https://www.facebook.com/groups/welovememoirs/

INTERVIEW WITH THE AUTHOR

What's it like living in Montefrio?
(home of "one of the best views in the world")

by Frank from mappingspain.com

Hi Sabina! Can you please tell me about yourself and on how you ended up moving to Spain?

I'm originally from Poland, but I have never worked in my home, at least not to build a career. I left Poland while I was a postgraduate student and completed my Master's degree in the Netherlands. Since then, I have lived in Sweden and the United Arab Emirates. It was in the UAE where I built my professional career as an EFL teacher and a textbook writer. While the expat life in Abu Dhabi can be very cushy, it can also become a trap. After nine years there, both my husband, Robert, and I felt that we were in a rut.

We decided to return to Europe and start from scratch here. Being EU citizens (it was in 2012, and Robert, who is British, was still able to travel freely around the EU) made it easy for us to choose the European country where we wished to live. We spent some time searching online for rural properties in countries with warm climates and stunning nature. We quickly realised that Andalusia had the most affordable property prices for our budget, and we loved the photos of the house patios shaded by grapevines, lush greenery, and stunning flowers.

We fell in love with the charming white cottages that are nestled among the tranquil olive groves in the region and decided to visit this part of Europe to see it for ourselves. In the summer of 2012, we arranged house sightings with several estate agents in the triangle between Malaga, Cordoba and Granada. I liked the idea of living in the mountains but still being close to the Mediterranean Sea.

The summer we bought our property was the first time we visited Spain. We spoke very little Spanish and were very naïve about house renovations and our future in this country. The house search led to many strange encounters, which I describe in my book *The Crinkle Crankle Wall: Our First Year in Andalusia*.

Neither Robert nor I like to overthink things, so instead of spending a lot of time making detailed plans and trying to anticipate any possible problems, we jumped right into it. Making life-changing decisions on the spur of the moment has been our life philosophy; it has often landed us in difficult situations, but it has also paid us dividends.

I heard you came to Spain and immediately bought an old house in Montefrio. Why Montefrio?

When we started our quest to find a suitable property in Andalusia, we were focused on finding a place in a peaceful location. Nature, the distance from the main roads or potentially noisy neighbours, and the possibility of growing our own fruit and vegetables were the main factors that informed our decision where to buy a house.

Montefrio was not initially on our radar at all. It just so happened that the cottage that we fell in love with was outside the village of Montefrio. Because we don't go out a lot and work from home, it did not really matter where exactly we lived. It's just an added bonus that Montefrio is a very picturesque white village with a typical Moorish castle at the top of the hill that overlooks the historical centre. It also has a few supermarkets that sell local fruit and vegetables, a health centre with very friendly and professional doctors and nurses, and for those who don't have a car, a daily bus connection to Granada.

I know Montefrio is one of 10 towns considered as having "the best views in the world" (by National Geographic). Does it get a lot of tourism?

When we first purchased our property, we decided to renovate it so that we would have two independent rural apartments for paying guests. This project took us two years to complete as we had to do a lot of DIY projects ourselves. Shortly after we opened our guest house, called *Cortijo Berruguilla*, National Geographic announced that the views of Montefrio's old Moorish castle perched on top of the mountain were worthy of it being ranked in the top ten of the most beautiful village views in the world. This has put Montefrio on the tourism map and has significantly boosted local and international tourism.

Because of this distinction, our local Town Hall has made many improvements to the appearance of the village and road signage. Several new bars and restaurants have opened to cater for the additional visitors. Since Montefrio has only one small hotel, many rural guest houses around the village, like ours, have benefited from the increased visibility. To see some photos of our guest house, Montefrio, and the surrounding nature, you can check out my pictures on Facebook @cortijoberruguilla or Instagram @cortijo.berruguilla.

Most tourists who stay with us enjoy the peace and tranquillity of the olive groves. They spend long days relaxing by the pool and enjoy the warm summer evenings drinking wine and eating delicious local cheese. Our neighbours make one of the best artisanal cheeses in Spain from their dairy in Montefrio. At night, the guests can admire the starry night and see all the constellations. But it's also a great location for day trips to Granada, to visit the amazing Alhambra, to Cordoba to see the old mosque called the Mesquita or to the beach in Malaga.

There are many smaller attractions nearby, including the stunning fortress in Alcalá la Real, the bat cave in Zuheros, an amazing hike across hanging bridges in Moclin, a dip in hot springs in Alhama de Granada, or a swim in the lake in Rute. On clear days, we also recommend the drive to the top of the Sierra Nevada mountains.

You're a busy person: besides running a guest house, you have a language school and also write books. Can you tell us about both?

While living in a rural part of Andalusia has many advantages in terms of getting a lot of physical exercise, good food, and close social connections with your community, one of the disadvantages is that the job market here is very limited. We have learned that to succeed, you must take charge of your life and keep your eggs in as many baskets as possible.

Tourism in Andalusia can be profitable but is limited to late spring, summer, and early autumn. The winter months can be quiet, and the weather can be unpredictable at that time. For this reason, I started teaching again at a local school. During my first year there, I was given the opportunity to buy the business, and so I decided to jump in. I write about this experience in my latest book, *Olive Leaf Tea: Time to Settle*, which is about growing roots in Andalusia and becoming part of the community.

Having a variety of income sources helped us survive the covid lockdowns, which were very strict in Andalusia. Without the language school, which we were able to keep running online, we would have had serious financial difficulties, like most of the tourism and hospitality industries in Spain in 2020.

In addition to my work with my guest house and language school, I also write EFL textbooks. This is a job that I have done since 2010. The good thing about writing is that you have a flexible timetable, but the drawback is that I usually work seven days a week.

I've enjoyed reading excerpts from your books; it somehow makes me think of Frances Mayes' "Under the Tuscan Sun" with its colorful stories of locals and life in the countryside. What motivated you to be a writer?

Writing non-fiction is my hobby. It's something that I enjoy doing even when I find it challenging. I have always been an avid reader, and I have always written little stories. But I never managed to finish a book until I wrote *The Crinkle Crankle Wall: Our First Year of Andalusia*. I suppose that the writing work was also a little therapeutic as some of the experiences of renovating a cottage and living in a house with no roof during the rainy months were quite stressful. I use humour and satire in my books as a way of distancing myself from these memories.

Amazon universal link to The Crinkle Crankle Wall https://bit.ly/CrinkleCrankle

Once I had published *The Crinkle Crankle Wall*, many readers wrote to me to tell me how relatable my story was. I think many people dream of doing something different with their life — renovating an old cottage in the middle of nowhere, moving to a different country, or travelling are universal themes. The positive feedback that I received from the first book motivated me to continue writing – the second book, *A Hoopoe on the Nispero Tree: Our Andalusian Adventure Continues,* describes our financial struggles in Spain and our search to figure out how we can live in the countryside without steady jobs.

Amazon universal link to A Hoopoe on the Nispero Tree https://bit.ly/A-Hoopoe

Montefrio is a small place (a population of 5,479, according to Google). Are you and your husband the only foreigners in town? Was moving here a bit of a culture shock? Were the locals welcoming?

Yes, Montefrio is a small village, but you should consider rural Andalusia, more generally, as a conglomerate of small villages and medium-sized towns — they all rely on each other, and people travel between them to do business. Many families live in the countryside and live off the land. But it's not an insular place. There are expats all around who live in the villages and in the countryside. We have friends from the Netherlands, Belgium, France, a few Americans, and several Brits. There is a significant expat community where we live.

The friendliness and openness of the local people have been one of the reasons we never hesitated when we bought our property. To give you an example, here's a fragment from *The Crinkle Crankle Wall* in which I describe how we met our neighbour who grew up in the house we bought:

"Juan Carlos grunted and repeated what I told him. He then looked at us and said something that sounded like *propietario*. I guessed that he was asking whether we were the new owners of the house on the hill and confirmed his deduction with multiple exclamations consisting of the word *si*. As I handed him the wine and the dates, his wrinkled face lit up. He inspected the bottle — it was a cheap Crianza, but it was all we had at hand when we ran out of the house. He seemed pleased with the vintage and called his wife. A petite lady with short dark hair came out of the house.

As soon as she saw us, she started to talk incessantly. There was a slight whine to her pitch, and we were not sure whether it meant anything. Juan Carlos showed her the wine bottle and the dates and repeated everything I told him about us. She kept on interrupting her husband's account with squeals of excitement and clasping her hands in front of her chest in joy as if she had just heard that they had won the lottery. She nodded and waved her arms while listening and then started telling us something. The only two words that we could distinguish were Gabi and *tia*. We remembered that *tia* means *aunt* and puzzled the rest together. Mercedes was Young Gabi's aunt. Her father had built our house, and she and her brother, Old Gabi, were born and raised there." From *The Crinkle Crankle Wall: Our First Year in Andalusia*

How is your Spanish? Are you now fluent? Has learning/speaking been a challenge?

When we purchased the house, we spoke twenty words of Spanish between the two of us, ten of which were numbers from one to ten. Even though I'm a language teacher myself, I don't particularly enjoy attending classes. After we bought the house and were fixed on settling in Spain, I listened to audio lessons and podcasts in the car during my commute to work. This was a good starting point when we moved, but it also led to many strange exchanges and humorous misunderstandings.

After nine years and running two businesses, I'd say my Spanish is 'intermediate', but I have not taken any tests yet. I've learned most of what I know about Spanish 'on the go'. I have picked it up by having to speak to clients at my guest house and language school. I also follow social media sites that are specific to our community and read the news and posts there in Spanish.

Here is a funny exchange from the summer when we bought the house:

"As we sat there, an elderly lady strolled in. Both women started kissing and squealing, which is a typical form of greeting in Andalusia. We were then introduced, or so we guessed we were since our names were mentioned, and the old lady proceeded to shake our hands. The women kept on talking to us and repeating the word that sounded like *cantar* in Italian. In my smugness, I took it upon myself to translate to Robert the one word that I thought I understood and told him that the old lady was asking him whether he liked to sing.

'*Cantar*, no? Play guitar,' Robert decided to engage in that topic. 'How do you say *I play the guitar*?' he asked, looking at me. I don't know what gave him the impression that I would know this. Still, it has subsequently become a particularly endearing habit of his to ask me to translate complicated English phrases while in the middle of a conversation with Spanish speakers.

'I have no idea,' I responded in a tone that told him that he was on his own with this topic, and so he continued to entertain the ladies on his own.

'I have GUITARS. GUITAR,' he mimicked played the guitar as he enunciated the word. The old lady and the estate agent nodded their heads, and both gave us a smile reserved for mentally ill relatives who have convinced themselves that they are Napoleon.

'Yes, sure you are. Now go and take your pill, please,' the smile said. It took me another year before I figured out that people in

Andalusia were not asking me whether I liked singing whenever they met me. I have to admit that I started to wonder why people who have just met me kept on bringing this topic up, but I assumed that they must really love music very much. I don't remember the exact moment when I found out what the word really meant, but it revived my memory of the discussion about music in the estate agent's office and made me feel quite stupid. What they were saying was *encantada* which means *Nice to meet you!* and not *Do you like to sing?*" From *The Crinkle Crankle Wall: Our First Year in Andalusia*

You have some colourful stories of initially settling in town and building your home. It sounds like it was very challenging. Can you share a few stories?

I think living in the middle of a building site for many cold months was the most challenging. In hindsight, it was a mistake, but then I would not have had as many funny stories to write about.

"Living among the rubble with significant parts of the old house now demolished meant that we spent the late autumn being cold and dirty. The several months that it took to put the house's main structural parts back together were probably the most bitterly cold and miserable in our lives, both physically and emotionally. It was in mid-October that we experienced our first torrential rains in Spain. The first one took us by surprise. After nine years of living in the desert, I forgot that it rains in Europe in the autumn, even in sunny Spain.

That first rainy night, we spent most of it in wet pyjamas shoving rainwater from one place to another. Because there was no roof on the house at all, the rainwater was collecting on the floor of the second floor. Once it reached a certain depth, it started to run down the staircase and into our living room, cascading like a spring waterfall. We scooped up water in buckets and dumped them out of the house. The task closely resembled the manic speed and desperation of people trying to get the water out of a sinking boat. It was a futile endeavour. As I stood on the staircase trying to control the waterfall, I looked up at the black sky and the torment above. 'What are we doing?' I wondered for a second, but really, there was no time to moan and complain.

After an hour of scooping up the water streaming down the staircase onto the sweeping pan and into a plastic bucket, we were desperate for a break. As was inevitable, we started to argue and question each other's technique of catching water. Harsh words were exchanged — not the first or last time that terrible autumn. I got angry and kept sweeping water in silence with heavy rain still falling on my back. That's when Robert dropped the mop and left the house into the cold, stormy night." From *The Crinkle Crankle Wall: Our First Year in Andalusia*

What advice would you give anyone thinking of moving to Spain and buying a cortijo in rural Andalusia?

One of the biggest struggles we have experienced in rural Andalusia is the water shortage. Since we moved here nine years ago, we have experienced many years of drought. We rely on our well to supply us with water, and unfortunately, there have been many summers when it has run dry. If I could travel back in time and give myself some advice, it would be to ensure you have a secure water source. Perhaps drilling a borehole, deepening our well, or installing more water tanks to store the water when it rains should have been our first step once we had moved in.

Over the years, we have come up with some creative solutions to supply our house with water, but it can be very stressful, especially during years of drought.

You've lived in many places in the world. Do you sometimes feel those nomadic urges to move on and live somewhere new? Or is Montefrio where you wish to be for the foreseeable future?

I have indeed lived and visited many places in Europe and Asia, but I feel at home in Andalusia. I would like to explore South America, but I can't imagine myself leaving Spain. I think we've made it home now.

To keep in touch, readers can follow me on Instagram @sabina.author or Facebook @sabinawriter

Thank you so much for inviting me to your blog!

Thank you for doing this interview Sabina!

Visit www.mappingspain.com or join their Facebook group to read interviews with other expats and to get tips and advice about relocating to Spain.

ACKNOWLEDGMENTS

I would like to thank all the people who follow me on my social media and post friendly comments and send encouraging messages about my writing. This support really means a lot to me. The best way an independent author can promote her work is through word of mouth, so I really appreciate it when readers share my books with their friends and family.

Many readers and fellow writers have helped me during the editing stages of this book. I would like to thank Claudia Kiburz, Dan Costinas, Elora Canne, Jacqueline Vincent, Julie Haigh, Kathy Handren Hobbs, Kim Miller, Libertad Anderson, Pat Ellis, Sue Bavey, Sue Raymond, and Veronica M. Moore for their valuable time and effort in reviewing the final drafts of the book. Your comments and feedback have significantly improved this story.

Also, a huge thank-you to friends and readers: Aidan and Christine Thorne, Alison Cole, Céline Begley, Claire Howe, Julie Ross, Katherine L. Hall, Rosana Matos de Araujo, and many others for your continued support. I apologize in advance for not mentioning everyone.

Finally, this book would not have been possible without my husband, Robert Ryan, who not only provides us with an endless source of new adventures but has also edited the final copies of all of my books and added his own delicate touch in certain places.

Cortijo Berruguilla, August 2023

Printed in Great Britain
by Amazon

41437571R00179